THE VALUE OF SOLITUDE

STUDIES IN RELIGION AND CULTURE

Frank Burch Brown, Gary L. Ebersole,
and Edith Wyschogrod, *Editors*

THE VALUE OF SOLITUDE

THE ETHICS AND SPIRITUALITY OF
ALONENESS IN AUTOBIOGRAPHY

JOHN D. BARBOUR

UNIVERSITY OF VIRGINIA PRESS

CHARLOTTESVILLE AND LONDON

UNIVERSITY OF VIRGINIA PRESS
© 2004 by the Rector and Visitors of the University of Virginia
All rights reserved
Printed in the United States of America on acid-free paper

First published 2004

1 3 5 7 9 8 6 4 2

Library of Congress Cataloging-in-Publication Data
Barbour, John D.
The value of solitude : the ethics and spirituality of aloneness in
autobiography / John D. Barbour.
     p.   cm. — (Studies in religion and culture)
Includes bibliographical references and index.
ISBN 0-8139-2288-7 (alk. paper) — ISBN 0-8139-2289-5 (pbk. : alk. paper)
1. Solitude. 2. Solitude—Religious aspects. 3. Autobiography—Religious
aspects. I. Title. II. Studies in religion and culture (Charlottesville, Va.)
BJ1499.S65B37 2004
128' .4—dc22
                                                          2004006229

For Graham and Reed

CONTENTS

ACKNOWLEDGMENTS

MEG OJALA and Ian and Deane Barbour read the entire manuscript and offered criticism, encouragement, and support. Particular chapters benefited from the suggestions of Kimberly Rae Connor, Sandra Dixon, Rick Fairbanks, Richard Freadman, Rosemary Rader, Douglas Schuurman, and Eugene Stelzig. I presented portions of this book to the St. Olaf College Philosophy Department and to United Theological Seminary, and I am grateful for their responses. Cathie Brettschneider's editorial expertise and enthusiasm for a book on solitude made it a great pleasure to work with her again. I am indebted to Ellen Satrom, Mark Mones, and Kathryn Krug for their superb editorial work.

I dedicate this book to my sons Graham and Reed. Although as teenagers they have had little interest in solitude, they may in the future. As I worked on this book they confirmed for me one of my central ideas: aloneness is only welcome and fruitful when it is part of a life that also contains relationships with others. My times of solitude would have been very different without their presence in my life.

O you singer solitary, singing by yourself, projecting me,
O solitary me listening, never more shall I cease perpetuating you.

—WALT WHITMAN, "Out of the Cradle Endlessly Rocking"

> There is a solitude of space
> A solitude of sea
> A solitude of death, but these
> Society shall be
> Compared with that profounder site
> That polar privacy
> A soul admitted to itself—
> Finite infinity.

—EMILY DICKINSON, no. 1,695

Let him who cannot be alone beware of community. Let him who is not in community beware of being alone.

—DIETRICH BONHOEFFER, *Life Together*

THE VALUE OF SOLITUDE

INTRODUCTION

SOLITUDE IS often feared or avoided because it is associated with isolation, abandonment, or loneliness. Yet for some people solitude is the occasion for the most serene, profound, or exhilarating moments in life. Being alone may provide the necessary setting for their spiritual search, their attempt to understand life's meaning and to be related to the ultimate sources of goodness and power. This book explores some ways in which experiences of solitude, both positive and negative, have been interpreted as religiously significant. I also interpret the ways in which solitude raises ethical questions, as writers reflect on their need for aloneness and discern implications for their understanding of the good life and their involvements in society. This book differs from previous studies of solitude in two main ways: my focus on the links between solitude, ethics, and spirituality, and my approach to the topic by studying autobiographies.[1] I will introduce and circumscribe the subject matter with three sets of reflections: on the nature of solitude, on spirituality and ethics, and on autobiography.

The Nature of Solitude

Some initial clarity in defining the topic, with a cautionary word about the limits of definition, will help focus this study. There are two principal components of solitude, physical distance from others and mental disengagement. In his philosophical analysis of solitude, Philip Koch defines solitude as, most basically, mental disengagement from other people: "Solitude is, most ultimately, simply an experiential world in which other people are absent: that is enough for solitude, that is constant through all solitudes. Other people may be physically present, provided that our minds are disengaged from them; and the full range of disengaged activities, from reflective withdrawal to complete immersion in the tumbling rush of sensations, find their places along the spectrum of solitudes."[2] According to this definition, solitude does not include consciousness of other people. However, Koch elsewhere uses the term solitude more broadly (as I shall) to encompass experiences when a person is mentally engaged with others. Persons who are alone spend much of their time remembering, thinking about, or longing for other people. If any memory or thought of others disqualified a period of time as being true aloneness, there would be very little if any solitude in human history. Disengagement is a relative matter, not an absolute condition. Solitude usually also involves physical distance from others, which is what we usually mean by "aloneness." Yet not every experience of being physically isolated is experienced as solitude, and the geographical requirements for solitude are sometimes measured in inches. Without too prescriptive a definition, we need to examine how different authors understand solitude, especially the two aspects of physical apartness and mental disengagement.

Solitude is not a simple alternative to engagement with others, but a more complicated matter of different kinds of involvement that are always changing. I may be related to other persons in terms of my perceptions, thoughts, feelings, or actions. I may be engaged and disengaged with others in different ways at the same time: I may be so intent on my own thoughts that I do not notice people in the same room, or I may be emotionally preoccupied with my lover while I am gardening alone. Experiences of aloneness are contained within webs of social relationship, and a solitary individual may become more or less aware of the background presence of other persons. There is no single clear boundary between solitude and encounter, but rather a range of degrees of involvement and detachment from other people.

We should not prescribe a certain amount of time or physical distance from other people as requisite for an experience to count as solitude. It is surprising how much contact with others was had by some of the most famous solitaries, for instance Thoreau during his two years at Walden Pond. On his supposedly solitary walks, Jean-Jacques Rousseau was usually consumed with fantasies about his enemies' plots against him, and with constructing defenses of his character against their imagined accusations. By some definitions these experiences lack the necessary detachment from other people to qualify as solitude. Yet Thoreau and Rousseau see solitude as crucial to the experiences that form the core of their autobiographical narratives. It would be absurd to establish arbitrary requirements for solitude by formulating a definition that specifies a necessary temporal duration of mental disengagement or a minimum distance of spatial separation from others. Let us rather examine the varieties of solitary experience, the diverse ways in which individuals understand what solitude is.

Solitude is easily confused with related concepts such as loneliness, isolation, alienation, and privacy, and these ideas are often blurred in autobiographical accounts. Philip Koch helpfully distinguishes these concepts. Solitude is not the same as loneliness, which is a painful emotion of longing for other persons. Although the positive qualities of solitude are often contrasted with loneliness, solitude itself is not an emotion but a condition. The state of being disengaged from other people may be accompanied by various emotions or by none at all. Solitude is not the same as feeling isolated, which necessarily involves consciousness of being separated from other persons. Nor is solitude identical to privacy, which includes a belief that one is entitled to keep something unobserved by other people. These concepts require a consciousness of other persons that solitude often lacks. I may be so disengaged from other people that I have no wish to be with them and no desire not to be observed.

Finally, solitude is not the same as alienation, the sense of estrangement from other people that twentieth-century social thinkers, following Hegel and Marx, see as a negative quality of modern societies. Alienation involves a sense of fractured relationship; as with loneliness, privacy, and isolation, consciousness of other persons is an integral part of the experience. Koch holds that when we confuse solitude with these other concepts, we prejudge crucial questions about the value of solitude: "We wish to know, finally, whether solitude is a good or an evil, how good or evil and how so. Now if you begin by defining solitude as loneliness, the inherent negativity of loneliness is going to lead you to stigmatize solitude; but then it will be unclear as to whether you have attained some bold new insight into the subject—or simply changed it."[3] A theory of solitude should not be confused with a diagnosis of the ills of contemporary society.

It would be just as erroneous, although natural in a study of spirituality, to assume that solitude is necessarily a positive or affirmative experience, or that it is the only or most authentic kind of religious experience. Paul Tillich contrasts loneliness as "the pain of being alone" with solitude, "the glory of being alone." Tillich holds that God "wants us to penetrate to the boundaries of our being, where the mystery of life appears, and it can only appear in moments of solitude."[4] William James, in his great work *The Varieties of Religious Experience*, studies "the feelings, acts, and experiences of men in their solitude," choosing to ignore "the institutional branch" of religion.[5] Alfred North Whitehead identifies solitude with religiousness: "This doctrine is the direct negation of the theory that religion is a social fact. . . . Religion is what the individual does with his own solitariness. . . . Thus religion is solitariness; and if you are never solitary, you are never religious."[6] But the way of solitude is not inherently good or bad; aloneness is neither a direct path to God or enlightenment nor the road to hell or alienation. All of these questions of evaluation must be left to the writers we will consider—and to each of us, as we make choices about the role of solitude in our own lives.

Spirituality, Ethics, and Solitude

Spirituality is an elusive term notoriously difficult to define. Reference to the spiritual dimensions of religion usually means the personal, experiential aspects, in contrast with an organized community's doctrines, institutions, and rituals. Spirituality may include such experiences as feelings of joy or serenity, appreciative awareness, openness to and acceptance of reality, a sense of life's goodness and unity, self-surrender, healing, and belief that one is in contact with the fundamental sources of life.

This book deals primarily with the spiritual experiences of Christians who interpret solitude using the classic symbols and beliefs of their faith tradition, and also with individuals who do not think of themselves as belonging to any faith community, but who find in their aloneness access to life-giving sources of meaning. Limitations of space and competence prevent my attending to solitude in other historic religious traditions, although in the conclusion I offer suggestions about directions for further study. I examine here the solitude of Christian believers in God and that of persons who find in the natural world or within themselves something essential to the meaning of their lives, some value, power, or ultimate concern that shapes their convictions and commitments. Spirituality involves encounter or intimate relationship with something outside the self, whether a part of the natural world, God, or the cosmos as a whole; it also entails self-discovery, self-acceptance, and new understanding of who one really is. These two components—knowing oneself more fully and being better related to an ultimate reality beyond the self— are often fused in spiritual experience, so that, in the paradoxical language of mystics, a person may speak of a new awareness of the divine both within the self and beyond it.[7]

Spirituality is linked to solitude in various ways. How one chooses to spend time alone often reflects a desire for spiritual experience, whether one kayaks, gardens, prays, paints, makes music, meditates, walks in a forest, or sits on a porch swing in order to catch up with what is happening inside and return to a sense of who one is. Intentional solitude is linked to spirituality in that both attempt to transcend normal social consciousness, the roles and routines that can leave a person feeling trapped, bored, or overwhelmed by the demands and expectations of others. Experiences of intimacy or solidarity with others, whether through personal relationship or participation in a larger community, can also be profoundly spiritual events. But for many people, involvements with others often become a matter of grudging tolerance, attempted manipulation, irritated tension, or open conflict. Solitude may then be sought as a means to move beyond these unhappy states. Aloneness may help one find contact with what lies beyond social routines and conventions, beyond the repetitiveness and superficiality that often characterize interactions among people. Solitude may be a way to resist the pressures of socialization, an attempt to create a time and space for self-transformation. This may be important even if one's experiences with others are primarily positive. Solitude is more than an antidote or corrective for negative social interactions; it offers its own distinctive blessings. Solitude allows a person to focus on certain experiences and dimensions of reality with a fuller attention, a more complete concentration, than is possible when one must also attend to the reactions of other people.

A return to solitude may allow one to recover the deep springs of personal identity, those memories, feelings, bodily awareness, and other aspects of one's being that are not always expressed in social roles. Being alone need not reflect dislike or contempt for others, for it may express a yearning to find a more meaningful form of relationship, an engagement motivated by desire and commitment rather than simply conformity to social pressure. Sometimes a person can only recover integrity, wholeness, and centeredness of character by establishing some healthy distance in relationships with others. Solitude becomes spiritual when breaking out of ordinary social interactions leads to a clearer knowledge of who one truly is and to a better relationship to reality in all its aspects, especially those that are perceived as most essential, valuable, and life-affirming. Restricting one's contact with other people is not inherently antisocial, any more than dietary discipline in the Jewish or Islamic traditions signifies disapproval of food, or celibacy in Roman Catholic piety necessarily implies a negative view of sexuality. Asceticism and self-discipline with regard to one's social interactions express the belief that this is a crucial area of the spiritual life affecting one's relationship not only with others but with God or with whatever a person considers holy.

The ethical dimensions of solitude involve three central issues. First, since solitude is a withdrawal from other people, it has always been subject to criticism as selfish, irresponsible, or dangerous. Therefore, those who write about solitude in depth often try to show its value. They may seek to demonstrate that it serves important social ends, or they may argue that there is a place in any human life for activities and pursuits that benefit oneself. Thus arguments about solitude and autobiographical representations of a solitary life raise crucial questions about the nature of the good life, particularly how a person's own well-being is balanced or integrated with social concerns. Second, solitaries are often drawn to aloneness because of dissatisfaction with aspects of their social existence. Explaining the reasons one wants solitude may therefore involve social criticism. And finally, solitaries often draw from their time of aloneness lessons or conclusions that they believe are significant for others, and this is an incentive for them to write about their experience. They believe that solitude teaches important truths about how life should be lived both alone and with other people, for instance with greater serenity, attunement to the natural world, or detachment from ambition. The ethics of aloneness encompasses, then, the moral justification of solitude, the use of solitude for social criticism, and solitude as a source of insight to be shared with others.

Solitude is too often regarded as antagonistic to the values of social relationship. In much of the writing about solitude and in the popular imagination, individuals are confronted with a dichotomous choice between solitude and community. This is a false dilemma, for any particular understanding of solitude reflects a culture's values, and solitude has deep meaning for those who may rarely be alone. We experience solitude in a distinctive way partly because we conceive of it in ways learned from our culture. Solitude is imagined, made possible, and sustained by particular cultural beliefs and institutions, as well as by the specific people and material conditions on which a solitary depends. Solitude stands in a liminal (marginal or boundary) position in relation to social institutions, helping to define them. This boundary-marking role makes solitude both controversial and necessary to any culture's conception of community. A hermit may reflect or challenge his society's values; to different observers, he may be a rejected outcast, a prophetic critic of his society, or a harmless eccentric. A period of solitude may function as a touchstone for someone who would influence or reform society. What is learned in solitude may be carried back to one's life in society and provide a crucial corrective or alternative to prevailing patterns of interaction.

The attitudes one learns alone—for instance, silence, stillness, appreciation of nature or sensory experience, or detachment from ambition —may be interpreted as virtues that should also be practiced in society, as analogous to the right attitude toward other people, or as insights that need to be integrated with the values of organized communal living. Solitude has ethical and spiritual significance not only for the person who chooses to be alone but also for those around her.

Solitude in Autobiography

Autobiography can be a powerful way of exploring solitude. A priori and abstract arguments about solitude are interesting and valuable, but they are usually too simple, too general, and unattentive to the many individual circumstances and differences of temperament that shape actual experiences of aloneness. The value of solitude is situational, dependent on a variety of circumstances that can be depicted and explored in narrative. Autobiographers describe and help us to imagine specific experiences of solitude, especially those aspects of aloneness that unfold in time and need to be plotted in a narrative. Personal writing also expresses the ambivalence that most people feel about solitude, the way one may both love and fear aloneness.

Autobiography shows how times of solitude fit into the whole of a person's life. Many studies discuss periods of aloneness out of context, as self-contained episodes. But solitude is always bounded, both temporally and spatially, by relatedness to other persons. Experiences of aloneness and social interaction influence each other profoundly. We need to understand how episodes of solitude take place within the larger temporal span of a person's life and within a particular social context. Autobiography provides a helpful way of doing this, even when a writer tries to isolate a period of solitude from the rest of his life, for instance in such classic works as Rousseau's *Reveries of the Solitary Walker,* Thoreau's *Walden,* May Sarton's *Journal of a Solitude,* and Richard Byrd's *Alone.* Even in these works devoted to close examination of a limited period of intense solitude, the writer reveals what led to the desire for solitude, how other people were present in memory or anticipation, and how the experience of aloneness affected his or her return to ordinary social life. Autobiography helps us to think about how solitude and social interaction can best be combined within a life, and of the advantages and disadvantages of different kinds and amounts of aloneness.

For many authors the process of writing an autobiography is itself conceived of as a form of solitude, as detachment from other people in order to discover or create a new sense of personal identity. Solitude is not just an occasion in the author's past but an aspect of the act of writing an autobiography, and often a significant event in the writer's life. Like my two earlier books on autobiography, this study examines authors' conceptions of the activity of writing autobiography in terms of the ethical and religious significance of this kind of self-scrutiny.[8] When knowing and representing oneself are understood as essentially solitary acts, this view shapes the kind of life writing that results. Because the genre of autobiography is shaped by solitude in terms of its form as well as its content, I am interested in how experiences of solitude influence an author's larger story and in how the way a story is told reflects ideas about solitude. For example, the metaphor of autobiography as a sort of soliloquy recurs in this genre, when an author presents a textual image of the self in isolation, unaware of those who will read his words. An author may worry about whether intensive writing about oneself risks the same dangers as solitude: self-absorption, alienation from others, even unintelligibility. Invoking the image of Narcissus, or voicing one's fear of solipsism, or using rhetorical strategies that try to bring the perspectives of others into one's narrative may all be motivated by a concern about the risks of solitary introspection.

Significant, too, in autobiography is the creation of what we might call fictions or myths of solitude. Authors may represent themselves as being or having lived in a condition of solitude that has little basis in terms of their actual daily life, yet significantly discloses something about their sense of self and their relationship to other persons. Modern autobiographers often lament their isolation even as they express the need to be detached from society as an essential condition of forging a distinct personal identity. The ways in which solitude is described and the images and metaphors that a writer uses to characterize aloneness reveal a great deal about what she dreads and yearns for, and about her spiritual condition. The fictions of solitude remind us that the depiction of aloneness in a text is constructed or imagined by an author for particular reasons; a writer's aloneness is as much a matter of perspective and rhetorical purpose as it is of geographical distance from neighbors.

Writing an autobiography is usually understood to be a solitary pursuit and, in the books I will examine, it is often explicitly conceived of as the practice of spiritual disciplines and activities that religious traditions have sought within solitude, such as asceticism, examination of conscience, private confession to God, repentance, meditative awareness, and the cultivation of particular forms of virtue.

Autobiographies that demonstrate a keen appreciation of solitude offer important insights into the authors' religious values and beliefs. In withdrawing from social interaction in order to write their lives, these authors reorient themselves according to their moral ideals and spiritual aspirations, which they often believe have been blunted or dissipated by ordinary social interactions.

Autobiography provides a manageable, focused subject matter for reflection on elusive but significant cultural changes. I will trace changing views of solitude from Augustine until contemporary writers. The narratives I study reflect social and intellectual currents much larger than the tradition of autobiography itself, for instance such changes in the Western understanding of the self as Charles Taylor analyses in *Sources of the Self: The Making of Modern Identity*. Solitude is closely related to such fundamental concepts as individuality, authenticity, and self-expression. Although it is important to reflect on the role of these major cultural ideas and developments, there is also a danger of over-generalization and abstraction in discussing them. I hope that analysis of particular individuals' life stories will keep my reflections concrete, specific, and rooted in human experience. We need conceptual analysis and philosophical argument about solitude, and also interpretation of the compelling witness of those who have lived through periods of aloneness and sought to express its meaning.

The study of autobiography is not simply analysis of texts or discourse but an assessment of how people articulate their values and their wisdom about life. I evaluate the insights of these writers as they explore the interrelations between solitude and social bonds. A life without times of solitude or a life lacking intimacy with others may be chosen by a few rare individuals, but for the vast majority of people, a satisfying, full life, a spiritual life, contains occasions of solitude along with love, friendship, and participation in groups. We need a balance between the active and the contemplative, between encounter with another person and the need to recollect one's sense of selfhood apart from others. Few would quarrel with this generalization, but the details about how we each do this in our own lives are as interesting and various as our differing temperaments and needs. Is there any wisdom to be gleaned from those who have thought deeply about the role of solitude in their own lives? I hope that close examination of particular lives will offer illuminating insights about how to combine the pleasures and rewards of solitude and those of social engagement, and to avoid the dangers of either self-absorption or the diffusion of selfhood in the various social demands and communities that claim a person.

The chapters are organized as follows. The first chapter explores Christian attitudes to solitude from biblical times through the medieval period, providing historical context and raising some of the basic issues explored by autobiographers. Then I turn to four chapters centered on classic texts dealing with solitude: Augustine's *Confessions*; works by the humanist thinkers Petrarch, Montaigne, and Gibbon; Rousseau's *Reveries of the Solitary Walker*; and Thoreau's *Walden*. In the sixth chapter I discuss the spiritual values shaping twentieth-century autobiographies that explore "the varieties of solitary experience." The last two chapters turn again to closer examination of a few key texts. I discuss the ways that the ethics and spirituality of solitude are explored in the autobiographical writings of Thomas Merton, who is probably the most famous hermit in Western history and certainly the most thoughtful modern Christian writer to reflect on solitude. I then interpret a brief memoir by contemporary writer Paul Auster, whose *The Invention of Solitude* connects experiences of solitude with family relationships and with the nature of artistic creativity. The conclusion summarizes my understanding of the role of solitude in autobiography and the ethical and spiritual value of solitude.

These autobiographies involve both each author's cultivation of solitude for spiritual ends and the author's ethical evaluation of solitude's virtues and dangers. Each of these dimensions of aloneness is crucial for contemporary readers who understand the importance of the values sought by solitaries, including autonomy, individuality, and authenticity, yet yearn also for community and shared identity. We need to discern both the spiritual value of experiences of aloneness and the dangers that arise when solitary pursuits are severed from the relationships, social activities, and religious context that give them much of their meaning and value. We need both an ethics of solitude and a spirituality of solitude, and I hope that these autobiographical narratives will offer insights and wisdom.

1

CHRISTIAN SOLITUDE

EXAMINING CHRISTIAN views of solitude provides a background and context for understanding Augustine and later autobiographers. There is not one simple Christian view of solitude, but a lively debate illuminating many dimensions of meaning of aloneness. This chapter explores the spiritual motives that have been expressed and the goals that have been sought in solitude by individual Christians, focusing on two issues. I first examine the origins of Christian attitudes to solitude and some basic religious and ethical concerns expressed by advocates and critics of solitude. Then, pursuing my interest in how solitude and social engagement may influence each other and be combined, I discuss several ways in which eremitical (hermit's) ideals have been significant for Christians who were not themselves solitaries. Since there is practically no autobiographical writing by solitaries before the Renaissance, our sources in this chapter are the collected "sayings" of the desert fathers, stories and legends about early hermits, and modern scholarship about Christian solitude. These sources reveal many of the spiritual and ethical issues that solitude raises, thus orienting our approach to the autobiographical works studied in the rest of this book.

Early Christian Attitudes to Solitude

Although solitude was first cultivated as a distinctive way of life and spiritual path by the desert fathers of the fourth century, the biblical tradition significantly influences Christian attitudes to solitude. In the Hebrew Bible, experiences of solitude are often the occasion for Yahweh's speaking to Israel's leaders and prophets. Moses is alone when he first receives God's call, and he spends forty days alone on

Mount Sinai at the time he receives the Torah.[1] Amos, like most of
the prophets, is an isolated figure, "a herdsman and a dresser of
sycamore trees" (Amos 7:14), when God reveals the powerful visions
that portend the fate of Israel.[2] Solitude is an important factor in the
prophets' marginal position in Israel, shaping their critical perspective and their sensitivity to injustices suffered by the less powerful
and by outsiders. Elijah's call narrative describes how, fleeing Ahab's
persecution, this prophet "went a day's journey into the wilderness,
and came and sat down under a solitary broom tree" (I Kings 19:4).
The lone tree under which Elijah sits when an angel appears symbolizes his own isolation. Later, still alone, Elijah perceives the Lord not
in the wind, an earthquake, or fire, but in "a sound of sheer silence"
(19:12). It is hard to hear the sound of silence in the presence of others.
Yahweh's call to form the community of Israel is often heard distinctly in a moment of solitude.

However, the prophet's solitude is a temporary state, and the condition of long-term isolation from other people is one viewed with
pity or horror in the Hebrew Bible and by most of later Jewish tradition. In the Creation account Yahweh makes a woman because "it is
not good that the man should be alone" (Genesis 2:18). Those who
do not observe the Torah, for instance by failing to observe the day of
atonement, are threatened with an isolation that is equivalent to
extinction: "For anyone who does not practice self-denial during
that entire day shall be cut off from the people" (Leviticus 23:29).
Ecclesiastes warns that solitude is dangerous: "For if they fall, one
will lift up the other; but woe to one who is alone and falls and does
not have another to help" (4:10). In many of the Psalms the speaker
laments his loneliness and sense of being an outcast from Israel, and
yearns for intimacy with God and restoration to his people. Solitude
is not in itself a desirable state in the scriptures, although suffering
the deprivation of human company sometimes helps a person to be
more attentive to God.

In the New Testament the example of John the Baptist was frequently invoked by later Christian tradition as a precedent for ascetic
practices and withdrawal from society. Jesus led an intensely social
life, but on several occasions the gospels show him withdrawing
from crowds and his disciples in order to rest or pray: "In the morning, while it was still very dark, he got up and went out to a deserted
place, and there he prayed" (Mark 1:35). He also retires to give his
disciples special teachings, telling them to "come away to a deserted
place all by yourselves and rest a while" (Mark 6:31). Jesus seeks
seclusion, but "when the crowds found out about it, they followed

him; and he welcomed them, and spoke to them about the Kingdom of God, and healed those who needed to be cured" (Luke 9:11). Such passages suggest a repeated pattern in Jesus's ministry of disengagement and return to society. However, solitude is never presented as a requirement for disciples or a central religious activity, much less as a way of life. Like the prophets, Jesus understands religious life as necessarily involved with other people, especially those on society's margins. Yet Jesus also resembles the prophets in his recourse to solitude in decisive moments such as his experience of temptations in the wilderness, the transfiguration scene, and the vigil at Gethsemane.

Neither the gospels nor the epistles consider solitude as a Christian way of life, although certain passages recommend solitude for a specific purpose. Jesus advises his disciples to pray alone to avoid hypocrisy: "Whenever you pray, go into your room and shut the door and pray to your Father in secret; and your Father who sees in secret will reward you" (Matthew 6:6). Jesus's approval of Mary, who sat at his feet to listen while Martha labored (Luke 10:38–41), was taken by Christian tradition as justification of a life of contemplation. The writer of the book of Revelation is clearly alone when he receives a series of visions, and Paul may have passed a number of years in relative isolation between his conversion experience and the beginning of his preaching (see Galatians 1:17–18).

In the first few centuries after Jesus's life certain individuals sought solitude as they fled from persecution by Romans or other Christian factions. Such solitude was endured but not cultivated for spiritual reasons. It was at the end of the third century in Egypt and Syria that solitude became a distinct commitment and spiritual path for Christians. It is no coincidence that this occurred soon after Christianity was recognized as the official religion of the Roman Empire following the conversion of Constantine in 312. One of the primary impulses behind the desire for solitude was the wish to withdraw from the temptations inherent in the increasing worldly success of the church. The early desert Christians believed that it was not possible to lead a fully Christian life in the social and economic world of the late Roman Empire. The meaning of the word hermit (from the Greek *erēmos*, desert) reflects the geographical location where solitude could best be found. Another term for the solitary, anchorite, is from the Greek verb *anachōrein*, which originally meant to evade taxes or military service by fleeing to a remote area. (During medieval times the term anchorite was reserved for solitaries who were permanently enclosed in cells attached to churches.) The first Christian hermits fled the cities for the desert wastes, hoping to recapture the spiritual commitment of the age of martyrs. They remembered the wilderness wanderings of Israel, the callings of the prophets, and the accounts of John the Baptist and Jesus in the wilderness. The desert was not a comfortable or safe place, not a pastoral retreat, but a place of harsh conditions where survival was difficult. Asceticism replaced martyrdom as the ultimate form of Christian commitment. The first solitaries practiced various forms of discipline, deprivation, and mortification of the body, and usually understood aloneness as a form of asceticism. A dedicated Christian needed only the divine presence, not food, sleep, shelter, possessions—or people.

This emphasis on self-denial could also express individuality and self-assertion, as early ascetics left the solidarity of the Catholic Church to find their own route to moral purity and to salvation. This paradox can be seen clearly in the account of the first influential Christian solitary, Antony of Egypt. Antony lived from approximately 250 to 356, spending most of his life as an ascetic in the Egyptian desert. His biography, written about 357 by Athanasius, established Antony as the father of Christian eremitism (solitary life) and asceticism. In the description of his call Antony is depicted as being inspired by the way of life of the Apostles in the Book of Acts, especially their renunciation of personal property, when he happens to hear the admonition of Matthew 19:21:

> As he was walking along, he collected his thoughts and reflected how the Apostles left everything and followed the Savior; and how the people in Acts sold what they had and laid it at the feet of the Apostles for distribution among the needy; and what great hope is laid up in Heaven for such as these. With these thoughts in his mind he entered the church. And it so happened that the Gospel was being read at that moment and he heard the passage in which the Lord says to the rich man: "If thou wilt be perfect, go sell all that thou hast, and give it to the poor; and come, follow me and thou shalt have treasure in Heaven." As though God had put him in mind of the saints and as though the reading had been directed especially to him, Antony immediately left the church and gave to the townspeople the property he had from his forebears.[3]

Antony took up a life of poverty and asceticism in the desert. He lived alone in an empty tomb for about fifteen years, and then withdrew to greater isolation in an old fort on the east bank of the Nile, where he remained for twenty years. His fame attracted many disciples who demanded to join him. Antony gave advice to these followers and made visits to other hermits, and the loose community that developed around him is usually seen as the first Christian monastery.

This way of life combined the solitary path and communal living: "So, then, their solitary cells in the hills were like tents filled with divine choirs—singing Psalms, studying, fasting, praying, rejoicing in the hope of the life to come, and laboring in order to give alms and preserving love and harmony among themselves. And truly it was like seeing a land apart, a land of piety and justice. For there was neither wrongdoer nor sufferer of wrong, nor was there reproof of the tax-collector; but a multitude of ascetics, all with one set purpose— virtue."[4] In this description of early monastic life the ideal of solitude is seen as not only compatible with, but contributing to, a community embodying justice.

Much of Antony's biography describes his conflicts with demons who tempt him with various pleasures or threaten him with harm. Military and athletic metaphors characterize his contests with these devils. Antony's victories represent heroic accomplishments, a new kind of martyrdom for an age when it was no longer necessary to be ready to die for one's faith at any moment. Athanasius presents Antony as "a daily martyr to his conscience, ever fighting the battles of the faith."[5] When Antony's devils are viewed as symbols of the desires and preoccupations that can dominate a person's attention and prevent a spiritual life, they become meaningful for contemporary readers.

Although Antony responds to the needs of others, he yearns for undisturbed solitude and greater concentration on the spirit's needs. He is portrayed as being ashamed when he must eat or sleep, for bodily needs distract him from a proper focus on God. Antony eats with other people with some ambivalence, "embarrassed because of them, yet speaking freely because of the help his words gave them. He used to say that one should give all one's time to the soul rather than to the body."[6] Solitude is desirable for this ascetic partly because he is ashamed when others see that his body's needs must be met. For Antony solitude provides the conditions for pursuing certain spiritual ends, and it is chosen partly because of concern with how others see him.

The links between solitude and the ascetic impulse raise many questions. Is solitude simply the setting for ascetic practice, or is it itself an expression of asceticism? Should solitude be understood as essentially a matter of deprivation and self-denial? Does it express a negative view of human relationships? Or is the real enemy not other people, but one's own preoccupation with them, one's need to have their approval? In my view, if solitude expresses a negative view of the material world and of the embodied and social nature of human existence, it seems not only unhealthy but a denial of essential components of Christian spirituality. In contrast, if we see Antony as trying to free his spirit from being chained to that which cannot bring true fulfillment, and from preoccupation with how he appeared to others, he has some permanently valuable insights about how ascetic discipline can enhance life.[7] As we explore autobiographical accounts of solitude, we should ask how the authors understand these issues, in particular the question of whether solitude is sought as an escape from social evils or the setting best enabling some people to pursue specific positive values.

There is a tension in the early hermits' attitude to the church. On the one hand, Antony was involved in theological controversies and ecclesiastical politics, and his pastoral concern for those who followed him into the desert led him to establish and direct a monastic community. Yet Antony obviously found both the urban and village environments of the early church incompatible with his conception of a life devoted to God. He was able to dispense with many elements of Christian life which seem inextricable from the church: celebration of the Eucharist and other sacraments, communal worship, and concern about the impact of the Christian faith on the broad course of history. For a hermit such as Antony, solitude represented both an attempt to deny the self's needs in order to better hear God's voice, and also an assertion of individual destiny and identity. Even if the religious truths the solitary realized were believed to be common to all humans, he or she came to these truths in a unique personal way. In their search for a personal religious path, the anchorites and recluses of the early Christian world were the ancestors of those in the contemporary world who want both to be grounded in Christian tradition and to search for spiritual insights growing out of individual character and experience.

The early monks' and desert fathers' most negative statements about human relationships are quite misanthropic. Their more tempered view is that secular society is not inherently evil, but simply less good than the ideal of total religious dedication to God. The first Christian solitaries shared an ideal of total commitment to God, which for them meant radical disavowal of anything that could distract them from God. Human society was sometimes seen primarily as a place of evil temptations involving wealth, sexuality, and power. Ordinary social life served as a foil against which the beauty of the spiritual life could be set off. The desert fathers believed that the false claims of ultimacy made by social institutions must be shattered. Because insistent demands from other people can make a person neglect spiritual practices, the advocates of solitude often make extremely harsh judgments about social existence. But the desert fathers speak very powerfully about the importance of human communion and fellowship, once an active spiritual life has set social relationships within the right order of priorities.

Christian tradition contains many points of view on solitude. If one views the essence of Christian life as prayer, then solitude may be idealized as the state in which a person may most completely fill his or her life with prayer. Critics of solitude, however, seize upon hermits' most antisocial statements as evidence of their inconsistency with basic tenets of Christian faith. From the early centuries until today, Christian opponents of solitude assert that since the essence of Christian life is love of the neighbor, a hermit turns his back on a crucial duty and joy of a life grounded in faith. Basil of Caesarea (329–79) was one of the most outspoken opponents of Christians living a solitary life. Basil made two main criticisms of solitude that recur through the ages. A Christian needs other people to protect him from the dangers of pride and self-delusion by pointing out error. And the Christian life necessarily demands communion with and service of the neighbor, concrete opportunites to practice the law of love. Although Basil lived as a hermit himself for some time, when he wrote an influential Rule for monastics he argued that the solitary life was distinctly inferior to the cenobitic (communal) form of monasticism.

Between the extreme views, the main stream of Christian tradition discerns a combination of benefits and dangers in solitude. The early hermits soon discovered their need of each other for practical necessities and religious guidance. Colonies of hermits, sometimes called sketes or lauras, developed, where periods of solitude alternated with communal worship, conferences, and shared labor. In the evolution of Western monasticism eremitical isolation became rarer.[8] Most of the monastic tradition (with some exceptions to be noted) basically affirms cenobitical existence as normative, and acknowledges solitude as a valuable if minor part of a Christian life. When cenobitical monasticism became the norm, the monk (from Greek *monos*, alone) became the model not of solitary life but of the ideal of fellowship and communal religious living.

Yet solitary life continued to be valued by some monastics, and was even idealized as the highest calling. Often the abbot of a monastery became a hermit when he retired from his administrative duties.

According to Saint Benedict's Rule, the solitary life is so difficult that it must be prepared for by many years of living in the discipline of a group: "The second kind [of monks] are the Anchorites or Hermits: those who, no longer in the first fervor of their reformation, but after long probation in a monastery, having learned by the help of many brethren how to fight against the devil, go out well armed from the ranks of the community to the solitary combat of the desert. They are able now, with no help save from God, to fight single-handed against the vices of the flesh and their own evil thoughts."[9] This brief remark implies that the solitary life is a hard and dangerous one for the inexperienced, but a very high calling and even the final goal of the Christian monk's life. Benedict offers no specific guidance, however, as to the steps a monk would take to become a hermit, and his Rule envisages the common life as the normal one for monks until death.

Communal forms of monasticism integrate some of the concerns of hermits, for instance through the use of silence. Benedict praises "the spirit of silence" and sees it as essential to monastic virtue: "Since the spirit of silence is so important, permission to speak should rarely be granted even to perfect disciples, even though it be for good, holy, edifying conversation; for it is written, 'In much speaking you will not escape sin,' and in another place, 'Death and life are in the power of the tongue.'"[10] Communal silence integrates into communal life the solitary's wariness about gossip, distraction, and idle conversation. Silence should be kept at many meals while monks concentrate on a reading. "Monks ought to be zealous for silence at all times, but especially during the hours of the night."[11] Later religious groups such as the Quakers have also found that collective silence can be a powerful religious occasion that combines aspects of solitary and communal experience.

The most significant early Christian thinking about solitude, the writings of the desert fathers, balances appreciative and critical views of solitude. The wisdom of these early solitaries and originators of communal life is collected in anthologies organized by topic or by author, known as "sayings of the fathers" (Apophthegmata Patrum).[12] These aphorisms and anecdotes do not yield a consistent philosophy of solitude but rather a great deal of practical wisdom and insight into the various roles that aloneness plays in different human lives. The abbas (fathers) and ammas (mothers) of early Christian tradition make statements about solitude that often appear contradictory. Since each statement is a response to a particular occasion, we must understand the situation in which the remark was made and avoid taking any one statement as the definitive view of solitude. Solitude may be healthy or harmful to a person depending on many things. The desert fathers are interested in what experiences of solitude reveal about a person, both for better and for worse. They assess particular instances of solitude flexibly, according to a range of values and concerns.

Sometimes the abbas praise solitude as the best route to intimacy with God: "Abba Alonius said, 'If a man does not say in his heart, in the world there is only myself and God, he will not gain peace.'" Abba Arsenius, asked for "a word" about solitude, responds in this way: "As long as a young girl is living in her father's house, many young men wish to marry her, but when she has taken a husband, she is no longer pleasing to everyone; despised by some, approved by others, she no longer enjoys the favour of former times, when she lived a hidden life. So it is with the soul; from the day when it is shown to everyone, it is no longer able to satisfy everyone." A critical attitude toward the power of the established church is revealed in an anecdote about Abba Apphy, who when he became a bishop lacked the strength to practice his former austerities as a monk. In prayer he asked whether he had lost God's grace, and was given this revelation: "No, but when you were in solitude and there was no one else it was God who was your helper. Now that you are in the world, it is man."[13] Many elders saw sitting in one's cell for long periods as the foundation of the disciplines of monastic practice and an essential condition for knowing oneself and encountering God.

Juxtaposed with these approving views of solitude are warnings about the proper understanding of aloneness necessary for it to be spiritually fruitful. Three stories each make an important point about the conditions in which solitude brings one closer to God. Abba Theodore addresses a hermit who thinks aloneness should bring tranquillity:

A brother lived in the Cells and in his solitude he was troubled. He went to tell Abba Theodore of Pherme about it. The old man said to him, "Go, be more humble in your aspirations, place yourself under obedience and live with others." Later, he came back to the old man and said, "I do not find any peace with others." The old man said to him, "If you are not at peace either alone or with others, why have you become a monk? Is it not to suffer trials? Tell me how many years you have worn the habit?" He replied, "For eight years." Then the old man said to him, "I have worn the habit seventy years and on no day have I found peace. Do you expect to obtain peace in eight years?" At these words the brother went away strengthened.[14]

According to Abba Theodore, solitary life is not an escape from the trials of life, but a different kind of struggle than the social one, and serenity is not its likely outcome. Theodore's acknowledgment of his own troubles has a consoling effect on the inquiring brother, who goes away "strengthened."

Another story suggests that the same virtues cultivated in solitude may be learned and practiced with one's fellows:

> One day Abba Longinus questioned Abba Lucius about three thoughts saying first, "I want to go into exile." The old man said to him, "If you cannot control your tongue, you will not be an exile anywhere. There-fore control your tongue here, and you will be an exile." Next he said to him, "I wish to fast." The old man replied, "Isaiah said, 'If you bend your neck like a rope or a bulrush that is not the fast I will accept; but rather, control your evil thoughts.'" (cf. Isaiah 58) He said to him the third time, "I wish to flee from men." The old man replied, "If you have not first of all lived rightly with men, you will not be able to live rightly in solitude."[15]

Controlling one's tongue and one's thoughts, the crucial virtues for Lucius, may best be practiced in the company of others. This is the usual contention of Christian critics of solitude: whatever virtues a solitary aspires to can be better learned in community life. Patience, self-control, humility, and compassion are all required for living in close proximity to others. The conclusion of this story resembles Benedict's view that solitude is a worthy pursuit that a person must prepare for by years of living in community.

A final story at first makes a contradictory point, advising a monk with an acerbic tongue to flee his fellows:

> A brother questioned Abba Matoes saying "What am I to do? My tongue makes me suffer, and every time I go among men, I cannot control it, but I condemn them in all the good they are doing and reproach them with it. What am I to do?" The old man replied, "If you cannot contain yourself, flee into solitude. For this is a sickness. He who dwells with brethren must not be square, but round, so as to turn himself towards all." He went on, "It is not through virtue that I live in solitude, but through weakness; those who live in the midst of men are the strong ones."[16]

Abba Matoes's counsel shares the emphasis of the other stories on the need for humility, warning a would-be hermit against the spiritual pride sometimes carried into the desert by those who would turn away from the vices and conflicts of social existence. In this story solitude seems a flight from problems that it would be better to overcome in the company of others; aloneness does not seem a positive end in itself but a less than ideal means of coping with weakness.

One scholar of the desert fathers holds that solitude and interaction were not seen as a dichotomy but as equally important aspects of Christian living: "Perfection is not found in alternating between complete solitude and the life of a community . . . and attaining perfection in each successively, but in combining a search for austerity and loneliness in the desert with free, gracious, and uncomplaining acceptance of disturbance, and of the responsibilities of teaching and entertaining others."[17] Most of the abbas' comments about the dangers of contact with other people are not inherently antisocial, but primarily concerned with the threats interaction may pose to ascetic practice. For example, the fathers frequently discuss the proper attitude of an ascetic toward the *agape* (common meal) and toward offering and receiving hospitality. When a monk did choose to flee other people, it reflected his inability to live with them and was often intended to protect them from his harmful influence, especially the sins of the tongue. Solitary monks were warned to overcome their ill will or hostility to others, particularly those who interrupt them. They required the continuing instruction and guidance of an elder, who usually directed them to seek reconciliation with anyone with whom conflict had driven them into solitude. In short, "the solitude of the cell and interaction with others through the *agape*, hospitality, and the other opportunities which were available for the pursuit of good relationships, were two aspects of a single, varied pattern of semi-anchoritic life."[18] The desert fathers praised "sitting in the cell" alone in order to confront temptations and learn reliance on God, but they were equally concerned with the value of relationships.

Just as important as specific advice in the stories about the desert fathers is the way each anecdote dramatizes an interaction between two monks, as an aspiring solitary seeks counsel, is instructed, and goes away strengthened by the wisdom of an abba. The narrative form of these stories shows a wisdom earned in both solitary meditation and social experience, and made fruitful in a concrete human encounter. The understanding of solitude that emerges in the writings of the desert fathers portrays the value of periods of aloneness for certain individuals but always sets these within the context of life with others.

Not only in the larger world of monasticism, but even within eremitical traditions, hermits were urged to identify with other persons and to be ever mindful of the whole church. Evagrius of Pontus (d. 399) formulated memorably the ideal of the hermit as being both "separated from all and united to all."[19] Peter Damien, an eleventh-century Italian hermit who became a bishop, wrote a famous response to a hermit who asked him whether a priest celebrating Eucharist alone should include the customary greeting "The Lord be with you." Peter said a hermit must say these words not only because they are an established part of the liturgy, but because they express the reality that the hermit is always with others in spirit. The anchorite's aloneness is a *"solitudo pluralis,"* a community or corporate solitude in which the whole church is symbolically present.[20] The written and oral traditions with which spiritual directors guided Christian solitaries have offered frequent reminders that a hermit must remain in spiritual communion with other human beings even when not with them physically.

In summary, we see at the origins of the Christian eremitical tradition a number of distinct spiritual impulses and tensions. Solitude was a protest against the ease of living as a Christian in a society where this religion was not merely tolerated, but rapidly becoming a means to worldly success. The desert fathers' lives of solitude were closely linked to ascetic practices, radical poverty, manual labor, and constant prayer. Solitude expressed the desire for intimacy with God, for a closer personal relationship with the divine than some individuals could find in the rituals of the church, the study of sacred books, or the busy activities of local congregations. At the same time as hermits sought to transcend worldly cares through radical self-denial, however, solitary life afforded opportunities for individual achievement and heroic renown. Appreciation of the dangers of isolation led the desert fathers and the mainstream of the monastic tradition to balance praise of solitude with cautionary warnings, and to contain periods of aloneness within a life that was primarily communal.

The Social Significance of Christian Solitude

One paradox of solitude is that this apparently antisocial state often has great significance for those who would never dream of spending their lives alone. Like the modern figure of the anarchist, the hermit proposes no practicable order for society. Yet his ideals may affect his contemporaries' view of their society, if only by making them dissatisfied with present arrangements. And in a number of ways solitude has influenced the institutions and corporate life of Christendom. Consideration of the social significance of Christian solitude will prepare us to consider the ways that autobiographers have seen their aloneness as having meaning for others.

Eremitical ideals have inspired certain monastic orders, such as the Carthusians, the Carmelites, the Hermits of Saint Augustine, and many smaller orders. These monastic foundations often began as small hermitages sited around a cloister, or as clusters of hermits who met for common worship. But the tendency toward growth and greater organization always threatened the original purpose of silence and obscurity. Just as Antony's fame drew disciples to form a community around him in the Egyptian desert, so the very success of a hermit or colony of hermits in living a devout life, should it become known, makes the solitary life harder to realize. Thus arises a repeated pattern in the history of Christian monasticism whereby eremitical groups are absorbed into the church establishment, producing a new incentive for hermits to disengage from increasing social complexity and conflict. The ideals of the solitary thus contribute to one of the ongoing rhythms of renewal in the life of the church.

The positive ideals of solitary religious life have often been an example for the larger church. The daily life of most Christian recluses and hermits focuses on prayer, reciting the daily office, and cultivating a sense of God's intimate presence. Some solitaries stress the centrality of ascetic life, usually understanding practices of mortification as sharing in Christ's suffering or as penance for their own and others' sins. For many hermits aloneness has been a necessary condition for the contemplative life, providing the interior peace and detachment for meditation and encounter with God. This is especially emphasized in Eastern Orthodox churches in the tradition of hesychasm, the cultivation of inner peace. When the goal of spiritual perfection is conceived in terms of the practice of certain virtues, solitude provides the setting in which one can avoid the vices associated with social life and cultivate the dispositions proper to a good Christian.

Protestants have usually disdained extended periods of solitude as a valuable spiritual practice, associating it with monasticism. Yet the appeal of solitude resembles one of Protestantism's central motifs: the desire to recreate the perfection of Christian life of the Gospels and the early church, before worldly establishment and success brought dilution and distraction from the essentials of faith. Solitude has been a recourse for all sorts of Christians wanting to recapture the original fervor and dedicated commitment of the apostles, and has been necessary for those labeled heretics and forced to flee persecution. Enforced isolation has been the crucial setting for many prison writings by Christian dissenters, such as John Bunyan's *Grace Abounding to the Chief of Sinners.* And some Protestants have found solace in periods of aloneness used for Bible reading, prayer, and the examination of conscience. Jonathan Edwards practiced solitary reading and study, devotional seclusion, and mental imaging of the self before God, drawing on the piety and theology of his New England Puritan heritage.[21]

Although Christians usually describe total devotion to God as the rationale and justification for solitude, writings by or legends about hermits often reveal other concerns that become central for later autobiographers including secular solitaries. For example, hermits are often keenly attuned to the natural world, to animals and plants and patterns of weather, and appreciative of the ways these things may have meaning for an individual. Except for a few wandering hermits, most of them could only preserve their solitude by remaining in one sheltered location. Their sense of place—their intimate knowledge, appreciation, and commitment to one locale—resembles one goal of the monastic vow of stability. In a society with increasing mobility and incessant restlessness, the hermit focuses on the movement and homing of the spirit.

Hermits usually lived in deserts or mountainous areas, and came to love the healing power of the wilderness. The silence, indifference, and rugged beauty of these harsh landscapes taught important truths about the Christian *via negativa,* the mystical tradition of seeking God by denial, in the stillness and emptiness beyond language and familiar images. Belden Lane analyzes the Christian tradition of seeking God in wild terrain and the paradoxical ways that unpopulated and inaccessible places, which seem so unfriendly to humans, can release a person from anxious striving, obsession with managing other people's opinions, and the endless clutter of inessential details.[22] This Christian tradition of wilderness sojourn includes many lovers of solitude who prefigure the modern varieties of solitary experience I will describe in chapter 6, as they sought healing, attunement to nature, encounter with wilderness, and recovery of hidden springs of vitality and creativity. Like Thomas Merton, whose Christian understanding of aloneness I analyze in chapter 7, the desert solitaries are also concerned with the return to community, as a sojourn in the wilderness reorients a Christian's identity and language and leads to renewed engagement with other people.

A Christian hermit usually had to work very hard. Although many hermits were affiliated with and supported by a nearby monastery or church, and some even had wealthy patrons, most solitaries voluntarily embraced a life of poverty, manual labor, and simplicity. The solitary life involves work, whether copying manuscripts, weaving mats, or gardening. Hermits usually advocate and praise the virtues of poverty. Both values, labor and poverty, were often protests against the laxness of current monastic practice. Hermits and recluses presented a silent challenge to other Christians to return to a simpler and more apostolic way of life.

The revival of eremitism during the eleventh and twelfth centuries illustrates how solitude is inextricably related to ethical issues. At this time hermits inspired the foundation of over fifty new monastic orders, including those at Grandmont, Grande Chartreuse, and Premontre in France, and at Camaldoli, Vallombrosa, and Fonte Avellana in Italy.[23] These semi-eremitical orders, like many hermits of this period, criticized the powerful Cluniac monasteries, with their elaborate performance of the liturgy, fine architecture, and involvement in European political affairs. The revival of solitary life during this period stressed poverty, asceticism, and manual labor at a time when a monetary expansion was changing the economy of Europe and tempting the church with avarice and simony (the selling of church offices). The emergence and success of the Cistercian order, which emphasized manual work, a more austere life, and greater separation from ordinary society, is partly attributable to the influence of eremitical ideals.

Solitaries influenced the larger monastic movement in several ways. From the early centuries, communal living began to displace the hermit's way of life as the central stream of monasticism, especially in Western Christianity. Yet monastic communities as whole entities aspired to the ideals of seclusion, contemplation, and austerity exemplified by hermits. Eremitical ideals were embodied in a monastic group's corporate solitude, its detachment from society. Solitude for such Christians did not mean being without fellow monks, but being separate from secular society. In this way some of the ideals of solitude were preserved, but integrated with the values of community living and service. Many historic and contemporary discussions of the essential meaning of monasticism resemble debates about the eremitical life, insofar as they address the inherent tension between two spiritual motivations of the monastic life: the impulse to withdraw from the secular world and the impulse to serve the world.[24]

Some monasteries kept alive the unique experiences and perspective of the solitary by establishing cells for hermits outside their walls. This was done partly in order to make possible the pattern suggested by Benedict, whereby training in community disciplines built up a monk's character and inner strength to undertake the demanding rigors of solitude. An eremitical life was not only envisioned as the state of perfection one might achieve at the end of cenobitic training; fluid cycles of solitary and communal living were allowed for by many monasteries, especially in Eastern Orthodox Christendom:

> In the practice of the Orthodox Church, no sharp line of demarcation is made between the solitary and the communal life. A hermit may be settled on the edge of an organized community—either a coenobium or a skete—returning to live in it for longer or shorter periods, and then going back into solitude. The degree of silence, enclosure and isolation varies greatly in the case of different solitaries, or at different periods in the same man's life. Such matters cannot and should not be made the subject of detailed legislation; freedom must be left to the conscience of the individual, guided by the Holy Spirit and by his spiritual father.[25]

Thus in much of monastic tradition there was no sharp either/or choice between solitude and living with others, but a varied practice shaped by awareness of individual needs and the relative advantages and disadvantages of various amounts of contact with others.

In Western canon law the life of hermits has been regulated more closely than in the Eastern Church, and numerous eremitic rules prescribe the structure and practices of such a life. Yet spiritual life has a way of eluding legislation, and solitude has always beckoned certain individuals to find new meaning in this experience. The lives of many Christian saints have been marked by cycles of solitary contemplation and public action. Martin, bishop of Tours (316–97) alternated between the exercise of his ecclesiastical office and protracted periods of solitude. Francis of Assisi (1182–1226) made many solitary vigils and wrote a rule for hermits. He established primitive settlements where he and his followers could retire for rest and prayer, places that became Franciscan hermitages. Ignatius of Loyola spent most of a year (1522) in Manresa, Spain, in solitary prayer and fasting, emerging from this experience with inspiring visions and a set of guided spiritual exercises that others could systematically practice.

Loyola's book, the *Spiritual Exercises,* became the basis of spiritual discipline for the Society of Jesus, the order of priests that he founded. This is one of the most important developments in the history of Christian solitude, for it authorized and institutionalized the practice of making a spiritual retreat. A retreat is a limited period of temporary isolation in order to withdraw from normal social interactions into silence, meditation, and prayer.[26] The ideal of a spiritual retreat made a short period of solitude possible and desirable first for non-monastic priests, and then for any Christian. Loyola's new order was not devoted to traditional monastic practices such as asceticism, special dress, and lengthy chanting of the daily hours of the divine office. Rather, the Jesuits focused on loving service of the community. In preparing for this service, Loyola saw the value of short, intensive periods of introspection and concentration under the guidance of a spiritual director. Loyola's method is different from some kinds of Christian solitude in that the experience of aloneness is under the close supervision of a spiritual director, and the retreat is highly structured, with an expectation that the individual will move through a prescribed series of insights growing out of meditations and visualizations of Christ's life, death, and resurrection. Loyola formulated a plan of solitude as not a permanent occupation but a regularly repeated experience that could be integrated into the life of any Christian.

The tradition of making a retreat is an important part of Roman Catholic spiritual practice. Lent functions as an annual retreat to solitude for some monastic orders, as contact with outsiders is interrupted and mundane interactions minimized. Lent can be a forty-day retreat into solitude to identify with Jesus's withdrawal into the wilderness and his Passion. Spiritual retreats are expected of priests in the Catholic Church, and many lay Catholics make a retreat for a certain number of days a year. In the practice of spiritual retreats, then, the ideals of solitude are made accessible to all Christians. Unfortunately, for many contemporary Christians, especially Protestants, solitude is seen only as an odd pursuit of eccentrics or as an antiquated "monkish virtue." And those who do make retreats often find it difficult to integrate their insights into these experiences with the return to ordinary life.

The spiritual meaning of Christian solitude is not simply a matter of the motivations of hermits but also involves how these individuals were supported by a cultural context and a web of social relationships. Solitaries depend on other people both for the physical necessities of existence and for recognition and confirmation of their social role as solitaries. Hermits are strengthened to persist when they believe they provide something valued by their contemporaries. Many hermits fulfilled such social functions as counseling, reconciling, settling political conflicts, and teaching. They conceived of their prayers as intercessory for their contemporaries, and of their lives as exemplary of repentance and virtue. Two specific examples will illustrate ways that solitude has been significant for a historic Christian community.

In Palestine, Syria, and Asia Minor during the late Roman Empire and early Byzantine period, the role of the holy individual was crucial in the organization of society. The holy man's power, both religious and social, was closely associated with his solitude. The ascetic mortifications of the holy man or woman may be understood, according to Peter Brown, as "a long drawn-out, solemn ritual of dissociation" making the solitary a stranger and outsider to his society.[27] A position outside society allowed such a person to function as judge, intermediary, and spokesman for God. Symeon Stylites, who spent the last thirty-seven years of his life on top of a pillar in Syria, is the most notable example of a widespread pattern. Living on top of a sixty-foot column seems the epitome of withdrawal from society. Yet Symeon's pillar was often surrounded by adoring crowds. He adjudicated village quarrels, defended the economic interests of rural peasants, and advised powerful churchmen and political leaders, including the Emperor Theodosius II, who would put up a ladder so that they could consult with him. The holy man's detachment from society served a social need: "For the society around him, the holy man is the one man who can stand outside the ties of family, and of economic interest; whose attitude to food itself rejected all the ties of solidarity to kin and village that, in the peasant societies of the Near East, had always been expressed by the gesture of eating. He was thought of as a man who owed nothing to society. . . . Perched on his column, nearer to the demons of the upper air than to human beings, Symeon was objectivity personified."[28] The holy men of late antiquity had such influence partly because of the erosion of Roman institutions that had administered justice, as well as because of waning faith in non-Christian wonder-workers and oracles. Brown holds that the holy man usurped the position of the oracle in the ancient world as "the bearer of objectivity in society." Holy men had this role until they were eclipsed by new institutions that commanded respect and reverence: Benedictine monasteries, the ecclesiastical hierarchy, and the tombs of the saints.

The pattern that Brown traces illustrates a larger truth about solitude. The fortitude of Christian hermits through the centuries has been sustained, and their energies harnessed to quite practical social purposes, because particular societies have found value in the position of those who live on its margins. Individuals may seek solitude because their society does not satisfy their spiritual needs, but they often persist in solitude because they feel supported by a community, and their insights and experiences are recognized as contributing something other people need. Paradoxically, a position outside normal social obligations and ties can become an established social role. Solitude is a liminal (boundary or threshold) position on the edge of social positions defined by law, convention, and morality. Such a status is often threatening to established conventions, for it calls into question their necessity. Yet solitaries are also celebrated because of their proximity to what transcends the limitations and definitions of a society: the holy. The marginal position of a solitary in relation to society is at once the reason for the ambivalence with which he or she is regarded, and the basis of the solitary's role as a potential mediator of the sacred.

The example of the ancient holy men also reveals the great sociability that is encompassed by what particular cultures define as solitude: "The lonely cells of the recluses of Egypt have been revealed, by the archeologist, to have had well-furnished consulting-rooms."[29] Hermits often allow themselves a very active engagement with other persons. Our search for exemplars of solitude through the ages must accommodate such interactions as part of the meaning of aloneness. Solitude is socially constructed, imagined by hermits and supported by others in the light of particular cultural and religious values.

A second example of solitude's social significance is the role of urban recluses in medieval Europe. Usually called anchorites, these solitaries walled themselves into small cells attached to a church. The fourteenth-century mystic Julian of Norwich was one of at least fifty known recluses in that city. Anchorites were also known as *inclusi* (meaning "enclosed"). Most of those who were enclosed were women, partly because of the greater protection provided by this form of solitude. The choice of solitude was one of the few ways that a woman in medieval Europe could have a significant degree of independence from male authority. For instance, in the twelfth century Christina of Markyate, who was being forced into marriage by her parents, was helped to run away and become a recluse by a network of hermits. Another factor in the frequency of enclosures was the expansion of agriculture and towns all over Europe, and the corresponding decrease of locations providing sufficient remoteness from human intrusion. (In medieval Europe mountainous regions replaced the desert as the favored geographical locale for those seeking physical isolation.)

A medieval urban recluse lived a very public sort of solitude, supposedly withdrawn from normal life but in fact constantly interacting with it. The goal of the solitary was to become "dead to the world," and the ceremony for enclosing her in a cell resembled a burial service. Ashes were sprinkled over the cell, symbolically making it a grave. The locked door was sealed or bricked up so that there was no exit. Such an extreme of solitude may seem incomprehensible to the modern sensibility, a morbid denial of the value of other human beings and of ordinary social life. Yet the inclusi were deeply involved with those around them and conscious of their role as a model of piety. A glimpse into the meaning of this form of solitary life is provided by the *Ancrene Wisse,* a work of instruction written around 1215–22 by an unknown English cleric for three young anchoresses. Linda Georgianna's study of this rule interprets the variety of human relationships in which an anchoress was involved and the social significance of this highly public solitude. The anchoress's intercessory prayers and struggles with the devil offered crucial religious services to the community. The author of the *Ancrene Wisse* tells each young woman that she is a model of sanctity for all Christians and a support for the whole church. The author takes the word "anchorite" to mean, according to its popular usage, that this calling provides an "anchor" for the whole church: "It is for this reason that an anchoress is called an anchoress, and anchored under a church like an anchor under the side of a ship, to hold it, so that the waves and storms do not pitch it over. So all Holy Church, which is called a ship, shall be anchored to the anchoress, and she shall hold it secure so that the puffings and blowings of the devil, that is, temptations, do not pitch it over."[30] Belief in her vital role as an anchor for the whole church must have sustained such a recluse through many a lonely period.

The cells of the English anchoresses each had three windows: one that faced inward toward the altar of the church, one into the parlor of the church, and one outward toward the town. Church services could be seen and heard; men and women called and delivered meals at the parlor window; and the bustle and commercial activity of the town constantly beckoned. According to Georgianna, the author of the *Ancrene Wisse* does not focus on the walls of the cell but rather on the windows, the enclosed one's point of connection with her religious and social world. The text's detailed instructions about proper conversation, the right attitude to the world, and such mundane matters as care of animals and pets, all reveal an astute consciousness of how inescapably an anchoress remains involved in the ordinary affairs of the world. She is not dead, nor buried alive, but still very much attracted to the world, and her attachments constantly tempt her to sin. The *Wisse* author urges frequent confession and turning one's heart toward God. According to this interpretation of the solitary life, "to become 'hidden' can no longer be considered to be the final goal of the solitary. She has entered the anchorhold not to escape the world, but to transform what could be her doom into her joy."[31] The solitary's task is not to flee the world but to provide a model of how a Christian conscience can recognize sin and be moved to repentance and a new kind of love for the world in the light of God's love. The medieval anchoresses enclosed in their cells are a fascinating example of how an individual's commitment to solitude may be spiritually significant for other people.

Christian societies need, sustain, and value solitaries. I think that every human society creates niches where solitude can be practiced. At the same time, solitaries are often criticized or dismissed as failures, cowards, or irresponsible eccentrics. In recent centuries it has become increasingly difficult to find a social validation for solitude. In later chapters I will look at the emergence of "secular solitaries" who assert at once their need for aloneness and the difficulty of actually practicing it in the modern world, given the disdain with which solitaries are viewed. The personal narratives of these solitaries often explain the ethical justification and affirm the spiritual value of solitude. First, however, I examine the most important Christian autobiography, the *Confessions* of Augustine, who was the first to link solitude, spirituality, and autobiographical writing.

2

BOUNDED SOLITUDE IN
AUGUSTINE'S *CONFESSIONS*

THERE ARE several relationships between solitude and spirituality in the text most scholars consider to be the first autobiography, Augustine's *Confessions*. Part of solitude's appeal to Augustine grows out of his awareness of how many of his sins were prompted by his intense desire to please other people. The most famous example of this is his analysis of how and why he and "a gang of accomplices" destroyed some pears in an orchard.[1] Augustine speaks of "the thrill of having partners in crime" and discerns how the company of friends enticed him to do something that he would never have done on his own: "This was friendship of a most unfriendly sort, bewitching my mind in an inexplicable way. . . . And all because we are ashamed to hold back when others say 'Come on! Let's do it!'" (2.9). A second form of sin related to his social interactions concerns Augustine's teaching career. A recurring topic for Augustine in discussing his twelve years of teaching rhetoric is the ways one may compromise the truth or entirely neglect considerations of substance in order to present a subject matter to other people in a pleasing way. He refers to himself as "a vendor of words" (9.5), to his teaching position as "the chair of lies" (9.2), and to his school as a "market where I sold the services of my tongue" (9.2). Augustine's revulsion from his teaching career reflects his remorse that for many years he gave priority to the arts of persuasion instead of the pursuit of truth. A third form of sin that reflects excessive attachment to other people is Augustine's guilty feelings about his sexual life, for instance his taking a second mistress after abandoning a first, the mother of his son. Recognizing how often his own sins grew out of inordinate attachment to other people impels Augustine to seek solitude as a refuge from further temptations.

Augustine also saw solitude in positive terms as a state of total commitment to God. This idealism is reflected in his fervent admiration of the first Christian hermits. In Augustine's account of the events that culminated in his conversion he explains how a man named Ponticianus told him the story of Saint Antony and his heroic asceticism in the deserts of Egypt. Ponticianus recounts how two of his friends were "filled with the love of holiness" (8.6) and instantly converted upon reading the life of Antony. Deeply moved by this story, Augustine is ashamed of his procrastination in committing himself to the Christian faith. Alone with his conscience when Ponticianus leaves, Augustine struggles to emulate the heroes of the narratives he has just heard: "I was overcome by burning shame, and when he had finished his tale and completed the business for which he had come, he went away and I was left to my own thoughts. I made all sorts of accusations against myself. I cudgelled my soul and belaboured it with reasons why it should follow me now that I was trying so hard to follow you. But it fought back" (8.7).

What Augustine desired was not exactly the same thing that Antony sought in the solitude of the desert. He admired Antony's dedication, but did not aspire to emulate his solitude. Augustine had a pronounced ascetic side, as revealed in his determination to take a vow of chastity when he committed himself to God. But his conception of the monastic life and of the place of solitude within it are quite different from what these are in the context of Antony's asceticism. Augustine would never choose solitude at the expense of community. Antony's story appeals to him as an account of "groups of monks in the monasteries, of their way of life that savours of your sweetness, and of the fruitful wastes of the desert" (8.6). He is equally drawn to a monastery at Milan led by Ambrose. Solitude seems an incidental part of Antony's appeal to Augustine, an example of dedication to God but not necessary or even desirable for every Christian.

Augustine's view of solitude must be considered in the context of his ideal of the Christian life in the years leading up to the writing of the *Confessions*. When he was on the brink of conversion, living in Milan in the year 386, Augustine proposed to establish a community of like-minded men who would devote themselves to prayer and study (6.14). After he went back to North Africa as a Christian, he established a monastic community at Tagaste during the years 388–91. In 391 he was pressed into service as a priest, contrary to his desire to live a contemplative life with his friends. Augustine wept through

the ordination ceremony. As a priest and bishop in Hippo, he continued to live as a monk in the community he had established there. In
these early Christian communities, Augustine lived and wrote
about the ideal Christian life at a time when the meaning of monasticism was just being formulated and was not clearly distinct from
other vocations such as asceticism and the priesthood.[2]

Certain aspects of Augustine's ideal religious life were incompatible with solitude. For the early desert fathers, wisdom had little to do
with formal study. Antony responds to those who criticized his lack
of schooling by asking "Which is first, the mind or letters? . . . One
who has a sound mind has no need of letters."[3] In contrast, a love of
learning was an essential part of Augustine's conception of Christian
life, and sharing one's learning with other people was a crucial part
of this ideal. Furthermore, Augustine was strongly attracted to the
vision of communal living and shared ownership of property suggested in Acts 4:32: "Now the whole group of those who believed
were of one heart and soul, and no one claimed private ownership of
any possessions, but everything they owned was held in common"
(NRSV). Later in his life Augustine wrote a letter to nuns which was
influential in establishing the communal form rather than the eremitical one as the primary strain of monasticism. The so-called Rule
of Saint Augustine stresses the ideal of a community of love and the
duty of a Christian monk or nun to render practical service in the world,
as well as a life of learning and sharing with others.[4] Augustine's
understanding of monasticism went beyond the ascetic ideals of
chastity, fasting, poverty, and protracted prayer and reading of scripture. Equally important for him were communal activities: learning
and the discipline of a life shared with others in the service of Church
and world. His own conversion drew him closer to other people, not
away from them, and for this he praises "You, O God, who bring men
of one mind to live together" (9.8). Because of Augustine's recognition of the essentially social nature of human beings, he would never
advocate the hermit's life, however much it might appeal to him in
moments of revulsion from his past way of life.

Augustine's explicit comments on solitude are sometimes positive
and sometimes negative. His early work *The Ways of the Catholic
Church*, written in Rome and Tagaste soon after his conversion,
defends the desert fathers from the reproach that they are useless
members of human society. Augustine sees benefits for others in the
prayers and exemplary lives of the hermits. His main reservation
about the solitary way of life is not that it is deficient in any way but
that it exceeds normal human capacities.[5] This view resembles that

of the sixth-century Benedictine Rule: the eremitical life offers a more demanding and difficult form of Christian commitment that should be prepared for by years of training in communal living.

At other times Augustine portrays solitude quite unfavorably in comparison with communal life. In Augustine's commentaries on the Psalms he notes approvingly several passages that make this contrast, such as "Woe to the solitary man" and "Look, how good and pleasant it is when brothers dwell together." Commenting on the latter, Augustine asserts: "This is the psalm which has brought the world its monasteries; at the sound of it those brothers leapt up who desired to live together. This verse was a trumpet call for the assembly, and sounded over the whole world; and those who were living in separation from one another came together."[6] Augustine's intriguing interpretation of the Greek word for monk stresses unity, not aloneness: "It is true that the word *monachos* came from *monos*, but that must not necessarily mean 'alone,' it can also mean 'one,' and can refer to that one heart and soul which are a necessity if people are to live together in one house."[7] Augustine sees monastic "oneness" in the light of the ideals of the apostolic community described in Acts: "'One alone' is correct usage for those who live together in such a way as to make one person, so that they really possess, as the Scriptures say, 'one heart and one soul' (Acts 4:32)—many bodies but not many souls, many bodies but not many hearts."[8] Augustine's reinterpretation of the term *monachos* symbolizes the fundamental shift in the understanding of the monastic life that he helped effect: the distinguishing mark of the monk's "oneness" is no longer aloneness but the oneness of unity with his fellows.

Yet solitude retained a powerful appeal for Augustine, and it is a more central concern in the *Confessions* than his theoretical view of it would allow. The *Confessions* are shaped in four ways by his ideas about solitude. First, the plot depicts a crucial episode of solitude. This scene stands out partly because solitude is so rarely referred to by Augustine, as Peter Brown notes: "Having read the life of this extremely inward-looking man, we suddenly realize, to our surprise, that he has hardly ever been alone. There have always been friends around him. He learnt to speak 'amid the cooing of nurses, the jokes of laughing faces, the high spirits of playmates.' Only a friendship could make him lose 'half my soul,' and only yet more friendship would heal this wound. Seldom do we find him thinking alone: usually he is 'talking on such subjects to my friends.'"[9] There is one significant exception: the climactic scene of conversion in Book 8. Augustine leaves Alypius to take refuge in a garden "where no one could interrupt that fierce struggle, in which I was my own contestant, until it came to its own conclusion" (8.8). He is precise in reconstructing his exact placement in relation to Alypius, and the details of this situation have a more than circumstantial significance.

In this scene Augustine creates what I will call the image of bounded solitude, an image that reconciles his attraction to solitude with his reservations about it. His solitary situation in near proximity to Alypius symbolizes his view of the proper place of solitude in the Christian life. Augustine shows that the value of solitude is situational, dependent on a number of circumstances that are best explained in narrative. He dramatizes the necessity of solitude for experiencing and resolving certain forms of spiritual turmoil. Yet Alypius is always close at hand: "His presence was no intrusion on my solitude, and how could he leave me in that state?" (8.8). In the conversion scene Augustine experiences a protected solitude, a time and space in which his aloneness is circumscribed by the loving presence of his closest friend. For several chapters (8–11) Augustine turns to an analysis of the divided will, explicating the internal conflicts that paralyzed him as he struggled to make a whole-hearted commitment to God. Solitude is necessary for him to work through this conflict: "In this way I wrangled with myself, in my own heart, about my own self. And all the while Alypius stayed at my side, silently awaiting the outcome of this agitation" (8.11).

Augustine moves further away from his friend when he is overcome by tears: "I stood up and left Alypius so that I might weep and cry to my heart's content, for it occurred to me that tears were best shed in solitude" (8.12). Here we see another attraction of solitude for Augustine, for it is when he is alone that he can experience to the fullest the overwhelming emotions that were shameful to him and yet so determinative in his life. Similarly, in his account of Monica's death in Book 9, he describes being unable to cry for his mother while he is with others by her grave, or later at the baths. Again he stresses the relief of shedding tears when he is by himself, "as I lay alone in bed": "The tears which I had been holding back streamed down, and I let them flow as freely as they would, making of them a pillow for my heart. On them it rested, for my weeping sounded in your ears alone, not in the ears of men who might have misconstrued it and despised it" (9.12). Solitude is necessary for Augustine to plumb the depths of feeling that he is ashamed to reveal before others and yet sees as crucial in understanding himself and his relationship to God. Revealing his emotions is for Augustine as difficult, because as shameful, as it was for the ascetic Antony to eat in front of other people. In a culture where shame and honor are central ethical values, solitude plays an important role in preserving and protecting a person's sense of self-worth. In Augustine's case, of course, there is a fascinating paradox in the fact that he was also extraordinarily skilled at revealing to others the depths of emotion that swayed him, including grief, sexual desire, and other shameful passions. What he is ashamed to show before his best friend, and needs solitude to experience to the fullest, is displayed before all the world in the *Confessions*.

In Book 8, Augustine's solitude in the garden is interrupted by the voice of a child crying "Take it and read, take it and read." Remembering how Antony had been converted by a chance encounter with words from the gospel of Matthew, Augustine rushes back to Alypius and opens the Bible to the first passage he sees, Romans 13:13–14: "Let us live honorably as in the day, not in reveling and drunkenness, not in debauchery and licentiousness, not in quarreling and jealousy. Instead, put on the Lord Jesus Christ, and make no provision for the flesh, to gratify its desires" (NRSV). In an instant, says Augustine, "it was as though the light of confidence flooded into my heart and all the darkness of doubt was dispelled" (8.12). George Lawless argues that the significance of this particular Pauline passage lies partly in the way it recalls Roman literature criticizing the vices of avarice, sensual indulgence, and worldly ambition, and partly in the way it adumbrates what would become the threefold vows of the Christian monastic: poverty, chastity, and obedience.[10] Augustine's full conversion to Christianity is marked by his attaining the confidence to commit himself to a form of monastic life that does not include solitude. Alypius, too, finds a passage that he applies to himself, as the human chain of influence and imitation stretching back through Ponticianus and Antony, and back through Simplicianus's story about Victorinus (8.2–5), continues forward through Alypius to others, including, Augustine hopes, the reader.

Solitude was critical for Augustine in working through the conflict that had held him back for so many years. Several scholars speculate that Augustine's portrayal of his conversion in Book 8 condenses into one dramatic scene a process that may actually have taken considerably longer.[11] In coming to a firm commitment to Christian faith Augustine must have needed both continuing interaction with friends and mentors and intervals of solitary reflection and struggle. But the exact nature of Augustine's actual experience of solitude is not what is most significant about this passage. Rather, I suggest that Augustine's portrayal of his conversion scene symbolizes his normative view of the place of solitude in Christian life. Solitary prayer and conscientious self-scrutiny can occasion an experience of communion with God and precipitate the most pivotal event in a person's lifetime. Augustine approves of solitude for only a limited time, however, as a momentary experience rather than a settled state. Augustine removes solitude from the context of lifelong asceticism. It is no longer just a monastic vow, a special duty and permanent condition for the few Christians called to struggle toward perfection and holiness. Rather, Augustine suggests that a time of solitary disengagement may be crucial for any Christian, an opportunity for self-discovery, emotional catharsis, and encounter with God.

The boundaries of solitude are spatial, or relational, as well as temporal. That is, Augustine dramatizes his solitude as bounded and supported by relationships with others, and set within a larger context of life with Alypius, Monica, lovers, students, and many others. Augustine suggests that one must always be attentive to interruptions of one's solitude, for the voice of a crying child may be the neighbor or God calling one back to human society. A person's disengagement from others must always be tentative, prepared for new encounter. Solitude is a moment within the plot of a larger narrative and a situation located within a web of human relationships. The details of the conversion scene represent symbolically Augustine's normative view of bounded solitude, reconciling his desire for solitude with his scruples concerning it. This image of a Christian's bounded solitude contrasts with the vision of Plotinus, who saw the "flight of the alone to the alone" as the ideal, and with the intense social striving Augustine experienced in Rome and Milan, where he had lost awareness of God and himself in the boundless company of others and the vices that attached him so desperately to other people.

There is a second sense in which the *Confessions* links solitude and spirituality: not by representing incidents of solitude but by presenting the very writing of this text as an alternative means of realizing some of the same goals sought by the hermit or recluse. It is highly significant that the first autobiography was written at the same historical moment as the beginning of the monastic movement. Both this form of writing and monasticism may be interpreted as responses to the establishment of Christianity as first tolerated, and then the official religion of the Roman Empire. With the increasing acceptability of Christianity and its adoption for reasons of social, political, and economic expediency came a new worldliness and status that were utterly different from the earlier church's position as a persecuted sect. Many scholars of Christian monastic tradition trace its origins to a desire to withdraw from the temptations and laxity of established Christianity and to recover the purity and rigor of commitment of the early church, when to be a Christian meant being willing to die at any moment for one's faith.

In a similar way, Augustine's *Confessions* reformulates the meaning of Christian commitment at a time when the church's worldly success exposed it to trends that some Christians felt to be corruptions. Augustine discriminates among various kinds of motivation for joining the church and different levels of commitment, and he creates a literary form that dramatizes tensions and conflicts inherent in the new life of faith: "The Christian's worst enemies could no longer be placed outside him: they were inside, his sins and his doubts; and the climax of a man's life would not be martyrdom, but conversion from the perils of his own past."[12] The writing of autobiography and the monastic movement are analogous responses to the new situation of Christianity in the post-Constantinian era. Each involves a limited and partial withdrawal from direct engagement with others, with significant ethical implications and consequences.

Solitude is an important element in both the monastic movement and the autobiographical impulse that produced Augustine's *Confessions.* The central activities of monastic life—praising God and meditating on one's sins—are also central to the kind of writing Augustine initiates. Although these spiritual practices may be engaged in either alone or with other people, certain persons find solitude to be most conducive for them. The writing of the *Confessions* certainly required large blocks of solitude, and many of Augustine's comments on the process of composition emphasize the solitary nature of autobiographical reflection. For instance, in his analysis of memory in Book 10, Augustine discusses the work of the mind as a process of gathering, collecting, and recollecting. When memories recede, "I have to think them out again, like a fresh set of facts, if I am to know them. I have to shepherd them out again from their old lairs, because there is no other place where they can have gone. In other words, once they have been dispersed, I have to collect them again, and this is the derivation of the word *cogitare,* which means *to think* or *to collect one's thoughts*" (10.11). This process of recollecting one's memories involves intense work, a demanding and focused activity best undertaken in solitude.

A third connection between solitude and Augustine's confessional activity is his striking awareness of his audience as he represents himself writing in solitude, or rather in solitude engaged with God. His continual second-person address to God makes his book a sustained prayer. He is, at the same time, highly conscious of his audience, and the hoped-for good effects of his writing on them authorize his spending so much time and energy on prolonged introspection. This double awareness—of himself alone with God and of himself in relation to his fellows—shapes the basic rhetorical strategy of the *Confessions*, which is presented as the outpouring of a solitary person who is accidently overheard by others. In a revealing remark in Book 9, Augustine describes how he wishes that the Manichees could hear him reciting the Psalms. He is "burning to echo them to all the world, if only I could, so that they might vanquish man's pride" (9.4). However, he does not want simply to preach the Psalms to the Manichees (or his *Confessions* to the reader). He wishes that others would eavesdrop as he speaks to himself; this would be the ideal rhetorical situation to convince others of his sincerity:

> I wished that they could have been somewhere at hand, unknown to me, to watch my face and hear my voice as I read the fourth Psalm. They would have seen how deeply it moved me. . . . How I wish that they could have heard me speak these words! And how I wish that I might have been unaware that they could hear, so that they need have no cause to think that my own words, which escaped from me as I recited the Psalm, were uttered for their benefit alone! And it is true enough that I would not have uttered them, or if I had, I should not have uttered them in the same way, if I had known that they were watching and listening. And if I had uttered them, the Manichees would not have understood them in the way that I spoke them. They would not have understood how this cry came from my inmost heart, when I was alone in your presence. (9.4)

Augustine wishes to be overheard so that the listener will not suspect him of trying to produce an effect, and so that he can plumb the depths of his heart as he only can when he is unconcerned about what others might think, not worrying about how best to deploy the arts of persuasion. Augustine reveals both the rhetorician's wish for a rhetoric that disarms all suspicions of design on the audience, and a genuine yearning for solitude in order to fathom, retrieve, and articulate the deep workings of his spirit. This passage expresses eloquently Augustine's ambivalent feelings about solitude: on the one hand his longing for the sincerity and depth of emotion that come when he stops calculating his effect on others, and on the other hand his desire that his words and his life serve God in the world. Augustine seeks the effect of being overheard in solitude throughout the *Confessions*. The way he presents this work—as a soliloquy, the "cry from the innermost heart" of a man who thinks he is alone but is overheard by his audience—expresses and resolves his conflicts about solitude.

The fourth way in which Augustine's *Confessions* reflects its author's thoughts about solitude is its self-critical reflections on the dangers and difficulties of knowing and assessing one's own life. He defends his autobiographical writing from the same criticisms as were made of Christian solitaries. Saint Basil opposed the eremitical life because it gave no opportunity for direct expression of love of neighbor and because the solitary did not have a spiritual master to rebuke his faults. These basic criticisms of the early hermits, which recur through the ages in Christian opposition to solitude, can also be made against the activity of autobiographical writing. Augustine asserts that his narrative does indeed serve the neighbor, by moving readers to love God in the way that Augustine was moved by the examples of others: "When others read of those past sins of mine, or hear about them, their hearts are stirred so that they no longer lie listless in despair, crying 'I cannot.' Instead their hearts are roused by the love of your mercy and the joy of your grace" (10.3). Augustine resolutely asserts the social usefulness of his solitary act of writing and his intention to inspire the reader's heart just as he himself was powerfully affected by the force of example.

The hermit and the autobiographer alike are exposed to the dangers of overestimating their achievements and of spiritual pride. Augustine's constant scrutiny of his efforts at self-understanding, his watchfulness for pride, self-deception, and complacency, resembles the kind of self-examination requisite for a solitary who has no fellow monk or superior to point out his sins. Augustine acknowledges the difficulties of self-knowledge, pleading with God to help him plumb the depths of his soul: "It is you, O Lord, who judge me. For though 'no one can know a man's thoughts, except the man's own spirit that is within him,' there are some things in man which even his own spirit within him does not know" (10.5). Throughout his narrative Augustine confesses "both what I know of myself and what I do not know" (10.5) and stresses his constant reliance on God and the scriptures to guide him as he searches his soul. The analysis of memory and temptation in Book 10 returns frequently to the vast size, confusing contradictions, and mystery of the inner world: "The powers of my innerself are veiled in darkness which I must deplore. When my mind speculates upon its own capabilities, it realizes that it cannot safely trust its own judgement" (10.32). Augustine's scruples about writing his life story resemble the two most frequent criticisms made of hermits: the solitary life is essentially selfish, and a person cannot know himself alone. He cautiously hopes that with the help of God his confessions will surmount these dangers of solitary attempts at spiritual knowledge.

At the end of Book 10, Augustine concludes his examination of his own life before turning in Books 11–13 to analysis of the first chapter of Genesis. He recalls his desire to flee into the solitude of the desert. He renounced this desire, sacrificing his yearning for solitude and contemplation, and took up the endless tasks of service in the church that brought him to his present role as bishop of Hippo: "Terrified by my sins and the dead weight of my misery, I had turned my problems over in my mind and was half determined to seek refuge in the desert. But you forbade me to do this and gave me strength by saying: 'Christ died for us all, so that being alive should no longer mean living with our own life, but with his life who died for us'" (10.43). This quotation from Paul's second letter to the Corinthians suggests not merely the duty but the joy of a life freed from concern only with oneself, a life to be shared gladly with Christ and with one's fellows.

Although Augustine decided not to seek solitude in eremitical life, he found a permissible form of solitude in writing the *Confessions*. We have seen four ways in which this book reflects Augustine's complex thoughts and feelings as they relate to solitude. In his description of his conversion in Book 8, Augustine symbolically depicts his normative view of bounded solitude, showing how a time of aloneness can precipitate a life-changing conversion but should be temporary and set within the context of human relationships. Second, he conceives of writing the *Confessions* as a spiritual activity with many affinities to the vocation of the Christian solitary, in particular meditation on sin, praise of God, and discernment and practice of a more intensive form of commitment than the average Christian finds necessary. Third, he presents his autobiographical reflections in the *Confessions* as the utterances to God of a solitary individual whom the reader happens to overhear. Thus the basic rhetorical strategy of the book is shaped by his self-representation as a man temporarily suspended from enmeshment in many human relationships, including one with the reader. Not only the conversion scene but the entire narrative is conceived of in terms of a situation of bounded solitude, with the reader eavesdropping on Augustine as he speaks to God. Finally, Augustine's scruples and anxieties about the dangers and difficulties of self-knowledge in autobiography are the same as the reservations that critics in the early church had about those who sought to live their lives alone, and he attempts to defend his *Confessions* from these charges. In all of these ways, Augustine's conception of his autobiographical project and its religious significance is shaped by his view of solitude's value and its dangers.

3

THE HUMANIST TRADITION

PETRARCH, MONTAIGNE, AND GIBBON

THE HUMANIST tradition of thought about solitude influences auto-biography as much as Christian ideas, and is most vividly expressed in the works of Petrarch, Montaigne, and Gibbon. These three writers are all deeply indebted to the classical legacy of ancient Greece and Rome. Greek philosophers offered an ambiguous view of solitude, viewing it favorably or unfavorably in different contexts. Plato and Aristotle both presented contemplation of the supreme reality as the highest human good, an activity that seems to require and justify withdrawing from ordinary social interaction. At the same time, the political and ethical thought of each philosopher holds that the individual's first duty is to the state. In the *Republic* Plato sees the life of the philosopher-king as involving contemplation of the eternal Forms, yet this activity is apparently reserved for only a few individuals, and it is not clear how they would combine the pursuit of wisdom with ruling society. Aristotle defines human beings as social animals, and in the *Politics* (1, 2) denounces the solitary person as either less or more than human, either a beast or a god.

The schools of Greek and Roman philosophy, especially the Epicurean and Stoic, debated the same basic questions: How can one reconcile the ideal of a detached, contemplative life with the equally important ideals of service and the public good? Is the solitary less than fully human, and hence unworthy of respect, or does he represent the furthest range of human aspiration to divinity? Roman orators and rhetoricians such as Cicero and Seneca tried to reconcile the demands of public service with the contemplative life. They added a new emphasis on the attractions of retirement to a country estate; the favored place for solitude was not desert wilderness but a well-maintained rural residence. Like the Christian debate about solitude, the classical tradition found mediating positions, such as the view that solitary study should eventually benefit others, or that country retirement was a justified reward for long years of public service.

Roman poets celebrated the pleasures of solitude in a safe and secure rural retreat. In the pastoral tradition begun by Horace and Virgil, solitude is associated with relaxation, study, and rest. Solitude is not motivated by misanthropy or religious devotion but by the wish to enjoy the pleasures of life outside the cares of the city. This ideal life did not require absolute aloneness, for servants and slaves took care of physical needs, and congenial friends visited. Withdrawal from the cares of public life was valued not primarily as an escape from other people but rather as an opportunity to cultivate leisure and enjoy the pleasures of mind and spirit, especially literature and philosophy. This vision of cultured retirement was not opposed to the main ideals of Roman society, but understood as the fruition or consummation of that society's values, a vision of the true purpose and dignity of human life when free from the drudgery of mundane toil.[1] The Latin tradition of lyrical poetry praising the freedom and rest provided by solitude informs the views of the three autobiographers to be considered in this chapter.

Petrarch

The first autobiographer for whom solitude is a central concern is Francesco Petrarca (1304–74), or Petrarch, as he is usually known by English-speakers. Petrarch was the first person to devote an entire book, De Vita Solitaria (The Life of Solitude), to the topic of the pleasures of solitude, and to link experiences of solitude to the development of individual character. Solitude also figures prominently in two other autobiographical works he wrote, as we shall see. Petrarch astonished his contemporaries by retiring from his work at the papal court in Avignon to a secluded country estate at Vaucluse. His subsequent life involved periods of travel, public life as an ambassador or secretary, and seclusion at Vaucluse and other places. He always yearned for solitude and praised it in letters and poems. His love of Vaucluse and the association of that place with many of his literary works helped establish rural retreat as fashionable for literary writers, and he may be seen as the first in a tradition of country-dwelling humanist authors stretching through Montaigne to the present day. Petrarch's life and the legends about him were as important as his books in establishing the conventions of literary solitude, an author's retirement to compose written works.

The Life of Solitude is an epistle to Petrarch's close friend Philip, Bishop of Cavaillon, the diocese in which Vaucluse was situated. Petrarch began writing the manuscript in 1346 and worked on it intermittently for twenty years. The form of *The Life of Solitude* is an essay with two parts: a philosophical defense of solitude and an encyclopedia of examples of notable solitaries. The first book undertakes a sustained contrast between the happiness of the solitary man and the misery of "the busy man": "It seems to me that I can demonstrate the blessedness of solitude by exhibiting the troubles and afflictions of a populous environment, reviewing the actions of men whom one kind of life preserves in peace and tranquility and the other kind keeps agitated and careworn and breathless. For there is a single idea underlying all these observations, that one kind of life is attended with happy leisure and the other with grievous worry."[2] For Petrarch, the value of solitude is its distinctive pleasures: "For it is not the mere name of solitude but the good things which are proper to it that I praise. And it is not so much the solitary recesses and the silence that delight me as the leisure and freedom that dwell within them. Nor am I so inhuman as to hate men, whom I am instructed by divine commandment to love as I love myself, but I hate the sins of men, especially my own, and the troubles and sad afflictions that reside among crowds" (108). What Petrarch values most about solitude is its freedom from the demands of others and its provision of the conditions for a person to choose his own way of life. He loves not simply being alone, but free time to pursue his work, pleasing interludes in the natural environment, and a moderate life of pleasure without dissipation or self-indulgence.

Half of Petrarch's apology for solitude is satiric criticism of the acquisitive, anxious, and exhausting life of an urban businessman in hot pursuit of wealth. There is a strong element of social critique in Petrarch's contrast between the individual who has found a consistent and self-directed plan for his life and the typical city dweller, whom he portrays as driven by envy, resentment, imitation of the latest fashion, and gratification of sensual appetites.[3] But Petrarch is not a misanthrope; he would "flee from crowds and not from friends" (162). Paradoxically, at least for most modern understandings of solitude, one of the greatest pleasures of solitude as Petrarch defines it is enjoying it with those he loves: "I would share my solitude like everything else with my friends, believing that Seneca spoke with true humanity when he said that 'no good thing is pleasant to possess without friends to share it'" (165). His aloneness is always interrupt-ible by the pleasures and claims of friendship, although probably not by the call of religious or civic duty: "No solitude is so profound, no house so small, no door so narrow but it may open to a friend" (292).

The second part of *The Life of Solitude* is an encyclopedia of famous examples of solitude. Petrarch devotes chapters to Old Testament figures who he says cultivated solitude (Adam, Abraham, Isaac, Jacob, Moses, Elijah, and Jeremiah) and to monastic founders, saints, popes, and other notable Christians. He catalogues ancient philosophers, orators, poets, emperors, military leaders, and even "Brahmans" and "Hindoos" who pursued a solitary life. He approves of solitude not only for Christian prayer and meditation, or even for broadly religious devotion; he applauds any individual's choice of aloneness to achieve a central purpose, to answer an irresistible call to some higher end. Petrarch attributes nearly every great accomplishment to an experience of being alone. It is his failure to probe the dark side of solitude, its excesses and dangers, that is the chief limitation of *The Life of Solitude.*

The Life of Solitude defends solitude but it is not autobiographical; it does not describe the role of solitude in the author's life. Petrarch's primary significance in relation to the development of autobiogra-phy is the document called the *Secret,* a series of three dialogues between Augustine and the character "Petrarch" which analyzes the latter's desires, vices, and ambitions.[4] The dialogue between these two speakers scrutinizes the poet's literary ambitions and his devo-tion to Laura, the woman with whom Petrarch fell in love when he first saw her in a church in 1327, and whom he continued to love after she was married. Augustine's words function as the voice of Petrarch's conscience, condemning his worldliness and calling for the kind of conversion that Augustine went through, but which seems unattainable to Petrarch. The work is not a straightforward confession, yet it discloses the poet's inner conflicts, especially his inability to renounce the world as he believes is a Christian's highest calling. Petrarch's *Secret* is a dialogue between two sides of the poet, a deeply introspective work that probes his internal division and ends somewhat inconclusively, with the poet hoping for a conver-sion but still very much drawn to the world.

This autobiographical document presents an intriguing picture of its author in solitude. In the "proem" prefacing the *Secret,* Petrarch says that his book "is not intended for wide circulation, but will remain among my private papers—in keeping with its title. For it is a private conversation."[5] Petrarch claims that he wrote the book for his future private reading pleasure, "to experience as often as I want, by reading it, the joy I experienced when we had the conversation." This work was not published until after Petrarch's death, and scholars do not agree as to the date of its composition. Petrarch was well aware that the book would see the light: "The very existence and refined formulation of the work betray its author's concern that whatever fresh understanding of his own nature he has come to in it should be known also to others. Unlike Augustine, Petrarch is addressing his secular confession not to God, but to men."[6] Petrarch places the reader in the same position that Augustine in his *Confessions* described as the ideal rhetorical situation: the reader overhears a solitary person deliberating with himself. The author's soliloquy seems to guarantee the honesty and truthfulness of his self-disclosure.

There is another important Petrarchan autobiographical text that links solitude, self-disclosure, and religious experience. In 1336, the year before he retired to Vaucluse, Petrarch climbed Mount Ventoux, a peak northeast of Avignon. On his return he wrote a famous letter to the Augustinian friar who was his confessor.[7] This friar had introduced Petrarch to Augustine's *Confessions*, giving him the copy of that book that he carried to the top of the mountain. In his letter Petrarch explains how, like Augustine, he opened his book at random and read the first passage he saw. These words from the tenth book met his eyes: "And men go to admire high mountains and mighty waves of the sea, and the great flowing rivers, and the edge of the sea, and the course of the stars, and forsake themselves." Petrarch describes the scene in terms that recall Augustine's similar reading of a text, and interprets his experience through the lens of Augustine's conversion. But whereas Augustine is finally moved to a wholehearted act of faith, Petrarch turns not to God but to continuing self-examination. Although his brother and two servants accompanied Petrarch on the climb, he has little interaction with them, and on the descent he withdraws into virtual solitude. He keeps his brother at a distance, just as Augustine had placed himself in relation to Alypius, in order to confront his conscience:

> I was astounded, I confess. I asked my brother, who wanted to hear more, not to disturb me. I closed the book, angry with myself that I should still admire earthly things when long since I should have learned from the pagan philosophers themselves that nothing is to be admired except the soul, beside whose greatness nothing is great.
>
> Happy by now and even sated that I had seen the mountain, I turned the eyes of the mind on myself and from that moment on no one heard me speak until we reached the bottom.[8]

This experience turns Petrarch toward profound introspection. He takes Augustine's advice to heart, meditating on "how great was men's foolishness who, neglecting their most noble part, diffuse themselves in many things and vanish in vain spectacles, looking on the outside for what could be found within."[9] When they return to their inn Petrarch immediately retires to write the letter in which he describes this experience.

Both the letter describing the ascent of Mount Ventoux and the *Secret* focus on the spiritual problem of Petrarch's loving the world more than he believes he should according to Augustine, the voice of conscience rebuking his weakness. In both cases detachment from other people helps the poet enter into a deeper communion with his internalized spiritual guide, who calls him to account for excessive love of the world in the form of lovely views, Laura, or literary fame. In these two autobiographical texts solitude is directly linked to the inward turn necessary for repentance, shame, and the somewhat in-conclusive, even half-hearted hope that in the future God will help him to renounce the world's attractions. Petrarch seems stuck at a point Augustine dramatized in his process of conversion, when the person conscious of his sins wishes fervently for God's salvation—but not quite yet, please. Each of these texts, the *Secret* and the letter, describes a past experience of introspective self-scrutiny and presents the act of writing as a reentry into solitude in order to effect the still-hoped-for religious conversion. Implicitly the reader is called on also to enter into solitude, there to recognize the soul's yearning for God.

The Life of Solitude does not involve this kind of direct self-disclosure. It reveals Petrarch's personality and values indirectly, however, as he describes the various uses of solitude. Although the spiritual worth of Christian solitude is dutifully praised, Petrarch becomes more animated and enthusiastic when he speaks of books, study, and authorship. Without books he would not want to be alone: "Isolation without literature is exile, prison, and torture; supply literature, and it becomes your country, freedom, and delight" (131). Petrarch's own temperament and values emerge clearly whenever he discusses the use to which he put his own solitude.

The Life of Solitude represents a crucial stage in the development of ideas about the role of solitude in a person's life. Petrarch justifies the pursuit of solitude in terms of the individual personality's right to realize its distinctive qualities. The central idea of the book, according to its translator, is "the establishment of self-cultivation as an adequate guiding motive in life."[10] Petrarch links the choice of solitude to individual fulfillment and personal choice: "I am not so much proposing a rule for others as exposing the principles of my own mind. If it commends itself to anyone, let him follow its suggestion. Whoever does not like it is free to reject it and, leaving us to our solitude, to embrace his own anxious cares and live to his own satisfaction in scorn of our rural retreat" (130). The life Petrarch recommends is not for everyone, but he defends it as justifiable for those who share his taste for it, concluding his book in this way: "I have treated these matters not in the spirit of one who lays down the law but as a student and investigator. . . . I know that the chosen few to whom I address myself will be on my side" (315). Jacob Zeitlin notes the novelty of this appeal: "The argument takes shape finally not as an ordinary didactic plea, a counsel of perfection to be generally applied, but as a vindication of the right of a particular individual to regulate his life according to the disposition and humor with which nature has endowed him and without any reference to the claims of his fellowmen upon him. In no moral treatise before this do we find the writer's own experience and character made the ground of a plea for the human personality."[11] Petrarch's *The Life of Solitude* adumbrates the basic justification of solitude by later autobiographers who appeal to personal interests and the variety of individual character. Solitude, like many other aspects of life, will become a matter of individual choice rather than being determined by a single prescriptive moral standard for all humankind.

This ethical justification of solitude, based on the value of discovering and expressing one's individual temperament, represents a crucial stage in the secularization of solitude. According to one scholar of "the cult of solitude" in the early modern period, "Petrarch revolutionized the terminology of the solitude debate, replacing the terminology of right and wrong, morally superior and inferior, more and less pleasing to God (terms familiar from medieval debate over the active and contemplative lives), with a new terminology of personal will, individual nature, and more and less pleasing to self."[12] He praises solitude not only when it leads to salvation or moral perfection but because of its pleasures, in his own case those growing out of literary pursuits. At one point Petrarch discusses Christian solitaries who have sought a mystical vision of God, and asserts his belief that for some persons it is indeed possible to "hear the chorus of angels singing harmoniously in heaven and behold in an ecstasy of mind what he is unable to express when he comes back to himself" (148). He immediately goes on to disclaim this as his own goal, pleading inadequacy, and warms to his real passion: "But what can I know or say about all these things, unhappy sinner that I am, dragging about with me the ball and chain of my iniquities? My love of a spot favorable to literary leisure springs no doubt from my love of books, or perhaps I seek to escape from the crowd because of an aversion arising from a discrepancy in our tastes, or it may even be that from a squeamishness of conscience I like to avoid a many-tongued witness of my life" (148). Petrarch does not seem truly contrite about admitting his personal weaknesses but rather relieved that they excuse him from tedious public duties. Although he acknowledges the importance of religious devotion, his heart is really in "the more obvious pleasures" of literary solitude.

If Petrarch stands at the origin of the secularization of solitude, in what respect can we speak of solitude as spiritual in his work? Petrarch uses the language of moral duty and religious veneration to describe his chief pursuits:

> to devote oneself to reading and writing, alternately finding employment and relief in each, to read what our forerunners have written and to write what later generations may wish to read, to pay to posterity the debt which we cannot pay to the dead for the gift of their writings, and yet not remain altogether ungrateful to the dead but to make their names more popular if they are little known, to restore them if they have been forgotten, to dig them out if they have been buried in the ruins of time and to hand them down to our grandchildren as objects of veneration, to carry them in the heart and as something sweet in the mouth, and finally, by cherishing, remembering, and celebrating their fame in every way, to pay them the homage that is due to their genius even though it is not commensurate with their greatness. (151)

The literary life is not simply a matter of personal ambition, but of reverence and devotion to exemplary figures. This motif of fidelity to the past is a central theme in the humanist tradition, distinguishing its aims from the emphasis on personal creativity and originality stressed by most nineteenth- and twentieth-century solitaries.

Scholars debate whether Petrarch's humanism represents a departure from Christian tradition because of his worldly interests and individualism, or a creative synthesis of Christian and classical themes characteristic of the emerging Renaissance. Zeitlin sees the Christian elements as perfunctory: "There is more in his attitude of Horace and of Epicurus than of the moralist or Christian mystic. . . . It is with a rather awkward gesture that he tries to wrap his superiority in a mantle of religion and humility. . . . Of Christian mysticism one discerns scarcely a trace."[13] Charles Trinkaus speaks of Petrarch's religious egoism in advocating a primary focus on one's own character rather than the needs of the neighbor. Responding to the usual accusation that solitude makes a person irresponsible to other people, Petrarch asserts that the best he can do is to pray for others and attend to his own sins and need for salvation:

> I would admit . . . that whoever is in a place of safety sins against the law of nature if he does not offer what aid he can to the struggling. But for me, who have hitherto been struggling as in a great shipwreck, it is enough to pray for the aid of him who is alone able to provide aid in our need. . . . I could wish to have everybody, or at least as many as possible, gain salvation with me. But in the end what do you expect me to say? It is enough for me, yea a great cause for happiness, if I do not perish myself. But for those who profess themselves guardians of the helpless sheep, alas, how much I fear that they are wolves eager to rend them alive. (130)

Michael O'Loughlin describes the thrust of this passage as a "transformation of humility into egoism, of abnegation into indulgence. . . . The acknowledgement of Christ's power seems, potentially at least, to dispense the writer from the communal responsibilities of being a Christian."[14] All three of these scholars see Petrarch's approach to solitude as a movement away from Christian tradition.

I think this view overstates Petrarch's secularization. Petrarch's reasoning is in some respects similar to that of the desert fathers and Christian contemplatives who believe that God calls them to a special task that can not be accomplished in the midst of human company. Although Petrarch's primary motivation is not to be more devoted to God, there is a significant religious dimension to his pursuit of literature. Petrarch admired Augustine partly because of the way the great theologian used examples and metaphors from ancient literature in his apologetic efforts to convince others of Christian truths.[15] Petrarch's Christian humanism is based on the faith that God works in many ways in the world, and that a person may achieve salvation even in the midst of such worldly attractions as poetry and love. In this he not only embodies the emerging faith of the Renaissance humanists but prefigures one impulse of the Protestant Reformation, although the reformers stressed the need for worldly vocations more directly to serve the neighbor.

For Petrarch a literary life is as valid a commitment as religious devotion. In the first words of *The Life of Solitude* Petrarch offers religious faith, self-knowledge, and intellectual friendship as alternative routes to the "repose" that is the desire of all humans. He recommends solitude as the best setting for all three pursuits: "I believe that a noble spirit will never find repose save in God, in whom is our end, or in himself and his private thoughts, or in some intellect united by a close sympathy with his own. . . . But whether we are intent upon God, or upon ourselves and our serious studies, or whether we are seeking for a mind in harmony with our own, it behooves us to withdraw as far as may be from the haunts of men and crowded cities" (105). This passage defends solitude for pursuits that have nothing to do with religion. Yet these individual pursuits—self-knowledge and friendship—are given a meaning and significance such as we now associate with the term spirituality.

Petrarch is a crucial transitional figure in his understanding of the spiritual meaning of solitude. The opening statement of *The Life of Solitude* suggests that a similar spiritual impulse is at work both in officially sanctioned religious activities and in certain apparently worldly pursuits. The "repose" to which Petrarch refers recalls the rest that Augustine asserts humans seek in all our restless striving: "You made us for yourselves and our hearts find no peace until they rest in you" (1.1). There is a crucial difference: Augustine believes we can only find rest in God, whereas Petrarch suggests that it can be attained in several ways. Petrarch thinks that the same human energies and passions motivate both religious and secular activities. He discerns a common spiritual impulse at work in all the ways that individuals seek fulfillment and serenity, and he holds that solitude offers the repose that will in each case satisfy that seeking. Certain worldly pursuits, above all the literary life, have attained a standing of equal worth with traditional Christian practices insofar as both may satisfy the basic human quests for meaning and for peace of mind and spirit. All uses of solitude seem worthwhile spiritual practices to Petrarch, and contrast with the restless, anxious, and debilitating life of the busy man of the city.

In evaluating solitude so positively, in linking it with individual choice and self-fulfillment, and in justifying the use of solitude for literary pleasure as being equally propitious as religious piety for satisfying the human desire for happiness, Petrarch formulates an early humanist understanding of solitude. *The Life of Solitude*, however, is largely a matter of theoretical argument and example rather than direct self-disclosure; the latter appears two centuries later in the essays of Montaigne.

Montaigne

On his thirty-eighth birthday, Michel de Montaigne (1533–92) had painted on the wall of his library the following inscription (in Latin) commemorating his retirement from the cares of public life: "In the year of Christ 1571, at the age of thirty-eight, on the last day of February, anniversary of his birth, Michel de Montaigne, long weary of the servitude of the court and of public employments, while still entire, retired to the bosom of the learned Virgins [the Muses], where in calm and freedom from all cares he will spend what little remains of his life now more than half run out. If the fates permit he will complete this abode, this sweet ancestral retreat; and he has consecrated it to his freedom, tranquillity, and leisure."[16] He began to spend a great deal of time reading in the tower library of the family manor at his country estate near Bordeaux. Soon he started to write the essays that he worked on until his death. Montaigne's withdrawal into solitude had several motivations. He had been a member of the Bordeaux Parliament for thirteen years. Now he sought a place from which he could view from afar the struggles, the false appearances, and the vanity of public life. Montaigne initially saw solitude as both an escape from public affairs and a vantage point from which to observe them. He continued to be involved in politics, however, serving as mayor of Bordeaux for four years and becoming involved in important negotiations. Montaigne's final essays reveal a complex understanding of solitude in relation to the social bonds that he affirmed as a crucial part of his life. I will trace the evolution of Montaigne's view of solitude, beginning with the understanding that shaped his withdrawal to his tower.

Montaigne's retirement was not simply an escape or secession from the world, but had positive goals. The commemorative statement refers to the pursuit of "freedom, tranquillity, and leisure." Montaigne sought not ease or idleness but the ideal conditions for the pursuit of wisdom. He wanted serenity in order to direct his attention as he wished. Choosing his library as the site of his solitude, he desired to be alone in order to read and write. In this he resembles Petrarch, although Montaigne's initial goal was study rather than literary production, and oriented toward philosophical wisdom rather than aesthetic beauty. He had carved into his library walls some fifty Greek and Latin maxims, many of them comments on human ignorance and vanity. He sat alone, surrounded by these epigrams from the classical literary sources he loved, constantly reminded of one of his favorite themes.

Philippe Ariès, editor of a massive study of "the history of private life," links the development of a sense of the individual self to an architectural innovation during the Renaissance: the private study. Prior to the Renaissance, houses were not so clearly divided into separate rooms used for specific purposes. Ariès sees the modern senses of privacy and individualism as being formed by this new location, where a person could be alone and read. A new kind of literary culture was linked to these developments, as the ways people read and wrote changed, for instance by silent reading, which allowed individuals to form their own interpretations more readily. Montaigne's description of his study and his reflections on how his third-floor tower room gave him a perspective—both spatial and intellectual—may be understood in the light of Ariès's study.[17]

At thirty-eight years, Montaigne avails himself of one of the standard justifications of solitude, old age. His dedicatory inscription declares his right to "what little remains of his life." Old age is a recurring theme in Montaigne's essays for a variety of reasons, including its granting him the privilege of looking back on and writing about his life.[18] His view of himself as an elderly man at a strikingly early age authorizes his retirement: "Solitude seems to me more appropriate and reasonable for those who have given to the world their most active and flourishing years. . . . We have lived enough for others; let us live at least this remaining bit of life for ourselves."[19]

Several recent encounters with death had a sobering effect on Montaigne, turning his thoughts toward his own mortality and what he ought to do with "what little remains of his life now more than half run out." His father died in 1568, his brother in 1569, his firstborn child in 1570 (the first of five of his six daughters to die within a few months), and he himself had a serious accident when he was knocked off a horse.[20] But it was above all the death in 1563 of his closest friend, Etienne La Boétie, that for many years colored Montaigne's thoughts in solitude. His friendship with La Boétie was Montaigne's warmest human bond, and his essay "Of Friendship" is a moving analysis of and tribute to their relationship. Montaigne had already devoted a great deal of his time to preserving the memory of his friend and promoting his literary reputation. He installed La Boétie's books in his library and for several years tried to model his character after the virtues of his friend. Montaigne's foremost biographer interprets the *Essays* as, among other things, "a compensation for the loss of La Boétie," and traces their origin to Montaigne's wish to find another such friend: "Montaigne's loneliness led him to write; the lack of his friend, leaving him no one to address in letters, made him seek a form of his own that would be both a testimony to his life and a means of communication which might bring him another good friend and thus fill the void in his heart."[21] The impulse to withdraw and that to communicate alike reflect his need to remember and mourn his friend. His essays are an attempt to recreate the intimacy of an ideal friendship. In the introductory note "To the Reader" that Montaigne attached to his first edition of essays in 1580, he describes his "domestic and private" purpose in writing: "I have dedicated it to the private convenience of my relatives and friends, so that when they have lost me (as soon they must), they may recover here some features of my habits and temperament, and by this means keep the knowledge they have had of me more complete and alive" (2). As he remembers La Boétie, so would Montaigne like to be remembered by his own friends and family, in both cases preserving the relationship with a literary memorial.

In this way Montaigne's solitary retirement is sustained and bounded by vital but vulnerable connections to past and future friends. Jean Starobinski describes Montaigne's withdrawal as an interlude between two moments of intimate communication:

> The writer's solitude is haunted and traversed by the internalized continuation of a lost "society," just as it is oriented by the expectation of a future "society," composed of other friends: the act of writing is intended to link Montaigne and his departed friend indissolubly in the public mind, in order to put across the living image of an author who himself will soon have no *place* to reside, no *body*, no "sponsor," other than his own book, offered as a gift to posterity. The period of studious retirement thus takes on meaning as the interval between two moments of "communication": the exalted communication with the chosen companion (which precedes the book) and the posthumous communication (achieved through the book) with those who will be the intimates of Seigneur de Montaigne. Whichever way we face in time, the essay works in relation to absence, in memory or anticipation of loss.[22]

Solitude and communion are closely interwoven in Montaigne's writing. Much of his solitary work is devoted to communication with other people about the ebb and flow of human relationship. He does not speak directly about loneliness or feeling isolated, yet he conveys to the reader a wisdom born of long periods of aloneness. His voice is intimate and personal, disarming in its candor about his yearning for solidarity with his readers. He hopes to find in the reader an ideal friend:

I hope for this other advantage, that if my humors happen to please and suit some worthy man before I die, he will try to meet me. I give him a big advantage in ground covered; for all that long acquaintance and familiarity could have gained for him in several years, he can see in three days in this record, and more surely and exactly.

Amusing notion: many things that I would not want to tell anyone, I tell the public; and for my most secret knowledge and thoughts I send my most faithful friends to a bookseller's shop. . . .

If by such good signs I knew of a man who was suited to me, truly I would go very far to find him; for the sweetness of harmonious and agreeable company cannot be bought too dearly, in my opinion. Oh, a friend! (749–50)

Montaigne conveys at once a sense of reserve and a deep desire for an intimate companion: "Oh, a friend!" Solitude and human connection constantly qualify each other in his writing. This passage, like many others, also recalls Augustine's reflections about the desirability of being overheard by others as one utters the most private and revealing thoughts and feelings. Montaigne's disclosures are presented as a soliloquy, a talking to himself that gives the reader the illusion of unmediated access to the speaker's consciousness, to an inner realm normally hidden from view.

"Of Solitude" is the explicit subject matter of an early essay written about 1572–74. Montaigne asserts that while a wise man can live anywhere, if given the choice "he will flee even the sight of a throng. He will endure it, if need be, but if it is up to him, he will choose solitude" (175). One should choose to be alone to secure freedom and serenity, "to live more at leisure and at one's ease" (175). Yet mental detachment and tranquillity are not obtained simply by removing oneself from others, for they are a matter of attitude. Montaigne quotes Horace's insight that "Reason and sense remove anxiety / Not villas that look out upon the sea." Solitaries often take their troubles with them, and "whatever the mind is wrapped up in, it is all wrapped up." True solitude is not simply physical isolation but a matter of one's orientation, and requires the avoidance of the vices of "ambition, avarice, irresolution, fear, and lust" (176). The spiritual value of aloneness for Montaigne emerges in these characterizations of solitude as transcendence of the cares that diminish human life in even the most favorable material conditions. But the way to escape from these vices is not the usual recourse of Christian faith, casting oneself on God's mercy. Religions and philosophies that advocate solitude may not avoid the vices: "They often follow us even into the cloisters and the schools of philosophy. Neither deserts, nor rocky caves, nor hair shirts, nor fastings will free us of them" (176). We may not escape our insatiable desire to control other people even when we flee their presence. Montaigne's meditation on solitude leads to a moral appeal to control the social passions: "It is not enough to have gotten away from the crowd, it is not enough to move; we must get away from the gregarious instincts that are inside us, we must sequester ourselves and repossess ourselves." The soul must withdraw into itself; "that is the real solitude, which may be enjoyed in the midst of cities and the courts of kings; but it is enjoyed more handily alone" (176).

Montaigne's reflections on solitude in this early essay are closely related to his avowal of the basic principles of Stoic philosophy. He recommends detachment from others as the best way to take control of one's happiness by making oneself invulnerable to loss. "Let us make our contentment depend on ourselves; let us cut loose from all the ties that bind us to others" (177). It is not necessary to renounce family, friends, and other relationships, but we should live with them, as with material possessions, without clinging or excessive attachment:

> We should have wife, children, goods, and above all health, if we can; but we must not bind ourselves to them so strongly that our happiness depends on them. We must reserve a back shop all our own, entirely free, in which to establish our real liberty and our principal retreat and solitude. Here our ordinary conversation must be between us and ourselves, and so private that no outside association can find a place; here we must talk and laugh as if without wife, without children, without possessions, without retinue and servants, so that, when the time comes to lose them, it will be nothing new to us to do without them. We have a soul that can be turned upon itself; it can keep itself company. (177)

Montaigne holds that recognizing the religious problem of finitude should incline a person toward solitude in order to achieve detachment.

Anticipation of death should affect human relationships by bringing a kind of love that will not be devastated by the inevitable losses life brings: "We must untie these bonds that are so powerful, and henceforth love this and that, but be wedded only to ourselves. That is to say, let the other things be ours, but not joined and glued to us so strongly that they cannot be detached without tearing off our skin and some part of our flesh as well. The greatest thing in the world is to know how to belong to oneself" (178). This statement may sound cold, aloof, indifferent. It was made by a person who had loved and recently lost father, brother, first child, and best friend. With the loss of La Boétie still a living sorrow, Montaigne's wisdom reminds us of Augustine's warning about loving a friend too much: "What madness, to love a man as something more than human!" (4.7). But whereas Augustine would have us redirect our ultimate love and loyalty to God, Montaigne speaks of self-control, of listening to reason, and of acceptance of the common human lot. He does not preach that we should find in God our only lasting support, but advises us how best to prepare ourselves for life's inevitable losses. He advocates self-reliance, self-possession, and mastering a smaller world of one's own making. Solitude is part of a larger philosophical program based on the Stoic's resolution to minimize suffering and to steel the will to endure what is unavoidable. We shall see how this way of understanding solitude changes as Montaigne ages.

One other theme in "Of Solitude" deserves comment: the use of aloneness for literary pursuits. One of the chief attractions of solitude should be its freedom from the anxieties of worldly ambition. How, then, can a person devote his solitude to the quest for literary fame? Montaigne jokes about a pedant who sacrifices his health for grammar: "This fellow, all dirty, with running nose and eyes, whom you see coming out of his study after midnight, do you think he is seeking among his books how to make himself a better, happier, and wiser man? No such news. He is going to teach posterity the meter of Plautus' verses and the true spelling of a Latin word, or die in the attempt" (177–78). Montaigne criticizes two Roman writers, Cicero and the younger Pliny, who advocated the study of letters in order to gain a reputation, and the dedication of solitude to winning immortal fame. Such men only retire from the world halfway, and "by a ridiculous contradiction they still aspire to reap the fruit of their plan from the world when they have left it" (180). They still seek glory, a goal incompatible with the detachment and serenity that are Montaigne's own end:

> Now, as for glory, the goal that Pliny and Cicero set up for us, it is very far from my reckoning. The humor most directly opposite to retirement is ambition. Glory and repose are things that cannot lodge in the same dwelling. As far as I can see, these men have only their arms and legs outside the crowd; their souls, their intentions, are more than ever in the thick of it. . . . They have only stepped back to make a better jump, to get a stronger impetus wherewith to plunge deeper into the crowd. (182)

"There are ways to fail in solitude as well as in company," and the "ostentatious and talky philosophy" of Pliny and Cicero is Montaigne's chief example of misused solitude. In this way Montaigne takes a critical stance toward the humanistic tradition of literary solitude that profoundly shaped his own life and work, as he devoted thousands of hours, thousands of pages to his essays. He criticizes those who use their solitude only to throw themselves, in the form of their books, back into the crowd. This awareness of possible dangers in his own favored use of solitude distinguishes Montaigne from Petrarch and Gibbon, whose celebrations of literary solitude largely ignore the ways that the same vices condemned in public employments can contaminate the supposed purity of a life devoted to letters. I see Montaigne as the counterpart within the humanistic tradition of the Christian tradition's wiser desert fathers, for he is equally appreciative of the benefits of solitude and its potential dangers and distortions.

Montaigne's solitude was not as purely enjoyable as he had expected when he retired to his library. In a crucial passage in the early essay "Of Idleness," he ponders the origins of his impulse to write, significantly linking it with his sense of his mind being out of control: "Lately when I retired to my home, determined so far as possible to bother about nothing except spending the little life I have left in rest and seclusion, it seemed to me I could do my mind no greater favor than to let it entertain itself in full idleness and stay and settle in itself, which I hoped it might do more easily now, having become weightier and riper with time." Unfortunately, he found (quoting Lucan) that "idle hours breed wandering thoughts," and that his mind, "like a runaway horse . . . gives itself a hundred times more trouble than it took for others, and gives birth to so many chimeras and fantastic monsters, one after another, without order or purpose, that in order to contemplate their ineptitude and strangeness at my pleasure, I have begun to put them in writing, hoping in time to make my mind ashamed of itself" (21). Here we see the significant conjunction of an experience of solitude and the incentive to write autobiographically, but in a different form than in the case of Augustine or Petrarch. Montaigne's hope for calm and orderly reflection was disappointed and he was appalled by the unruly horde of monsters produced by his wandering mind. He writes to "contemplate" these fantastic images from a distance and eventually, he hopes, to make his mind "ashamed of itself." This passage marks a change in his conception of his essays; beyond simply recording his reactions to his reading, he now turns toward making a portrait of himself in all his complexity and an "assay" that he hopes will influence his moral character for the better. Fifteen years later he would write: "I have no more made my book than my book has made me" (504).[23]

References to monsters and to his dismay at his mind's anarchy reveal Montaigne's fear of madness. Another passage from the first edition of his essays also links writing to a negative experience of solitude that he associates with melancholy: "It was a melancholy humor, and consequently a humor very hostile to my natural disposition, produced by the gloom of the solitude into which I had cast myself some years ago, that first put into my head this daydream of meddling with writing. And then, finding myself entirely destitute and void of any other matter, I presented myself to myself for argument and subject" (278). Montaigne invokes the medical theory of the four humors, which was generally accepted in the sixteenth century. Melancholy was one of four basic personality types that were believed to be caused by blood, bile, phlegm, and black bile, the substance predominating in the melancholic.[24] Montaigne shared the contemporary view that melancholy individuals were drawn to reading and writing books. Like Robert Burton, who explored melancholy for hundreds of pages in *The Anatomy of Melancholy* (1621), Montaigne saw solitary individuals as tending to be melancholic in temperament. Prolonged solitude could also induce melancholy in other types of disposition. Burton concludes his massive tome with this succinct advice to the melancholic: "Be not solitary, be not idle."[25] With Burton, Shakespeare, and many other thinkers of his time, Montaigne was fascinated by melancholy, the humor associated with most of the mind's extreme states: the ecstacy of religious inspiration, the creative flights of genius, and the delirium of insanity. "As a man subject to melancholy, Montaigne could hope for genius and fear lunacy."[26]

Montaigne believed that he was a mixture of the melancholic temperament and the jovial, sanguine humor that brought hope and assurance. He worried that spending a great deal of time alone would increase his susceptibility to melancholy. The "gloom of solitude" was not for him a fixed destiny, but a constant possibility influenced partly by his own behavior. Being alone could modify his mood and subject him to the darker side of melancholy: suspicion, anxiety, and misanthropy. Writing a book is a dangerous pursuit for such an individual, for it risks accentuating the negative effects of melancholy. Yet writing is also, for Montaigne, a way of coping with the disordered mind's monsters and chimeras, an attempt to regain control. Idle minds need a task, a direction: "Unless you keep them busy with some definite subject that will bridle and control them, they throw themselves in disorder hither and yon in the vague field of imagination" (21). In analyzing the motivation for his literary project Montaigne describes both his susceptibility to the gloom of his dark humor and his resolve to oppose this tendency by giving his mind a series of set tasks. In the way he considers the subject of each essay, too, Montaigne resists the dangers of solitude, always testing and tempering his own views by consulting the opinions of others. He does not simply gaze within but compares his experiences and views with those of historical and literary figures. He withdrew into solitude in order to write his way out of solitude. He peopled his time alone with the best company he knew.

Montaigne's understanding of solitude developed considerably during the years he was writing his essays, which extend from when he was about forty until his death at fifty-nine. Modern editions of the *Essays* are printed to distinguish three kinds of material within the final text: "a," material published in the first edition of two books (1580); "b," material published as Book 3 and some six hundred additions to books 1 and 2 (1587); and "c," material added by Montaigne in the margins of the so-called Bordeaux edition, which went into the final edition of his work published after his death. Much modern scholarship on Montaigne explains apparent inconsistencies in the *Essays* as reflecting his evolving ideas. The most influential account of this development in English is Donald Frame's work, which describes a shift from a Stoic to a Skeptical to an Epicurean vision of life.[27] Montaigne's evolving understanding of solitude is closely related to this larger course of his ideas. So far we have considered only the first strata of his work, the "a" material in the first two books. In the "b" and "c" material, solitude is seen less as a permanent condition of retirement than as part of a natural rhythm in human life of engagement, disengagement, and return to the world. In a passage from "Three Kinds of Association," Montaigne asserts that solitude is a recurring need of his nature:

> There are private, retiring, and inward natures. My essential pattern is suited to communication and revelation. I am all in the open and in full view, born for company and friendship. The solitude that I love and preach is primarily nothing but leading my feelings and thoughts back to myself, restraining and shortening not my steps, but my desires and my cares, abandoning solicitude for outside things, and mortally avoiding servitude and obligation, and not so much the press of people as the press of business. Solitude of place, to tell the truth, rather makes me stretch and expand outward; I throw myself into affairs of state and into the world more readily when I am alone. At the Louvre and in the crowd I withdraw and contract into my skin; the crowd drives me back to myself. (625)

When Montaigne is alone his mind seeks contact with a larger world, projecting itself into the surrounding space; when his involvements with the world threaten to dissipate his sense of identity and integrity, he shrinks back into private meditations. Montaigne's description of solitude in this passage asserts his need for alternating intervals of openness to the world and reserve, for fresh contact with external reality and internal consolidation and freedom to reflect.

Solitude and sociability are equally necessary for Montaigne, provided that he has some choice in their timing: "By nature I am not an enemy to the bustle of courts; I have spent part of my life in them, and I am built to get along cheerfully in large companies, provided it is at intervals and at my own times. But that indolence of taste that I have been speaking of attaches me forcibly to solitude, even at home, in the midst of a numerous household and as many visitors as anywhere" (625). In this passage Montaigne's discussion of solitude merges with another central theme of his thinking, the disjunctions between one's public role and one's private consciousness of self. This topic becomes a dominant motif in his last discussions of solitude.

In the opening paragraph of the same essay, "Of Three Kinds of Association," he contrasts the flexible, versatile person he admires with those whose subjection to a humor makes them narrow, rigid, and only half alive: "We must not nail ourselves down so firmly to our humors and dispositions. Our principal talent is the ability to apply ourselves to various practices. It is existing, but not living, to keep ourselves bound and obliged by necessity to a single course. The fairest souls are those that have the most variety and adaptability" (621). Montaigne would surely extend this assessment to those who can only be comfortable when they are either alone or with company. His assertion of the need to rise above our humors reflects Montaigne's recognition of the dangers of his own attraction to solitude, and his considered advice to himself. He values both sociability and solitude; his ideal is a versatile and adaptable soul with many interests, many talents, and many kinds of association with the world, including those best nurtured in solitude.

Although Montaigne does not analyze it at length in any of the essays in Book 3, solitude is an important dimension of his reflections on several other topics. It is an essential aspect of the "movement" that Jean Starobinski traces throughout Montaigne's thought. Starobinski discerns a basic sequence of three stages in Montaigne's thinking about a variety of issues, including friendship, death, freedom, the body, love, language, and political life. Montaigne loves triads and three-part structures; his essays are full of examples. He usually begins by denouncing the dissimulation and hypocrisy surrounding a topic. From uncritical acceptance of prevailing notions, from immersion in a world of false appearances, Montaigne withdraws. He tries to be self-sufficient, autonomous, truthful according to his own standards. In a third phase, Montaigne typically realizes that to define and realize himself, an individual needs other people and received ideas. He therefore returns to various forms of relationship with other people, and to participation in conventions, in a more complex and detached way.

The second phase of Montaigne's "motion" is essentially a movement into and through solitude. By withdrawing from public conventions, the individual seeks to define his own world. Disengagement is a crucial phase of experience, from which a person returns with an altered sense of relationship to the external world. In Starobinski's analysis of the self's relation to others, he describes Montaigne's three-part motion in terms suggestive for our study of solitude: "The break with the world, the withdrawal into individual existence, can only be an intermediary phase between two styles of 'relating to others': the first, a consequence of one's social roots and customary attachments, is experienced in an almost unconscious manner, connected with the specious need for prestige, and directly determined by the surrounding environment; the second, much more far-reaching, implies that one is fully in possession of oneself and virtually open to the universal, which is acknowledged and accepted with full clarity of mind. Thus one's relations to others run the gamut from blind dependence to self-mastery."[28] After severing his bonds to the family, the state, or the local community, Montaigne returns to these relationships neither estranged from nor absorbed by them. Instead he can evaluate his connections in a detached way, both critical and appreciative. After dependence and an attempt at total autonomy by separating oneself from relationship, "in a third phase a full legitimacy is restored to the bond, woven of concrete obligations and duties, that unites us to our surroundings."[29] Thus Montaigne moves from uncritical dependence to attempts at self-sufficiency, and finally to a disciplined and principled relationship based on choice and commitment.

Unlike the view that Montaigne moved from Stoic to Skeptic to Epicurean in a linear process over the years, this interpretation sees Montaigne as repeatedly going through the motion of withdrawal and return. The need for disengagement is not an intellectual stage that one leaves behind once a final balanced position is achieved. Rather, Montaigne discerned a continual dialectical movement in life as an individual seeks to define a personal identity and establish a satisfactory relationship to the social world. There are countless areas of life in which a person may realize that he is being ruled by the opinions of others, attempt to think critically about the terms of relationship, and return to social involvements in a more free, relaxed, even playful manner. Solitude can facilitate the moment of disengagement and critical detachment from the social environment.

As an example of how Montaigne's thinking about a specific issue incorporates the motion of withdrawal and return, consider the late essay "Of Husbanding the Will," which treats his involvements in public affairs. For a person who loved solitude, Montaigne's political commitments were extensive. Although he had resigned his position in Parliament and retired to his estate, Montaigne was involved in numerous political negotiations during the bitter religious warfare and dynastic struggles of his era. In spite of his reluctance, he was elected mayor of Bordeaux and served for two terms. "Of Husbanding the Will" begins with Montaigne's assertion that he has been engaged in, but not possessed by, public affairs: "In comparison with most men, few things touch me, or, to put it better, hold me; for it is right that things should touch us, provided they do not possess us" (766). Self-containment does not mean that he does not care about or serve others but that there is always a limit: "We must lend ourselves to others and give ourselves only to ourselves" (767). The central thrust of this essay is the need to maintain a free spirit, a free soul, in the midst of one's engagements. He mocks those who are "seized and carried away" by little things as well as large, and those who "seek business only for busyness" (767). Such fussy and overcommitted persons forget their duties to the self: "You have quite enough to do at home; don't go away." Montaigne is extensively involved in public affairs and actively concerned about other people, but he will not ruin his health or peace of mind for them: "If people have sometimes pushed me into the management of other men's affairs, I have promised to take them in hand, not in lungs and liver; to take them on my shoulders, not incorporate them into me; to be concerned over them, yes; to be impassioned over them, never" (767). He will "look to" public affairs but not "brood" over them. The memory of his father, "his soul cruelly agitated by this public turmoil," is a constant reminder of the danger of overcommitment. Although Montaigne admires his father's altruism and self-sacrifice, he will not imitate these qualities. His father was heedless of his own wellbeing in serving the public good, believing that "the individual was not to be considered at all in comparison with the general" (769).

Montaigne seeks to establish a more harmonious balance between private happiness and the common good.

Detachment does not prevent one from doing one's public duty, Montaigne found. It may actually help one to deal with others more efficiently and impartially, for "we never conduct well the thing that possesses and conducts us" (770). Montaigne recommends that we play our part in the social world conscious of the deceptive appearances attached to social roles. The masks that he had begun by criticizing as hypocritical lies are now seen as necessary to the drama of human interaction: "We must play our part duly, but as the part of a borrowed character. Of the mask and appearance we must not make a real essence, nor of what is foreign what is our very own. We cannot distinguish the skin from the shirt. It is enough to make up our face, without making up our heart" (773). Montaigne's style of political leadership reflects this attitude: "The mayor and Montaigne have always been two, with a very clear separation" (774). When he needs to lose his temper or display anger, he can "borrow it and wear it as a mask" (782).

While Montaigne had conservative political beliefs, it is wrong to condemn him, as some have done, as merely an advocate for the status quo whose only real interest was protecting his own privileged position in society. His insights into public life apply to all partisan allegiances. Montaigne holds that political commitments, however well-intentioned or ethically justifiable, do not subsume the whole of our being or satisfy all the soul's longings. He would perform his appointed tasks without identifying his whole being with them or resting his entire happiness on the outcome. We must don our masks, but never confuse them with our private consciousness; we must do what is required with decency and fairness but not sell our souls. Montaigne does not retract his earlier criticisms of the hypocrisy behind many of society's false appearances, but he has learned that it is in this world that the individual must act, define himself, and perhaps even learn to enjoy himself. Summing up his assessment of his political career, Montaigne declares himself satisfied with modest accomplishments: he had a tranquil administration with no crises or heroic achievements. To those who would criticize his service as lacking in zeal or activity, he admits his limitations—and more: "I had published elaborately enough to the world my inadequacy in such public management. I have something still worse than inadequacy: that I hardly mind it, and hardly try to cure it, in view of the course of life that I have designed for myself. I did not satisfy myself either in this undertaking, but I accomplished about what I had promised myself" (784). Montaigne's attitude to public life thus reflects his insistence on detachment, disengagement, and withdrawal not as a permanent condition but as part of a natural rhythm in a person's relation to the social world. No longer does he choose solitude primarily to protect himself from life's trials and losses, but to face them with an inner strength.

In his most mature reflections in Book 3, Montaigne's cheerful affirmation of solitude shows a distinctive wisdom and spiritual orientation. A fine passage from "Of Experience" places solitude within the context of his view of Nature as at once guiding moral norm and beneficent source of pleasure: "When I dance, I dance; when I sleep, I sleep; yes, and when I walk alone in a beautiful orchard, if my thoughts have been dwelling on extraneous incidents for some part of the time, for some other part I bring them back to the walk, to the orchard, to the sweetness of this solitude, and to me. Nature has observed this principle like a mother, that the actions she has enjoined on us for our need should also give us pleasure; and she invites us to them not only through reason, but also through appetite. It is unfair to infringe her laws" (850). The desire for solitude reflects both an essential human need and an inexhaustible source of enjoyment for Montaigne, and making a place for it in one's life is a part of wisdom: "It is an absolute perfection and virtually divine to know how to enjoy our being rightfully" (857), and the knowledge of how to enjoy solitude, how to use it well, is one aspect of the wisdom his essays convey.

Montaigne's view of solitude is closely related to his "Epicurean" affirmation of nature and sense experience, which have been variously interpreted in relation to Christian tradition. Some, emphasizing his skeptical epistemology, see him as departing from orthodox beliefs and moving away from Christianity. In contrast, M. A. Screech speaks of Montaigne's "Christian Epicureanism" as the first attempt to work out a spirituality for lay Catholics.[30] At the close of his final essay, Montaigne speaks of God as Creator of the natural world that we should enjoy and appreciate:

> As for me, I love life and cultivate it just as God has been pleased to grant it to us. I do not go about wishing that it should lack the need to eat and drink, and it would seem to me no less excusable a failing to wish that need to be doubled. . . . I accept with all my heart and with gratitude what nature has done for me, and I am pleased with myself and proud of myself that I do. We wrong that great and all-powerful Giver by refusing his gift, nullifying it, and disfiguring it. Himself all good, he has made all things good. . . . There is no part unworthy of our

care in this gift that God has given us; we are accountable for it even to a single hair. (854–56)

The context of these words is Montaigne's affirmation of the body and his criticisms of dualistic philosophies and religious views that denigrate the physical basis of human existence in order to exalt our spiritual nature. The passage articulates the kind of balanced perspective Montaigne would also have offered as a corrective to those who claim too much for either solitude or social relationship. We need to know how to enjoy each kind of experience and to see it as a gift. The contours of a life are etched by continual movements between these equally important experiences. To be enslaved to either one's solitude or one's relationships is to miss an aspect of life's fullness and freedom—hence Montaigne's insistence on the capacity for detachment from whatever threatens to tether the soul's mobility. "It is for little souls, buried under the weight of business, to be unable to detach themselves cleanly from it or to leave it and pick it up again" (851). The capacity for enjoyment is as important to him as detachment, and bodily pleasures have a rightful place alongside the pursuit of wisdom and the stern demands of moral duty. Montaigne's view of solitude reflects this larger context of ideas about the need for balance between detachment and engagement, private consciousness and public role-playing, and the motives of duty and pleasure in the conduct of life.

Montaigne seems to me in many ways a model of a right understanding of solitude. He sees the rhythms of involvement and disengagement from other people as an ongoing part of life, and would not choose one at the expense of the other. The inner life of reflective meditation and the public life of outward action must each be given their due. No hermit or misanthrope, he avows that "he who lives not at all unto others, hardly lives unto himself" (769). He speaks frankly of his need for solitude even as he recognizes its dangers, the "monsters and chimeras" that can disorder an ordinary mind when dislocated from social interactions. He affirms the pleasures and duties of personal relationship and of public service; he also sees the waste of time and energy brought about by excessive, overcommitted busyness with what does not finally much matter. Montaigne knows that the best solitude is a matter of attitude as well as of location, requiring detachment from excessive concern. For Montaigne, the capacity for solitude reveals a person's fundamental orientation to life.

As does Augustine, Montaigne understands that solitude should have a definite but delineated place in a human life, limited in duration and sustained by social bonds. In contrast with Augustine, he sees solitude not simply as a momentary escape from the prying eyes of others, or as an occasion for communion with God, but as enjoyable for its own sake. He is less concerned than Petrarch about using solitude for positive social ends. Solitude need not be used for prayer or literary productivity, and its cultivation for its own sake can be an important instance of knowing "how to enjoy our being rightfully." While in his early Stoical phase Montaigne withdrew into solitude primarily because of apprehension about possible harm to himself, he learned to enjoy retirement with a more relaxed, cheerful, and affirmative attitude. This genial, appreciative, and celebratory mood discloses a new understanding of solitude. Yet Montaigne is not naive about aloneness because he knows its dark and melancholy side. His approach to solitude reflects his version of Catholic faith yet appeals to many readers with different beliefs but a similar desire to affirm the goodness of life in all its mixed and diverse complexity. The *Essays* that emerged from Montaigne's solitude reveal a person often fully engaged with the minds of others, and at other times allowing himself to be idle or to simply observe his world: "When I walk alone in a beautiful orchard, . . ." (850). His wisdom about aloneness draws the reader into a more alert awareness of one's own solitude at the same time that one is brought into relationship with Montaigne's unique individuality. Later writers will discover other aspects of solitude, and narrative accounts will explore in more detail how the meaning of solitude shapes and is shaped by a person's sense of personal history. For basic wisdom about the place of solitude in life, for insight into its value and limitations, Montaigne sets a standard by which to measure other thinkers.

Gibbon

When Edward Gibbon (1737–94) wrote his memoirs he concentrated on the experiences that enabled him to write *The Decline and Fall of the Roman Empire*. His public writings, he says, "can alone entitle me to the esteem and friendship of my readers."[31] Like Benjamin Franklin, Gibbon was one of the first persons writing in English to focus his life's story not on religious matters but on his secular work, treating his early years as the training-ground for adult achievement. Gibbon presents solitude as a crucial condition for his career as a writer, and his memoirs analyze the circumstances in his life that converged to make him a person with a strong desire for solitude.

The term "autobiography" did not yet exist when Gibbon experimented with six manuscript drafts of his life story, slowly working his way toward a satisfactory self-portrait. These six drafts were edited into a composite text by Gibbon's friend Lord Sheffield, and this version has been further revised by modern scholars restoring material that Sheffield emended or deleted to produce a more flattering impression of Gibbon. Passing over textual problems related to alternative versions of "Gibbon's autobiography," I will rely on a modern scholarly text based on Sheffield's version that contains the significant passages on solitude.

Gibbon was the only one of seven children in his family to survive infancy. His mother died when he was nine, and he was largely neglected by his father. He was raised by an aunt, Catherine Porten, for whom he expressed fondness, but much of his boyhood was spent alone. Gibbon was a sickly child whose small size and unathletic body led him to prefer books to playing with friends. "Instead of repining at my long and frequent confinement to the chamber or couch, I secretly rejoiced in these infirmities, which delivered me from the exercises of the school and the society of my equals. As often as I was tolerably exempt from danger and pain, reading, free desultory reading, was the employment and comfort of my solitary hours" (25). From an early age, Gibbon felt an "invincible love of reading, which I should not exchange for the treasures of India" (21). The future historian was allowed to read following his own interests, and this soon became his chief enjoyment: "the dynasties of Assyria and Egypt were my top and cricket-ball" (26).

Gibbon depicts himself as an autodidact whose native genius was fortunately spared the boredom of formal schooling. The central principle of his self-teaching was "vague and multifarious reading," following his own interests. Although satisfying his random curiosity did not teach him to think critically, what he appreciates most about his youth is his intellectual freedom:

A school is the cavern of fear and sorrow; the mobility of the captive youths is chained to a book and a desk: an inflexible master commands their attention, which, every moment, is impatient to escape: they labour, like the soldiers of Persia, under the scourge; and their education is nearly finished before they can apprehend the sense or utility of the harsh lessons which they are forced to repeat. Such blind and absolute dependence may be necessary, but can never be delightful. Freedom is the first wish of our heart; freedom is the first blessing of our nature: and unless we blind ourselves with the voluntary chains of interest or passion, we advance in freedom as we advance in years. (27)

When he was fifteen Gibbon was sent to Oxford University, where he spent fourteen months. His caustic remarks about "the bigots of Oxford" and "the monks of Magdalen," as he called his professors, reveal his contempt for sloth and subservience to religious ortho-doxy: "From the toil of reading, or thinking, or writing, they had absolved their conscience, and the first shoots of learning and inge-nuity withered on the ground" (33). He was not oppressed by the demands of Oxford, for his tutors hardly bothered to acknowledge his existence. Significant learning only happened when he followed the bent of his own mind. Every distinguished thinker, he writes, has two educations, "the first from his teachers; the second, more personal and important, from himself" (46). Gibbon's education did not come in Oxford's clubby and stultifying atmosphere but rather in the school of solitude.

While he was at Oxford, Gibbon went through a religious conver-sion to Roman Catholicism that led to his leaving the university. In retrospect "it seems incredible that I could ever believe that I believed in transubstantiation" (39). He attributes his conversion solely to the influence of reading controversial works of theology: "The blind activity of idleness urged me to advance without armour into the dangerous mazes of controversy; and at the age of sixteen, I bewildered myself in the errors of the Church of Rome" (38). Catholic controversialists persuaded him of the errors of Protestantism: "I read, I applauded, I believed" (39). Gibbon portrays himself as subject to a youthful "momentary glow of enthusiasm" and as sacrificing his personal interests to conscience. The whole process was effected within himself, and he had not met a Catholic nor been to a Catholic Mass when he made his decision: "I never conversed with a priest, or even with a Papist, till my resolution from books was absolutely fixed" (40).

His return to Protestantism happened in a similar way, as the result of solitary reflection and conviction. His father sent him to Switzerland to remove him from Catholic influences in England. In Lausanne, Gibbon was taken under the supervision of a Calvinist minister, Daniel Pavillard. Although Gibbon gives some credit to Pavillard, his conversion back to Protestantism "was principally effected by my private reflections; and I still remember my solitary transport at the discovery of a philosophical argument against the doctrine of transubstantiation. . . . The various articles of the Romish creed disappeared like a dream; and after a full conviction, on Christ-mas Day, 1754, I received the sacrament in the church of Lausanne. It was here that I suspended my religious inquiries, acquiescing with implicit belief in the tenets and mysteries which are adopted by the general consent of Catholics and Protestants" (46). "Acquiescence" with "implicit" belief in the articles of Christian faith was to remain his stance for the rest of his life. He indicates his indifference, even aversion, to further speculation; the differences between Protestant and Catholic beliefs, as well as how the Anglican Church compares to these, no longer seem to him significant as he writes.

Scholars differ as to whether Gibbon's position was simply a cover for the skepticism and outright cynicism that often emerge in his discussions of Christianity in the *Decline and Fall*, or whether Gibbon did hold many Christian convictions, even if he doubted the conclusiveness or utility of theological speculation.[32] Gibbon's hostility to Christianity in the *Decline and Fall* is partly attributable to his painful experience of enthusiastic religious commitment swaying him against his better judgment. Having once had the course of his life drastically changed by religion, Gibbon determined not to be so moved again by its emotional force or abstruse theological reasoning. He henceforth held himself aloof from religious controversy, surveying the role of religion in history but detached from any party and forgoing further personal searching. Although Gibbon presents his conversion, deconversion, and reconversion as coming about in solitude, he views himself as exceptional. In general he viewed religion as a social phenomenon, and he tried to protect himself from its dangers by preserving the stance of a solitary observer of history.

Five years in Switzerland contributed to Gibbon's sense of himself as a detached observer. When he arrived, "suddenly cast on a foreign land," he could not speak French, and found himself shut off from communication. He was "an exile and a prisoner," a castaway who had lost his country. But this period of separation from England brought substantial benefits in the long run, for during the years in Switzerland he learned French, Latin, and Greek and began to focus his intellectual interests on history. He developed the habits of dispassionate observation and ironic perspective that were to serve him well as a writer. What first felt like miserable exile, banishment, and disgrace turned out to be a fortunate fall: "Whatsoever have been the fruits of my education, they must be ascribed to the fortunate shipwreck which cast me on the shores of the Leman lake" (56). Had he remained at university, he would have been "steeped in port and prejudice among the monks of Oxford," and his knowledge of the world "confined to an English cloister." As it was, his experience of being an outsider was an excellent preparation for understanding another empire, another era. Displacement from England had a cost:

"poverty and pride estranged me from my countymen." By the time he returned from Switzerland, at age twenty-one, Gibbon "had ceased to be an Englishman" (56). He never laments the estrangements from family, religion, and nation that led him to develop so strong a sense of himself as a separate being, a singular individual. In this way he seems the antithesis of that other founding figure of modern autobiography, Jean-Jacques Rousseau, who constantly yearns for total transparency and identification with an ideal community. Yet in different ways, solitude helped each of these men discover a new form of writing and a new way of thinking about the self. For Gibbon and Rousseau, solitude seems a constitutive condition of the sense of singularity expressed in those writings that demarcate the origin of secular autobiography.

While he was in Switzerland, Gibbon fell in love with and became engaged to a Swiss pastor's daughter, Susan Curchod. His father would not permit the marriage, and Gibbon, afraid to lose his inheritance, broke the engagement: "After a painful struggle I yielded to my fate: I sighed as a lover, I obeyed as a son" (55). This incident has not won Gibbon many modern admirers; he seems to most readers an insufferably self-interested and self-contained person, and rather a cold fish. Gibbon must have realized that marriage would interfere too much with his freedom, his ambitions, and his prized self-sufficiency. He never again seriously considered marriage, even after he had become financially independent and a famous author. "A matrimonial alliance has ever been the object of my terror rather than of my wishes" (87). His irritation at the incessant minor demands of family life comes through clearly in the following description of his residence with his father and new stepmother after his return to England:

> At home I occupied a pleasant and spacious apartment; the library on the same floor was soon considered as my peculiar domain; and I might say with truth, that I was never less alone than when by myself. My sole complaint, which I piously suppressed, arose from the kind restraint imposed on the freedom of my time. By the habit of early rising I always secured a sacred portion of the day, and many scattered moments were stolen and employed by my studious industry. But the family hours of breakfast, of dinner, of tea, and of supper were regular and long; after breakfast Mrs. Gibbon expected my company in her dressing-room; after tea my father claimed my conversation and the perusal of the newspapers; and in the midst of an interesting work I was often called down to receive the visit of some idle neighbors. (62)

Gibbon contrasts the tiresome obligations of politeness with the joys of solitude, which he characterizes both as "a sacred portion of the day" and as a guilty, forbidden secret that must be "stolen" from others. He never admitted feeling lonely (until the very end of his life) and cautiously avoided any sort of attachment that would encumber him with irksome duties, whether to individuals, institutions, or communities.

He found his chief satisfactions in relation to ideas, and the reading and writing of books occupied in his life the central position that family or religious commitment did for others. In relation to books he could feel a measure of control and avoid being dominated by emotion or authority. Although his writings are often disdainful of the passion and enthusiasm characteristic of human sexuality and religion, he displays a great deal of intellectual passion, especially for the twenty-year project of writing *The Decline and Fall of the Roman Empire*.

Gibbon returned to England in 1758, at the age of twenty-one. The next decade was difficult, for in spite of his reserved temperament and studious habits he yearned for a definite role or standing in English life. He was financially dependent on his father until his death in 1770 and lived primarily in his father's home. The elder Gibbon had neglected his son as a boy, ill-advisedly sent him at fifteen to Oxford, exiled him from England for more than five years, barred his marriage, and now subjected him to various arbitrary decisions, requiring him to join the militia and to engage in tedious social visits. Gibbon watched helplessly as his father squandered part of his inheritance. Given eighteenth-century norms of propriety, Gibbon is explicit about his conflicts with his father.[33] As he approached thirty, he "began to feel the desire of being master in my own house" (87). He longed for independence from his father, for "such is the law of our imperfect nature, that we must either command or obey" (87). The roots of Gibbon's detachment and his need to establish an independent place for himself are entangled in his longstanding conflict with his father.

How can a person be independent, autonomous, and self-reliant without a secure social role? How can one "command" without other persons who will "obey"? As much as Gibbon wanted solitude, he wanted involvement in his society. This was his dilemma for a number of years. The image of solitude as a lonely and frightening situation of disconnection emerges as he recalls his feeling of inertia during this period: "While so many of my acquaintance were married or in parliament, or advancing with a rapid step in the various roads of honours and fortune, I stood alone, immovable and insignificant" (87).

He wanted financial resources not only to establish his independence but to help needy friends. Keenly interested in the difference money makes in life, Gibbon discusses his economic situation several times. Unlike many solitaries, he does not idealize poverty or the simple life, but finds the best position to be a middle station: "In circumstances more indigent or more wealthy, I should never have accomplished the task, or acquired the fame, of an historian; . . . Few works of merit and importance have been executed either in a garret or a palace" (96). His father's death finally gave him, at the age of thirty-three, the means to define himself on his own terms. He does not hide the brevity of his grief or his relief at finally coming into his inheritance, for his father's death was "the only event that could save me from an hopeless life of obscurity and indigence" (96).

Gibbon alludes to certain personal attributes that he links to his choices to live in solitude and to express himself primarily in writing. He was slightly less than five feet tall and rather fat; by the end of his life he had great difficulty in walking. Many acquaintances thought him rather ugly. He dressed ostentatiously and had a number of irritating mannerisms. Jokes were frequently made at his expense and many of his contemporaries, including Johnson and Boswell, disliked him. His physical appearance and the teasing and ridicule he must have suffered as a boy help explain why from a very early age he tended to keep to himself. In addition, Gibbon was a timid speaker. He admits this in describing his silence during his years in Parliament: "After a fleeting illusive hope, prudence condemned me to acquiesce in the humble station of a mute. I was not armed by nature or education with the intrepid energy of mind and voice. Timidity was fortified by pride, and even the success of my pen discouraged the trial of my voice" (98). In letters Gibbon confesses to a feeling of humiliating failure at his inability to speak publicly.[34] Because of his awkwardness in speaking, Gibbon put his energy into expressing himself in writing. The connection between his physical and psychological limitations and his solitary studiousness emerges in a revealing passage in the memoirs: "I had not been endowed by art or nature with those happy gifts of confidence and address, which unlock every door and every bosom; nor would it be reasonable to complain of the just consequences of my sickly childhood, foreign education, and reserved temper. While coaches were rattling through Bond Street, I have passed many a solitary evening in my lodging with my books" (60–61). Gibbon does not complain, but he weighs the costs and the benefits, comparing what he gave up with what he achieved through his choice of solitude.

Gibbon's foremost biographer has challenged the view of Gibbon as, among other things, an awkward recluse. Patricia Craddock documents that, especially after Gibbon became a celebrated author, he had many friends, was an able conversationalist, and enjoyed a busy social life.[35] Gibbon asserts that after his initial sense of isolation, "in each of the twenty-five years of my acquaintance with London (1758–83), the prospect gradually brightened; and this unfavourable picture most properly belongs to the first period after my return from Switzerland" (61). Yet Gibbon sees the capacity for solitude as central in his character, and recognizes that the foundations of character are laid in early years. In reconstructing his life, in trying to understand the experiences that gave him his most profound feelings about himself as an individual and his sense of direction, Gibbon links his mental and bodily limitations to his basic impulse to withdraw from active intercourse with other people and to concentrate his energies on writing. Whatever the anecdotal evidence from others about his social manner or apparent self-confidence, Gibbon's memoirs make clear his own sense of solitude as central to his identity, and in part a compensation for his limitations.

After his father's death Gibbon established himself in London and began the immense labor of writing the six volumes of his *Decline and Fall of the Roman Empire.* He had written very little before this, and selecting a topic had long preoccupied him. He wanted sole command of a new field, and therefore avoided the history of England, "where every character is a problem, and every reader a friend or an enemy; where a writer is supposed to hoist a flag of party, and is devoted to damnation by the adverse faction" (75). Although Gibbon describes his temper as "not very susceptible of enthusiasm," he reveals his deep feelings when exploring Rome for the first time: "At the distance of twenty-five years, I can neither forget nor express the strong emotions which agitated my mind as I first approached, and entered the *eternal city.* . . . Several days of intoxication were lost or enjoyed before I could descend to a cool and minute investigation" (84). One of two high points of the memoirs is Gibbon's portrayal of his realization, in solitary reflection, that he might undertake a history of the fall of Rome: "It was at Rome, on the 15th of October, 1764, as I sat musing amidst the ruins of the Capitol, while the barefooted friars were singing vespers in the Temple of Jupiter, that the idea of writing the decline and fall of the city first started to my mind" (85). The significance of this scene is not diminished but highlighted by the speculation of biographers that (like Augustine's conversion scene) it may never have happened.[36] Gibbon created a

moment of epiphany which symbolically placed him in the exact
position he would occupy as historian: detached and solitary observer
of a community perceived as waning in influence, surviving through
the inertia of past achievements, and destined for ruin. His situation
as solitary observer allows Gibbon to perceive Christianity's role in
the modern world as analogous to the role of Rome in the ancient
world.

His feelings when he finally completed the last volume, some
three thousand pages and two decades later, are conveyed in equally
compelling terms:

> I have presumed to mark the moment of conception: I shall now com-
> memorate the hour of my final deliverance. It was on the day, or rather
> the night, of the 27th of June, 1787, between the hours of eleven and
> twelve, that I wrote the last lines of the last page, in a summer-house in
> my garden. After laying down my pen, I took several turns in a *berceau*,
> or covered walk of acacias, which commands a prospect of the coun-
> try, the lake, and the mountains. The air was temperate, the sky was
> serene, the silver orb of the moon was reflected from the waters, and
> all nature was silent. I will not dissemble the first emotions of joy on
> the recovery of my freedom, and, perhaps, the establishment of my
> fame. But my pride was soon humbled, and a sober melancholy was
> spread over my mind, by the idea that I had taken my everlasting leave
> of an old and agreeable companion, and that whatsoever might be the
> future date of my *History*, the life of the historian must be short and
> precarious. (114–15)

The climactic moments of Gibbon's autobiography describe the genesis and completion of his *magnum opus*. These scenes replace the
religious confession's drama of conversion, each condensing into a
highly charged emotional event the meaning of the author's life. For
Gibbon, as for many spiritual autobiographers, the climactic moments
of his life are represented as solitary experiences. He indicates in this
symbolic way that the meaning of his life is bound up not only with
his work, but with the solitude necessary for it.[37]

Gibbon's attitude to his writing shows his need to shield himself
from the influences of other people. As he wrote the history he kept
the work to himself, having been "disgusted" by the responses of
those to whom he read the manuscript: "Some will praise from politeness, and some will criticize from vanity. The author himself is the
best judge of his own performance; none has so deeply meditated
on the subject; none is so sincerely interested in the event" (98). He

insists that his work is the product of his mind alone: "Not a sheet has been seen by any human eyes, except those of the author and the printer: the faults and the merits are exclusively my own" (115).

Gibbon's solitude influenced the literary qualities of the *Decline and Fall.* According to W. B. Carnochan, Gibbon's experiences of aloneness helped him to discover the proper narrative stance for historical interpretation. The narrator takes his stance "on a high Roman promontory" that enables him to command history, to see it entire and judge it morally. "This point of view has been called 'Olympian,' and accurately so, for Gibbon views history in a long prospect. Encouraging reflections on mutability and the insufficiency of life's enjoyments, the prospect situation enables him to preserve, though with a difference, the utterance of the traditional moralist who watches the turns of Fortune's wheel."[38] Gibbon's private experience of solitude nurtured the qualities of irony, skeptical reserve, and temperate satire that mark his style as a narrator of history. His literary vision in the *Decline* reflects qualities of his inner life that were developed in solitude and allowed him to contemplate as if from a high prospect the reversals of individual destiny in history.[39]

Historical exemplars of solitude are treated in revealing ways within the *Decline and Fall.* Gibbon had little sympathy for the ascetic desert fathers, diagnosing Saint Antony's influence in this way: "a hideous, distorted and emaciated maniac, without knowledge, without patriotism, without natural affection, spending his life in a long routine of useless and atrocious self-torture, and quailing before the ghastly phantoms of his delirious brain, had become the ideal of nations which had known the writings of Plato and Cicero and the lives of Socrates and Cato."[40] Yet while solitude used for self-mortification is repulsive to Gibbon, a capacity for solitude is a notable attribute of many of the historical figures he admires, shaping his portraits of the scholar Barlaam, Julian the Apostate, the Empress Theodora, and "Mahomet."[41] Referring to arguments about Mahomet's sole authorship of the Koran, Gibbon writes that "conversation enriches the understanding, but solitude is the school of genius; and the uniformity of a work denotes the hand of a single artist."[42] Gibbon's own love of solitude colors his view of the founder of Islam, and his description of the Koran suggests one of the virtues of another book whose integrity comes from a solitary thinker: *The Decline and Fall of the Roman Empire.*

The final stage of Gibbon's life was spent in Lausanne, where he returned in 1783 and lived, except for visits, for his remaining years. He presents his change of residence as a withdrawal into solitude.

The opinion of the world "unanimously condemned this voluntary banishment," by which Gibbon broke his "English chain" to return to Switzerland. Recalling the words of Horace, he bade farewell to "the smoke and wealth and din of Rome" (111). When he wrote his memoirs he had been living in Lausanne for seven years. As he summed up his life since completing the *Decline,* he felt a need to defend his way of life in his new home. Lausanne provides solitude when he wants it, yet he can still emerge from the privacy of his library as an acclaimed author in great demand. Besides the cheaper cost of living in Switzerland, Gibbon enjoys his greater relative social standing: "in London I was lost in the crowd; I ranked with the first families of Lausanne" (112). Although social life is one of his pleasures, he is inclined to share "companionable idleness" rather than any more demanding interaction: "after the morning has been occupied by the labours of the library, I wish to unbend rather than to exercise my mind; and in the interval between tea and supper I am far from disdaining the innocent amusement of a game of cards" (112). Even though he undertook no extensive writing project after the *Decline* except for his memoirs, Gibbon by now viewed other people habitually as a light diversion to refresh his mind for the morrow's labors. He did have two close and lasting friendships. In Lausanne he lived for several years with his old friend Georges Deyverdun, whose conversations "would have reconciled me to a desert or a prison." When Deyverdun died Gibbon felt a loneliness that he had never known: "I feel, and with the decline of years I shall more painfully feel, that I am alone in paradise" (120). Gibbon also had a long and deep friendship with John Holroyd, Lord Sheffield, who edited the memoirs. With many other acquaintances and relatives he carried on more modest interactions. It was with his intellectual work that Gibbon had the deepest engagement, the most intense involvement.

There is a paradox in a person's choosing solitude in order to write books, addressing an audience and hoping for renown. Gibbon never comments on the irony of this situation, which so struck Montaigne. Montaigne warned that the ambition to achieve literary fame is a social passion as destructive of the soul's serenity as any of the more obvious ones. Gibbon, in contrast, recalls fondly an early endeavor at writing when he first heard "the music of public applause" (36). He acknowledges his need for critics and judges of his work at an early stage of his career: "A writer can seldom be content with the doubtful recompense of solitary approbation; but a youth ignorant of the world, and of himself, must desire to weigh his talents in some scales less partial than his own" (65). He is disgusted by authors who

complain that fame is fleeting and illusory, and relishes his own literary reputation, proudly asserting that it has been enough in itself
to make his life worthwhile. The *Decline and Fall* "has given me a
name, a rank, a character, in the world, to which I should not otherwise have been entitled" (123). In the closing passage of his memoirs, he frankly admits his hope that future generations will read his
works and respect his name: "In old age, the consolation of hope is
reserved for the tenderness of parents, who commence a new life in
their children; the faith of enthusiasts, who sing Hallelujahs above
the clouds; and the vanity of authors, who presume the immortality
of their name and writings" (124–25). There is something refreshing
about Gibbon's frank pronouncement of the basis of his self-esteem.
Yet he seems overly attached to a highly elusive judgment from others,
as even he recognizes by deprecating the "vanity" of his hope.

Gibbon's significance for the present study is that he so clearly ties
the meaning of his life to work that could only have been completed
in solitude. Unlike Montaigne and others who defend an elderly man's
retirement to solitude after a career of public service, Gibbon does not
feel the need to earn the right to withdrawal, and chose it at a very
young age. His cultivation of aloneness is inextricably bound up
with his sense of his singularity and individuality.[43] Gibbon's belief
in the distinction of his work is a bedrock value, a core conviction,
his court of last appeal as he assesses his life. With Benjamin Franklin
and Jean-Jacques Rousseau, Gibbon inaugurates in the eighteenth
century the modern quest for unique individuality that soon becomes
a form of spiritual search, replacing the search for God as the central
task of life. In spite of his professed Christian beliefs, he has little
awareness of or desire for relationship to God or for demanding spiritual practice. Gibbon represents, then, a further stage on the road to
secularization—both of autobiography and of solitude—that we have
traced in Petrarch and Montaigne. Unlike them, he has no interest in
justifying his writing or his solitude in Christian terms. The significance of his life, both for his readers and for himself, is his having
written a masterpiece of history. All his experience is interpreted as
preparation for this supreme achievement. He showed in his memoirs that *The Decline and Fall of the Roman Empire* could only have
been written by a person with a great capacity for aloneness, someone whose qualities as a narrator were honed in solitary reflection.
When he wrote the six drafts of his memoir, Gibbon was especially
interested in the various influences and events that predisposed him
to solitude; he focused the climactic scenes on his solitary thoughts
and feelings as he conceived and delivered his literary offspring; and

he stated forthrightly why he believed that the lack or sacrifice of many ordinary human relationships was finally worthwhile to him.

These three autobiographers, Petrarch, Montaigne, and Gibbon, share a humanistic view of solitude related to but distinct from the Christian tradition. They have much in common, as well as some significant differences. All three are deeply nourished by the literary and philosophical works of ancient Greece and Rome, and wish to bring aspects of the classical worldview into their contemporary culture. They all turn to what we would now call the humanities to find consolation, wisdom, and inspiration as they faced loss, loneliness, and death. Solitude is valuable for them because it provides some of the necessary conditions for literary study and creativity. Petrarch and Montaigne also celebrate the enjoyment of the natural world when one is alone, while Gibbon's solitude is an indoor and intellectual experience. Petrarch and Gibbon each present a central experience of solitude as the dramatic climax of their life, as did Augustine; Montaigne's thematic and digressive approach to self-portraiture reveals his desire for regular intervals of solitude throughout his life. Montaigne is far more aware than the other two of the dangers of solitude, and more concerned to integrate the virtues of solitude with ongoing relationships to others. The spiritual dimension of solitude in these three writers becomes increasingly distinct from Christian rhetoric and values. For each of them solitude is not simply a luxury but a necessity, an imperative related to the need to affirm one's identity and individuality. This threefold linkage of solitude, writing, and the call of an individual destiny is the legacy of the humanist tradition and becomes a central theme in many modern autobiographies.

4

ROUSSEAU'S MYTH OF SOLITUDE IN *REVERIES OF THE SOLITARY WALKER*

A MYTH OF solitude shapes both Rousseau's view of religious experience and his understanding of autobiographical writing. Rousseau's ideas about solitude are tantamount to a religious myth in that they underlie and shape all of his thought, they determine his normative evaluation of many issues, and they have a narrative contour, structuring the way he plots human experience in time. For Jean-Jacques Rousseau, solitude is both our origin and our end: the natural human condition and the only way we can attain happiness. His last work, *Reveries of the Solitary Walker,* reveals Rousseau's final convictions about solitude and its relation to religious experience and autobiography.

Rousseau's biographers describe his long history of estrangements from friends and benefactors, his fear of real and imagined plots against him, and both the great admiration and hostility he aroused in the public. When *Emile* and the *Social Contract* were officially condemned in 1762, he was forced to flee France. In 1763 his idealized home city, Geneva, also rejected him, and he began a period of wandering and frustrated attempts to justify himself and his ideas. Rousseau saw himself as a man of the people working to reform society, and yet all of his altrusitic efforts seemed to bring him enmity and persecution. He took refuge in England, Switzerland, and various places in the French provinces, and in 1770 was finally allowed to settle in Paris provided that he not publish any of his books.

There were also more personal reasons for Rousseau's testy relationships with others. He suffered from a painful urinary ailment and was frequently embarrassed by the urgent need to urinate. He wore an odd Armenian outfit to disguise the catheters he needed at all times. His common-law wife was of low social status, had no education, and was a rather coarse person; Rousseau was somewhat ashamed of her and faced many awkward situations in the course of his wanderings. Rousseau's childhood helps explain the sources of his complex character, his extreme sensitivity to others' opinions, his ideal of perfect trust, honesty, and transparency, and his constant disappointment, frustration, and blaming of everyone except himself for the lack of intimacy. Rousseau's mother died shortly after he was born, and his father chose to leave Geneva after a quarrel when Rousseau was ten. He was virtually an orphan after that, never received a formal education, and always felt a foreigner in France, an outsider in the artistic and intellectual circles to which he aspired, and a simple peasant in a corrupt society. These biographical facts, while they help us understand the origins of Rousseau's sense of being an outsider, do not account for the way that he persuaded so many readers to share his views, and specifically to value solitude as he did. To understand why and how Rousseau valued solitude, we turn to his autobiographical writing.

During the last years of his life Rousseau worked on three autobiographical works: the *Confessions*, the *Dialogues* (also known as *Rousseau, the Judge of Jean-Jacques*), and the *Reveries of the Solitary Walker*. These works were written during a time of exile and adversity, when Rousseau desperately wanted to redeem himself before public opinion and justify himself to his own conscience. One of the main reasons why Rousseau turned to autobiography was the anonymous publication in 1764 of a pamphlet actually written by Voltaire. This work exposed the secret that Rousseau had given five children to an orphanage. With his image as a virtuous reformer in jeopardy, Rousseau decided to present his own life story. His shrill, whining, or pompous rhetoric and his constant self-defensiveness often become tiring, and it is all too easy to dismiss him as paranoid, narcissistic, or simply insane. Yet his works continue to exercise a unique fascination over many readers. In the *Confessions* he created what most critics see as the first truly modern autobiography, powerfully dramatizing his ideas about individual identity, the sources of creativity, and morality. At the heart of many of Rousseau's ideas is his understanding of solitude. Rousseau was a crucial source of the Romantic idea of the solitary creative genius, which I discuss further in chapter 6. He saw himself as a lonely genius who longed for intimacy and communion but lived in a degraded society that does not understand or accept his unique vision and talents. Rousseau's understanding of himself as a persecuted solitary genius shapes all his autobiographical works.

Solitude became an increasingly insistent theme in Rousseau's works as he felt himself rejected by society. Believing in the goodness of the natural man prior to socialization, Rousseau called first for a radical transformation of society. When this change did not come, and when his writings and reputation were assailed by others, he began to praise solitude. He defended the idea of withdrawal to a more pristine and isolated state of harmony, usually alone or with a few choice soulmates. Rousseau adopted the role of a solitary to prove his sincerity and the seriousness of his critique of society. If communal life is radically evil, then withdrawal is the only moral recourse. Jean Starobinski sees the adoption of the stance of a solitary as a central theme in Rousseau's life after he began to criticize his society's vices:

> Rousseau's rebellion, directed as it was against the very essence of contemporary society, was so sweeping that it made sense only as the rebellion of a man who had excluded himself from that society. The only way to guarantee the seriousness of his challenge to the status quo was to take a stance—alone and against all others—somewhere outside hypocritical society. Evil and society being one and the same, fraud and hypocrisy would exist wherever human society was found. It was therefore necessary to flee society at all costs and to become a *belle ame,* or beautiful soul.[1]

Rousseau wanted his whole life to witness to his ideas. He intended his solitude to demonstrate his willingness to suffer for his beliefs. When he was alone, Rousseau was fully embroiled in struggle with others.

Solitude is the explicit subject matter of Rousseau's final book, the comparatively little-known but fascinating *Reveries of the Solitary Walker.* Composed between the autumn of 1776 and spring of 1778, this work was unfinished when Rousseau died on July 2, 1778, and published in 1780. The *Reveries of the Solitary Walker* is divided into ten brief sections entitled "Promenades" or Walks. Several sections describe actual perambulations, but in many of them the walk is largely metaphorical, an occasion for Rousseau to express a wide range of opinions and reflections and to wander in memory and imagination though his past and present. Because it is a solitary excursion, he can go where he pleases without following a preconceived plan or conforming his movements to the demands of others. His autobiographical writing reflects the unstructured, even shapeless, character of his life alone: "These pages will be no more than a form-less record of my reveries. I myself will figure largely in them, because a solitary person inevitably thinks a lot about himself. But all the other thoughts which pass through my mind will also have their place here. I shall say what I have thought just as it came to me, with as little connection as the thoughts of this morning have with those of last night."[2] He will take "barometer readings" of the soul, record-ing fluctuations "without trying to reduce them to a system" (33). The term *reverie* indicates Rousseau's interest in the subjective states of mind induced by his wanderings, and his desire to reach a serene and visionary condition beyond internal division or concern with his effect on others.

Of course, Rousseau is intensely conscious of how he presents himself to his audience. Eugene Stelzig holds that "For Rousseau, to be is to be perceived, and his image meant everything to him. He was obsessed with a celebrity fueled by the legend of the natural sage utterly indifferent to celebrity. . . . From first to last, the essence of his being was a function of how others looked at him, and his three autobiographies are a thoroughly calculated attempt to control and manipulate those looks."[3] From the outset, the rhetoric of the *Reveries* is based on the situation of a solitary person speaking to himself. This is the same ideal stance of an autobiographer in relation to read-ers who happen to overhear him as was wished for by Augustine. Rousseau contrasts his writing with that of Montaigne, who he says "wrote his essays only for others to read, whereas I am writing down my reveries for myself alone" (34). Rousseau would have us believe that we are not reading an apology, but overhearing a soliloquy.

"So now I am alone in the world, with no brother, neighbour or friend, nor any company left me but my own" (27). Thus begins the First Walk, as Rousseau repeats the familiar complaint in the *Con-fessions* and the dialogues *Rousseau, the Judge of Jean-Jacques* that he is the victim of a vast conspiracy and has been cast out of society against his own will: "The most sociable and loving of men has with one accord been cast out by all the rest. With all the ingenuity of hate they have sought out the cruellest torture for my sensitive soul, and have violently broken all the threads that bound me to them" (27). His aloneness is presented as innocent, Christ-like suffering. But the cruel fate he complains of also opens new possibilities for self-knowledge, "a road that leads from them to myself." Solitude provides the setting and impetus for an attempt to know himself in a new way: "detached as I am from them and from the whole world, what am I?" Rousseau alternates between lamenting his solitude and claiming that it has finally brought him to a condition of "complete calm and absolute tranquility" (31). Whereas with his *Confessions* he had hoped to win the esteem of his contemporaries and his *Dialogues* sought to persuade a future generation of his goodness, he now claims that he has resigned himself to living with the hatred of humankind. Solitude has brought him both suffering and quasi-divine transcendence of the world: "Everything is finished for me on this earth. Neither good nor evil can be done to me by any man. I have nothing left in the world to fear or hope for, and this leaves me in peace at the bottom of the abyss, a poor unfortunate mortal, but as unmoved as God himself" (31).

A crucial statement in the First Walk explains two ways in which solitude prompts autobiographical writing and has a spiritual dimension. Both motives of duty and pleasure impel the writing of the *Reveries:*

> Alone for the rest of my life, since it is only in myself that I find consolation, hope and peace of mind, my only remaining duty is towards myself and this is all I desire. This is my state of mind as I return to the rigorous and sincere self-examination that I formerly called my *Confessions.* I am devoting my last days to studying myself and preparing the account which I shall shortly have to render. Let me give myself over entirely to the pleasure of conversing with my soul, since this is the only pleasure that men cannot take away from me. If by meditating on my inner life I am able to order it better and remedy the faults that may remain there, my meditations will not be entirely in vain, and although I am now good for nothing on this earth, I shall not have totally wasted my last days. The free hours of my daily walks have often been filled with delightful contemplations which I am sorry to have forgotten. Such reflections as I have in future I shall preserve in writing; every time I read them they will recall my original pleasure. Thinking of the prize my heart deserved, I shall forget my misfortunes, my persecutors and my disgrace. (32)

Rousseau interprets the *Reveries* as a continuation of the examination of conscience begun in the *Confessions.* He hopes to improve his character through earnest moral self-assessment, and to put his soul in order before he must render an account of it to God. In addition to the goal of moral self-improvement, Rousseau admits his pleasure in writing about his solitary walks, not only as a distraction from his misfortunes but as a reliving of the most enjoyable experiences of his life. In the future "I shall recall in reading them the pleasure I have in

writing them and by thus reviving times past I shall as it were double
the space of my existence" (34). Writing about solitude will reveal
what has given him the greatest happiness in life and make possible
more pleasure, both in the writing process itself and in his anticipated
enjoyment of rereading his autobiographical work. Rousseau's account
of the pleasures and duty of solitude reveals his ultimate values and
spiritual orientation. Solitude promises not only pleasure but also
spiritual bliss; it is not simply morally permissible behavior but
rather the best path to virtue and moral truthfulness.

Pleasure and Ambivalence

The Second, Fifth, and Seventh Walks present the most positive
views of solitude in the *Reveries,* and each relies heavily, although in
different ways, on religious imagery and ideas. Rousseau begins the
Second Walk with the assertion that only in the freedom provided by
solitude can he truly be himself: "These hours of solitude and meditation are the only ones in the day when I am completely myself and
my own master, with nothing to distract or hinder me, the only ones
when I can truly say that I am what nature meant me to be" (35). It is
not easy to transcribe "the moments of rapture and ecstasy which I
sometimes experienced during these solitary walks. . . . Surrounded
by such riches, how was I to keep a faithful record of them all?" (36).
The reveries of solitude, like the heights of religious experience, are
ineffable, defying attempts to put them in language. Nonetheless,
Rousseau goes on to describe an autumnal ramble in the countryside
near Paris. He enjoys the plants still in flower, the "impression of
solitude and impending winter" given by the landscape, and "mixed
feelings of gentle sadness" evoked by thoughts of his own mortality.
Reviewing his life, he sighs over his limited accomplishments and
lost attachments to others, yet he enjoys his melancholy and is
pleased with the day's "peaceful meditations."

In the midst of this reverie he is knocked down by a large dog, in-
jured, and loses consciousness. On awakening he experiences a wonderful feeling of total immersion in the present moment and in the
world around him:

> This first sensation was a moment of delight. I was conscious of noth-
> ing else. In this instant I was being born again, and it seemed as if all I
> perceived was filled with my frail existence. Entirely taken up by the
> present, I could remember nothing; I had no distinct notion of myself
> as a person, nor had I the least idea of what had just happened to me. I
> did not know who I was, nor where I was; I felt neither pain, fear, nor

anxiety. I watched my blood flowing as I might have watched a stream, without even thinking that the blood had anything to do with me. I felt throughout my whole being such a wonderful calm, that whenever I recall this feeling I can find nothing to compare with it in all the pleasures that stir our lives. (39)

For a time Rousseau cannot remember his name and address. His delight when awakening and in recalling this incident, and the metaphor of being "born again," reflect his belief in the goodness of human beings innocent and ignorant of their social identity. The narrative thus far depicts one of Rousseau's chief themes: the goodness of the individual in the state of nature, as he enters the social world with no prescribed role or ambitions.

This Walk dramatizes another of Rousseau's sustaining ideas: the "fall" into evil that inevitably attends life in society. A few days after the accident Rousseau learns that rumors are circulating that he has died. An Avignon newspaper makes comments that seem to him "a foretaste of the tribute of insults and indignities" in store for him when he really dies. He imagines possible plots against him, and his serenity is destroyed. The end of the narrative offers several incidents as evidence of the "universal conspiracy" against him. Rousseau concludes by resolving to bear his sufferings in silence, for God must have ordained that he endure all this: "God is just; his will is that I should suffer, and he knows my innocence" (45). The Second Walk justifies Rousseau's withdrawal from society in order to attain religious detachment from the world. He tries to choose solitude rather than feeling it forced on him, to reach a state of resignation to innocent suffering, and to find tranquillity in the midst of calumny. Thus he reinterprets the misery of being isolated and persecuted as the passion narrative of Jean-Jacques Rousseau. The final purpose of his suffering, however, is not the salvation of anyone else but the vindication of his reputation in the future: "sooner or later my turn will come" (45).

The overall movement of the Second Walk reflects Rousseau's myth of solitude, dramatizing a fall from solitude into society and a return to aloneness. The blissful solitude of an autumn stroll and an innocent birth into human society give way to the anxiety and paranoia that always haunt his interactions with others. The Second Walk projects a future in which the author withdraws from persecution into a different kind of solitude and silence, this time sanctioned by God. The plot of this Walk thus enacts Rousseau's central myth of solitude as the origin of selfhood and the end to which we should return after our fall into the corruptions of social existence. Most of the other walks follow the same narrative pattern, beginning with a description of Rousseau contentedly alone, developing into an account of grievances and complaints about injustice, and concluding with a resolution to find inner peace by withdrawing from the world.

The Fifth Walk is the most serene and moving of the ten promenades and the most convincing in its portrayal of solitude as a positive spiritual experience. Rousseau describes the high point of his spiritual life, his visionary trances while on the Island of Saint Pierre in the Lake of Bienne. He fled to the Island of Saint Pierre in 1759 after his house in the village of Motiers was stoned by local peasants stirred up by a pastor angry at the religious views expressed in *Emile*. Rousseau was fascinated by islands all his life; his favorite book was *Robinson Crusoe*, the fictional autobiography of a stranded mariner. Both the island's physical isolation and this temporal interlude in his stormy life differentiate this period of sweet solitude from the antagonism and strife of social existence. His two months on the island were "the happiest time in my life, so happy that I would have been content to live all my life in this way, without a moment's desire for any other state" (83). Alone in a boat, he would lapse into a dreamlike state: "There, stretching out full-length in the boat and turning my eyes skyward, I let myself float and drift wherever the water took me, often for several hours on end, plunged in a host of vague yet delightful reveries, which though they had no distinct or permanent subject, were still in my eyes infinitely to be preferred to all that I had found most sweet in the so-called pleasures of life" (85). The noise of the waves and the movement of the water induced a semi-hypnotic trance that filled him with unutterable contentment: "The ebb and flow of the water, its continuous yet undulating noise, kept lapping against my ears and my eyes, taking the place of all the inward movements which my reverie had calmed within me, and it was enough to make me pleasurably aware of my existence, without troubling myself with thought" (86–87).

Analyzing the conditions of this reverie, Rousseau attributes it partly to his lack of consciousness of time, as "the present runs on indefinitely but this duration goes unnoticed, with no sign of the passing of time, and no other feeling of deprivation or enjoyment, pleasure or pain, desire or fear than the feeling of existence, a feeling that fills our soul entirely" (88). The "feeling of existence" is for Rousseau the pinnacle of human happiness, "a sufficient, complete and perfect happiness which leaves no emptiness to be filled in the soul" (88). It involves escape from awareness of temporality and transcendence of any sense of need or desire, attributes of mystical experience. In such a state, free from earthly passions, striving, and awareness of time, enjoying only "the feeling of existence unmixed with any other emotion," Rousseau feels "self-sufficient like God" (89).

Although he still yearns for this lonely island, he claims that he could enjoy this kind of reverie anywhere—even in the Bastille—by transporting himself in imagination to the past. In fact, he takes even greater pleasure in remembering and writing about the past than he had in the original experience. Composing his autobiography provides a more intense form of solitude than he had on the island or the boat:

> They cannot prevent me from being transported there every day on the wings of imagination and tasting for several hours the same pleasures as if I were still living there. Were I there, my sweetest occupation would be to dream to my heart's content. Is it not the same thing to dream that I am there? Better still, I can add to my abstract and monotonous reveries charming images that give them life. During my moments of ecstasy the sources of these images often escaped my senses; but now, the deeper the reverie, the more vividly they are present to me. I am often more truly in their midst and they give me still greater pleasure than when I was surrounded by them. (91)

Autobiographical writing is not simply a record but itself a form of reverie, what Starobinski calls "a dream of a dream" or a "second reverie."[4] Rousseau makes a very exalted claim about the spiritual dimensions of the autobiographical act, although in other passages he laments the decline in his imaginative life that makes this experience less frequent.

In the Seventh Walk, Rousseau describes his joy while botanizing in terms that suggest another attribute of many mystical experiences, the feeling of being united with the cosmos: "At such times his senses are possessed by a deep and delightful reverie, and in a state of blissful self-abandonment he loses himself in the immensity of this beautiful order, with which he feels himself at one. All individual objects escape him; he sees and feels nothing but the unity of all things" (108). Such feelings are denied to those who view nature for utilitarian purposes, for instance by "considering plants only as a source of drugs and medicines" (109). So, too, says the author of many nature essays and a botanical dictionary, is the sense of harmony withheld from those who would turn their encounter with nature into a means of career advancement: "As soon as our self-interest or vanity are brought into play and we are concerned to obtain positions or write books, as soon as we learn only in order to teach, and devote ourselves to botany merely for the sake of becoming authors or professors, all this sweet charm vanishes, we see plants simply as the instruments of our passions, we take no real pleasure in studying them, we do not want to know, but to show that we know, and the woods become for us merely a public stage where we seek applause" (116). For Rousseau, as for so many nature writers after him, including the Romantic poets and American essayists from Emerson and Thoreau to Annie Dillard, the world of plants and wild places is a spiritual setting primarily when it is experienced alone. All of these writers follow Rousseau in linking full appreciation of nature to a state of detachment from social interests and projects (although they presumably exclude their own writing).

These positive images of solitude in the Walks alternate with many passages describing the falseness and discomfort of his involvements with other people. A great deal of the *Reveries* is devoted to showing the harmful consequences of the lack of solitude. Whereas solitude involves an escape from time into an eternal present, social involvements bring an intense and painful consciousness of time. Rousseau excuses some of his lies as due to embarrassment at having to suddenly explain his actions; if only he had enough time to compose himself, he would be the most honorable of men! In the Sixth Walk he shows how social entanglements compromise even his generous desire to do good. Asserting that he is naturally benevolent and takes pleasure in helping others, on several occasions he spontaneously offers a gift to a child. But once he has done a good deed, he balks when he is then expected to do so again and again: "I often found my good deeds a burden because of the chain of duties they dragged behind them; then pleasure vanished and it became intolerably irksome to me to keep giving the same assistance which had at first delighted me" (94). This pattern demonstrates his fundamental belief that organized human society corrupts the individual's natural goodness: "all our natural impulses, including even charity itself, can change their nature when we import them into society" (95). Rousseau believes that the pressures of moral demand and obligation undermine his freedom and stifle his immediate response of love. This accords with his understanding of human freedom as essentially negative, a matter of freedom from constraint: "I have never believed that man's freedom consists in doing what he wants, but rather in never doing what he does not want to do" (104). He feels so incapable of acting under the constraint of moral duty that "I have often abstained from a good deed which I was able and anxious to do, fearing the enslavement which I would bring upon myself" (98). Rather than resenting those to whom duty would bind him, he withdraws from society: "I would rather flee from them than hate them" (100). In this self-congratulatory way Rousseau comes to see his quietism and passivity as more virtuous than social responsibility.

Rousseau fantasizes about the godlike benevolence that he would have practiced had he been able to combine solitude and power: "If I had remained free, unknown and isolated, as nature meant me to be, I should have done nothing but good" (101). This fantasy is enacted in several incidents in the *Reveries* when Rousseau distributes gifts among a group. His generosity creates a bond in the group, while he remains detached, savoring the good feelings his gift has created but uncommitted to the group's future.[5] Thus Rousseau justifies his aloofness not simply as a quirk of character but according to moral principle. For he holds that the motives for good acts must come not from conformity to expectation but from within the self, as an expression of natural benevolence. Depending on others' approval and taking pride when one's good deeds become known corrupt the best aspects of human nature, our spontaneous affections.

A key distinction underlies Rousseau's positive view of solitude and his negative view of society. The individual in his natural solitary state feels an instinct of self-esteem that Rousseau calls "love of self" (*amour de soi*). In human society this instinct is transformed into "self-love" (*amour-propre*), which is a self-conscious view of oneself as compared to and as viewed by others. Self-love makes one dependent on the opinion of other people, producing vanity and competition and subjecting one to pain from others' indifference and contempt. "Whatever our situation, it is only self-love that can make us constantly unhappy" (130). Repeatedly through the *Reveries* Rousseau assumes the pose of a man who has finally abandoned all hope of obtaining the good will of others and returned to the natural self-reliance and self-respect that he says constitute love of self. "Insults, reprisals, offences, injuries, injustices are all nothing to the man who sees in the hardships he suffers nothing but the hardships themselves and not the intention behind them, and whose place in his own self-esteem does not depend on the good-will of others" (130). Thus Rousseau links solitude to a basic condition of human happiness: a firm sense of self-esteem independent of other people. He admits that in the past his writing exacerbated the evil tendency to self-love, but his intention henceforth to write only for himself promises freedom from "the tyranny of public opinion" (129). He tries to project an image of himself as stoically immune to slander and plotting around him, as happy and virtuous in his aloneness.

This positive image of his solitude is largely wishful thinking.[6] Rousseau's solitude is neither as solitary nor as pleasurable as he claims. He cannot achieve his ideal of aloneness because, even when he is physically isolated, his mind is obsessed with other people. Memories haunt him, bringing guilt, shame, and the desire to atone or mend broken relationships. Furthermore, Rousseau needs constantly to imagine that others are threatening him in order to persuade himself of his perfect self-sufficiency in solitude. Concluding the Eighth Walk, in which he proclaims his return to natural love of self from the anxieties and insecurities of self-love, Rousseau defiantly cries "I laugh at all their scheming and enjoy my existence in spite of them" (135). The First Walk, too, concludes with an assertion of his immunity from any harm others can do him: "Let them enjoy my disgrace to the full, they will not prevent me from enjoying my innocence and finishing my days peacefully in spite of them" (34). His paranoia about "them" and his constant assertion of phrases such as "in spite of" show that Rousseau has hardly escaped into solitude. He takes society with him. He needs to imagine the opposition of others to feel his selfhood to the fullest.[7]

Even his pleasures while supposedly immersed in the natural world are augmented by his desire to taunt his enemies. An expression of enthusiasm for botany betrays his wish to triumph over adversaries: "It is my way of taking revenge on my persecutors; I could not find any more cruel punishment for them than to be happy in spite of them" (106). Botanizing as the sweetest revenge! Surely there are few individuals who reveal as clearly as Rousseau how an experience of solitude can be thoroughly permeated with obsessive thoughts about other people. As much as he idealized solitude as his natural and happiest condition, he needed other people to give him a complete sense of himself. In his personal life and his writing, imagining another person's antagonism was necessary to fully arouse his creative and expressive powers. Rousseau was never able to move beyond this dilemma. He hated being dependent on the opinion of others, but his strong needs for self-assertion and self-creation required a false social image of himself to react against. For Rousseau, recognition by others is necessary for self-creation, yet it ultimately undermines one's love of self, *amour de soi.*

The only moments of undiluted joy that solitude brings Rousseau are the incidents I described in three walks. But even these three brief narratives also demonstrate Rousseau's intense consciousness of other people, his unhappiness while alone, and his yearning to be understood. In spite of what he asserts about the pleasures of solitude, what he actually demonstrates far more often is the pain of loneliness. Many passages present solitude as the second best recourse, a compensation for failure to find love and community. Even in the Fifth Walk, Rousseau describes his reveries on the Lake of Bienne as his only alternative to the ordinary satisfactions of social interaction: "An unfortunate man who has been excluded from human society, and can do nothing more in this world to serve or benefit himself or others, may be allowed to seek in this state a compensation for human joys" (89). Rousseau's bitter comments on social life sound like sour grapes: what he can't have must not be worth much. Solitude hardly seems to be the best possible condition but rather all that he can salvage from the destruction of his hopes for love. He withdraws from rebuff and contemptuous insult, reconciling himself to solitude rather than seeking it as a positive good.

Yet in spite of these ambivalent experiences Rousseau continued to idealize solitude as the surest way to happiness and peace of mind. His rosy view of aloneness created new possibilities for failure and remorse. Rousseau must have suffered a sense of shame for his inability to make his own solitude as fruitful as his ideal. When Diderot had held that "only the wicked man lives alone," Rousseau replied: "The wicked man's hell is to be reduced to live alone with himself, but it is the good man's paradise."[8] Rousseau must have wondered: if he could not find contentment and a peaceful conscience when alone, was this a sign that he was not as virtuous as he claimed?

The deep ambivalence underlying Rousseau's statements about the positive values of solitude and the evils of society is illustrated by an intriguing incident in the Seventh Walk. On a hike in an isolated part of the Swiss mountains, he discovers what he believes is the wildest place he has ever been. His description of his awe and terror at this dramatic spot exemplifies the eighteenth-century passion for the sublime, which involves a solitary person feeling overwhelmed by a vast natural setting. Rousseau speaks of both the beauty and the "horror of this solitary place" (118). Although he is alone, in reverie he imaginatively deepens his sense of solitude, thinking of himself as "the first mortal to set foot in this place" and "a second Columbus" (118). Suddenly he discovers, only twenty yards away, a stocking mill. The unexpected presence of other human beings evokes "confused and contradictory emotions": "My first reaction was one of joy at finding myself among human beings where I had thought I was quite alone, but this reaction, which came like a flash of lightning, quickly gave way to a more lasting feeling of distress at not being able, even in the depths of the Alps, to escape from the cruel hands of men intent on persecuting me" (118). Rousseau is spontaneously drawn to others and welcomes their presence, but the thought of possible conflicts with them and his aversion to any kind of obligation or restriction quickly drive him to flee from them, resolving to remain henceforth detached from all social interactions.

Rousseau loved and idealized solitude, and found in it his most important spiritual experiences, including the "conversion scene" on the road to Vincennes in 1749 described in Book 8 of the *Confessions*. He also feared and hated being alone, and sought understanding and solidarity with others both in his personal life and through his writing. He was wildly inconsistent about solitude, and I think some of his appeal is the way he articulates so powerfully his readers' ambivalent feelings about solitude.

Examination of Conscience

Rousseau justified solitude in terms of its pleasures and its promise of spiritual bliss, and also as a moral duty: the obligation to examine one's conscience in solitary introspection. Several walks focus on moral issues, and Rousseau drops even the pretense of describing a natural setting. We saw how in the Sixth Walk he analyses his motives in doing good, criticizing acts done from a sense of obligation but without spontaneous love. As always, he provides a fascinating spectacle of inconsistency, admitting at the outset that "the real and basic motives of most of my actions are not as clear to me as I had long supposed" (94), but then going on to proclaim confidently his essential innocence, and concluding with assurance: "I have done very little good, but never in my life have I harboured evil intentions, and I doubt if there is any man living who has done less actual evil than I" (104).

The Ninth Walk is also devoted largely to moral self-evaluation, this time prompted by Rousseau's guilty conscience about abandoning his own children. Reading an obituary that mentions that individual's pleasure in seeing children, Rousseau immediately launches into an elaborate defense of his love of children, despite his having placed five of his own children in an orphanage. In doing this he was not "an unnatural father and a child-hater" but was looking after their best interests by protecting them from their mother, "who would have spoiled them," and her family, "who would have made monsters of them" (139). He recounts several anecdotes about giving gifts to children, awarding himself a good deal of moral credit for the pleasure this brought him. Yet Rousseau demands gratitude; he cannot abide discontented or grumpy faces, and in unpleasant situations refrains from doing good to others. Again he justifies in moral terms his withdrawal to solitude, for his impressionable susceptibility to other people's pain subjects him to misery, destroying the all-important affections that are of supreme importance to him: "A sign, a gesture or a glance from a stranger is enough to disturb my pleasure or ease my suffering. It is only when I am alone that I am my own master, at all other times I am the plaything of all who surround me" (148). Given his extreme sensitivity to others and his belief that he must fiercely guard his independence, he asks a rhetorical question that is in essence the central theme of the *Reveries:* "Is it surprising that I love solitude?" (149).

When Rousseau defends his religious views in the Third Walk, his apology appeals to the truthful verdict of his conscience when he is alone. He recounts the origin of his convictions in the illumination that struck him on the road to Vincennes when he was forty. This incident, which he regarded as the turning-point of his life, occurred on his way to visit his friend Diderot in prison. Rousseau read a newspaper describing a prize for the best essay on the question of whether the arts and sciences had improved morals. Rousseau's decisively negative answer to that question in his *Discour sur les sciences et les arts* set his course for the rest of his life. The reorientation of his life according to "a new moral vision of the world" required a serious commitment to heed and follow his conscience: "a strict self-examination which was to order my inner life for the rest of my days" (51). It involved simultaneously a renewed appreciation of solitude: "It is from this time that I can date my total renunciation of the world and the great love of solitude which has never since left me. The task I had set myself could only be performed in absolute isolation; it called for long and tranquil meditations which are impossible in the bustle of society life" (52). For most of the walk, Rousseau explains why his religious beliefs have not changed from the ideas presented in his "Creed of a Savoyard Vicar" in *Emile*, and he defends himself from the charge that he has not learned anything new as he aged. This review of his religious convictions and justification of stasis in his thinking is determined by conscience: "My own mind, resting on the most solid foundations I was able to provide, became so used to remaining there in the shelter of my conscience that no strange doctrine, old or new, can any longer disturb my peace for a single moment" (60).

Starobinski points out that for Rousseau the ideal of truth means not knowledge of the world but stability, permanence, and a fixed identity: "The passion for truth is not 'disinterested.' It does not culminate in knowledge of the world. Rather, it inaugurates, in Jean-Jacques's life, a period of firmness of will and unshakable conviction. It is a way of putting an end to the instability from which he has suffered for so long."[9] Rousseau desires to settle his opinions "once and for all" on something more firm and fixed than his own vacillating moods: "Let me decide my opinions and principles once and for all, and then let me remain for the rest of my life what mature consideration tells me I should be" (53). His turn to solitude and attempt to live according to permanently valid convictions of conscience are both attempts to escape variability, to acquire a lasting identity, an inner unity that cannot be lost. He defends his indifference to new ideas by arguing that virtue is more important than knowledge. The best thing he can do is "learn to leave life, not better, for that is impossible, but more virtuous than when I entered it" (61). The central thrust of the Third Walk, then, is an apology for his religious convictions based on a defense of his isolation and disengagement with new ideas.

Rousseau devotes his Fourth Walk to "a self-examination on the subject of falsehood" (63). Immediately he brings up an incident (described in Book 2 of the *Confessions*) when he stole a ribbon and accused a fellow servant, Marion, of the theft. He excuses this deed as not issuing from calculated malice but rather "a moment of irresponsible folly" brought about by shame. The rest of this Walk analyses other incidents when he "cheerfully" lied in spite of his firm belief in his essential integrity and honesty. In a characteristic train of sophistic reasoning Rousseau explains that not telling the truth is only a lie if someone is thereby harmed. "How can one be unjust if one is injuring no one?" (67). In his personal relations and his writings he has always told the truth or constructed not lies but fiction: "To lie without advantage or disadvantage to oneself or others is not to lie; it is not falsehood but fiction" (69). In a tortured and self-serving analysis of his motives, Rousseau excuses several of his lies as reflecting timidity or embarrassment but never cruelty or ill will. It would be tedious to point out the many inconsistencies and rationalizations in Rousseau's special pleading. What is significant for this study is his firm belief that solitary reflection helps him to face his conscience and to live a more honest life in the future: "It is not too late to correct my judgment and regulate my will, for this is henceforth all that is in my power" (80).

Rousseau believes that he should listen only to his conscience, ignoring the perspectives of others, and that solitude allows him to attend closely to conscience. In this he is representative of two related misunderstandings: that taking conscience seriously means believing it can not make mistakes, and that in consulting one's conscience one need not consider others' perspectives. I have argued elsewhere that Rousseau's view of conscience resembles his view of autobiographical truth: both are to be judged solely according to the agent's intention, which in principle he insulates from correction by others.[10] The *Reveries* takes to its inevitably solipsistic conclusion the views of conscience and autobiographical truth underlying Rousseau's work.

Just as Rousseau's myth of solitude as a blissful experience is undercut by his complaints of loneliness and his yearning for company, so, too, his understanding of solitude as the occasion for truthful conscientious reflection is constantly betrayed by his actual deliberations. In spite of his claims to have reached a decisive verdict of conscience, he returns obsessively to the topics that haunted him all his life. Not only the reader but Rousseau himself recognizes that his pleas of exculpation do not touch the deepest sources of his guilt. For instance, although he tries to excuse the incident of the stolen ribbon, "remorse for a lie has continually tormented me these fifty years" (65). His conscience is never settled, never at peace, always wandering over the same terrain. Indeed, Rousseau's specific understanding of walking is an apt metaphor for his conscience, which rambles aimlessly and endlessly and yet never seems to get anywhere, never arrives at a stable or trustworthy judgment, even according to his own standard.

Asserting that only he can judge himself, Rousseau does not recognize how much the very nature of conscience is dialogical. Conscience imagines possible criticisms, appeals to common human experience, anticipates doubts, and argues with accusations that must be rebutted. Just as Rousseau takes with him into solitude all the antagonists he feels persecuting him, so his conscience needs to address the voices he imagines questioning his actions and motives. Although he assures himself that he alone knows the truth about himself, Rousseau's own practice contradicts his theory of conscience, for in solitude he imagines and addresses the perspectives of others, and he yearns for the confirmation of another even as he tries to dismiss this as unimportant. Some of the incoherence in his writing is attributable to the contradiction between what he tells himself about the way conscience should operate in solitude and the ways that conscience in fact functions, seeking information, challenge, and assent from others.

Assessing Rousseau's Myth of Solitude

Rousseau evokes powerfully several specific occasions when solitude was a positive experience, and makes many more abstract and less convincing pronouncements of the virtues of solitude. At its best, Rousseau's solitude is not simply the absence of other people but an opportunity for communion with the natural world, for self-awareness and self-examination, and for affirmation of the worth of his experience independent of others' opinions. Although Rousseau could never overcome feelings of isolation and loneliness, he tried to make his periods of aloneness not simply meaningful, but the most significant part of his life. In the *Reveries,* along with a great deal of posturing and wishful thinking, he succeeded in presenting several times in his life when solitude brought serenity: meditative walks in the country-side, botanizing excursions, and especially the reveries in the boat on the Lake of Bienne. When he referred to the shores of the Lake of Bienne he was the first French writer to use the term "romantique" as applied to scenery.[11] Part of Rousseau's significance lies in his link-ing solitude to the appreciation of nature. His communion with the natural world foreshadows the Romantic movement and influences its religious attitude to nature.

So, too, is Rousseau important in formulating the ideal of a private life combining solitude with human relationship. In the Tenth Walk, Rousseau portrays his life with Madame de Warens at Les Charmettes as an ideal combination of intimacy and solitude. Madame de Warens, whom he met when he was seventeen, was Rousseau's protector and later his lover for several years. Their life together was the high point of his life, the "one short time in my life when I was myself, com-pletely myself, unmixed and unimpeded, and when I can genuinely claim to have lived" (153–54). He describes a life that integrates the need for solitude with the claims of relationship to others, although he affirms only the bond with his lover, with no connection to a wider public world. Although this idyllic period is only briefly sketched, and nostalgia makes him omit tensions described in the *Confessions,* the ideal of relationship balanced by solitude set the standard by which he measured all his later attempts at happiness.

Just as significant are the distinctly spiritual ways in which Rous-seau describes solitude. The state of reverie which seems attainable only in solitude has many characteristics of mystical experience: total absorption in the moment, freedom from care and anxiety, the sense of unity with the world, and the feeling of one's own being as harmonious, unified, complete. "The feeling of existence" which makes us feel "self-sufficient like God" (89) is for Rousseau the greatest joy for human beings. This feeling of self-sufficiency is not communion with God but being like God, so Rousseau's spiritual orientation is in this respect profoundly at odds with Christian tradition. His desire for solitude is a longing to escape the constraints of finitude, to transcend desire, memory, and suffering. "The feeling of existence" involves a state of contemplation and deep feeling that is only possible when one is free from the inevitable comparisons, judgments, striving, and conflicts that accompany social relationships. Rousseau articulates the malaise of many in the modern era who feel that the organization of modern society conditions us to a busy and superficial life that closes us off to other dimensions of life that are ultimately more important. According to Rousseau, human beings in their primitive natural condition and in their moments of deep religious feeling are not anxious social creatures seeking to dominate each other in order to achieve some practical end; rather, we are contemplative and somewhat passive beings whose true felicity is to delight in "the feeling of existence." He saw solitude as the best hope for attaining this state of personal unity and contentment, and for being able to affirm life's goodness. In expressing this positive view of aloneness, in creating a myth of solitude as our origin and our end, he articulates forcefully an understanding of the spiritual potentiality of solitude that has had an enormous influence on Western literary and religious sensibilities. Although he is not the only source of this exalted view of solitude, in many ways Rousseau is the exemplary representative of the idealization of aloneness by secular solitaries.

Several aspects of Rousseau's view of solitude should be criticized. Although his problems were certainly due to many other things as well, Rousseau's understanding of solitude plays an important part in his thinking about many issues, and I think it contributed significantly to his own unhappiness.

There are three related problems with Rousseau's view of solitude. First, he dreams of finding a permanent state of solitude, a refuge where he will never again have to deal with other people. He was to remain perpetually miserable because he could never realize his dream of a permanent shelter from the cares and anxieties of relationship with others. When he did find solitude, he could not be content, and soon turned back to the social conflicts that were central to his sense of identity. Without recourse to biographical information, the *Reveries* provides ample evidence of his inability to be happy with either total solitude or immersion in society. Rather than Rousseau's either-or choice, we need a conception of human life that alternates between periods of solitude and social engagements.

A second and related issue concerns Rousseau's fundamental belief in the autonomy and self-sufficiency of the individual, which deeply shapes not only the *Reveries* and his other autobiographical works but also his political, social, and educational theories. His idealization of solitude plays a crucial role in his optimistic view of the goodness of the natural man, a central doctrine which Rousseau's critics have attacked. Rousseau's ideal image of human beings as most natural and authentic when alone denies the basic interdependence and sociality of human nature. He continually fought against and frustrated his own yearning for other people. Instead of accepting the need for aloneness and the need for social engagement as equally important dimensions of life, Rousseau constructed a myth of solitude that idealizes it as the condition in which an individual transcends false social instincts and yet somehow retains his original benevolence and spontaneous generosity.

Third, the fantasy of being autonomous, "self-sufficient like God," provides a theoretical basis for closing oneself off from correction from outside the self. Rousseau defended the fixedness of his religious reflections, and his view of conscience makes a person's judgment of his own intentions the final criterion of virtue. In the religious and ethical spheres of life, as well as in ordinary social relationships, Rousseau's thinking ends in solipsism, insulating the individual from challenge or correction from outside the self. Rousseau epitomizes the creativity and courage of those in our culture who would find sources of spirituality within the individual's own experience, and he represents the dangers that arise when this stance leads a person to reject the possibility that sustaining sources of truth and goodness might also be found outside oneself. Even his references to God are usually metaphors for describing himself—for instance his being "as unmoved as God himself" (31)—rather than attempts to imagine what transcends and might challenge Jean-Jacques Rousseau.[12]

Rousseau's significance lies also in the ways he links solitude to autobiography. In the *Reveries* Rousseau proposes that autobiographical writing is an attempt to relive or duplicate earlier experiences of solitude. Writing will preserve the reflections of solitude so that "every time I read them they will recall my original pleasure" (32), and even "double the space of my existence" (34). Relationship to his own words is envisaged as an alternative form of companionship: "In spite of men I shall still enjoy the charms of company, and in my decrepitude I shall live with my earlier self as I might with a younger friend" (34). In this way autobiographical writing becomes the surest means to achieve the pleasures of both solitude and relationship with a reality beyond the self: one's written work becomes a younger friend with whom to commune.[13]

Rousseau portrays the process of composition as, ideally, an experience like reverie: a pleasurable wandering in the spheres of imagination, freely following subjective impulse. Although he must have known the frustrations, dead ends, and anxieties that written expression entails for most authors, the hope for and occasional experience of an effortless flowing-forth of language sustained Rousseau through thousands of pages of writing, much of it directly or implicitly autobiographical. Like solitude, autobiography allowed him to imagine himself as essentially good and innocently suffering ill treatment at the hands of a corrupt society. Writing was not simply a record of solitude but another means toward the essential happiness attainable in solitude. Rousseau formulates an understanding of autobiography as offering a field for spiritual development as an author discerns the meaning of the past and finds new significance in experience. Unlike Augustine's *Confessions,* the *Reveries* portrays this task as undertaken in complete solitude, without awareness of either other people or God. Autobiography is a religious undertaking not because it may bring encounter with God but because it involves the self-sufficient contemplation that in Rousseau's view makes a person most like God.

Rousseau's anxieties constantly undermine this hopeful view of autobiography, for of course he does want to reach readers and doubts his efforts. James Olney interprets Rousseau's significance in literary history in terms of how Rousseau portrays the writer severed from community and turning inward to explore ambiguities of memory and narrative. Writing becomes compulsive and obsessional when it loses contact with a social context:

> This, in a general way, is what Rousseau did in the history of self-writing. He cut the self loose, leaving it without ties, anchor, or direction, and to modern descendants he left as starting point what, for him, was the endpoint: a free-floating self, uncentered except in itself, and quite unreal. (An instructive comparison could be made with Montaigne, who, like Rousseau, turned always inward but seeking there the general and universal *through* the particular and individual.) Rousseau's individual is both unique and insane, unjudgeable by the experience or the criteria of others. He is the hero or the protagonist of the narratives of Dostoevsky, Kafka, and Beckett.[14]

According to Olney, Rousseau speaks "incessantly but always and only to and about himself. This, one feels, is also where all the children of Jean-Jacques begin. And who, in our time, is not one of his children?"[15] If we are all in some sense Rousseau's descendants, it is autobiographers who most clearly address the problem of forging connections between one's solitary preoccupations and the reader, the community, and an actual social world.

Rousseau's view of solitude is representative of an important part of modern culture: the intellectual and artistic currents that idealize solitude as a protest and alternative to the values of conventional society and the pressures to succeed on its terms. The understanding of aloneness as a privileged mode of access to a person's genuine or authentic self owes much to Rousseau. Charles Taylor argues that Rousseau is a pivotal figure in the evolution of the modern idea of nature as not an external order but an inner voice, a source of deepest truth that lies within:

> Rousseau immensely enlarged the scope of the inner voice. We now can know from within us, from the impulses of our own being, what nature marks as significant. And our ultimate happiness is to live in conformity with this voice, that is, to be entirely ourselves. . . . The source of unity and wholeness which Augustine found only in God is now to be discovered within the self.
>
> Rousseau is at the origin point of a great deal of contemporary culture, of the philosophies of self-exploration, as well as of the creeds which make self-determining freedom the key to virtue. He is the starting point of a transformation in modern culture towards a deeper inwardness and a radical autonomy. The strands all lead from him.[16]

Rousseau articulates the characteristic modern sense of the self as having inner depths and as needing to discover itself apart from the constraints and other-regarding calculations of social life. In society we lose contact with natural impulses and become primarily concerned with pleasing others to gain some advantage. Rousseau speaks for all those in modernity who resent the constraints imposed on them by civilized society, and who believe that if only they were liberated from these constraints they would be more authentic, more creative, more fully alive. His influence leads to various proposals to reorganize society in radically egalitarian ways, from the French Revolution through various socialist and anarchist thinkers and political leaders. Paradoxically, the author of *The Social Contract* also inspires those who give up on changing society and decide that they must withdraw in order to cultivate their individuality, creative work, or spirituality. His heirs believe that they can detach themselves from corrupt society and, alone, discover or invent a new and better self.

What Rousseau says about the ideal of solitude is one thing; what his life actually shows is quite another. The *Reveries* reveal, and biographical information confirms, that solitude more often brought him misery than bliss. He brought his paranoias and obsessions with him, and filled his hours alone with fantasies about universal conspiracies against him and plots of revenge against imagined persecutors. Telling himself that he lived in serene detachment, he craved for his writings to be understood, as well as for simple contact with children and ordinary people. He idealized solitude and despaired because it so seldom lived up to his expectations. In both ways he is a paradigmatic figure. Rousseau's significance lies equally in his assertion of the importance of solitude for personal self-discovery and spiritual experience, and his dramatization of how difficult it is to find solitude and to make it meaningful.

The unfinished Tenth Walk of the *Reveries* symbolizes the impasse to which Rousseau's view of solitude leads. He wrote on Palm Sunday in 1778, "exactly fifty years since I first met Madame de Warens" (153). To this fateful meeting Rousseau traces much of his destiny; his love for her "determined my whole life and led inexorably to the fate that has governed the rest of my days" (153). Significantly, Rousseau attributes his love of solitude to this period of intimacy, when aloneness and affection enriched each other: "The taste for solitude and contemplation grew up in my heart along with the expansive and tender feelings which are best able to nourish it. . . . I need tranquility if I am to love" (154). Rousseau persuaded Madame de Warens to live in the country, and he claims to have been perfectly happy for five years. The Tenth Walk ends, and with it the *Reveries* and Rousseau's authorship, as he recalls how the desire to preserve and protect this rural solitude led to financial anxieties and ambition:

> I wanted nothing except that such a sweet state should never cease. My only cause of sorrow was the fear that it might not last long, and this fear, founded as it was on our precarious financial situation, was not unjustified.
>
> From then on I attempted both to distract myself from this anxiety and to find means of preventing the realization of my fears. I decided that a rich store of talents was the surest protection against poverty,

and I resolved to employ my leisure hours in making myself able if
possible one day to repay the best of women for all the help she had
given me. (154–55)

It may be pure coincidence that this is as far as Rousseau got on
this Walk; he died only a few months later, and a change of residence
preoccupied him during this time. That the Tenth Walk remains unfinished, however, seems a fitting commentary on Rousseau's irrec-
oncilable attitudes to solitude. Solitude is an essential component of
the ideal life he lived with Madame de Warens, which combined
time alone and the communion of lovers. Yet because supporting this
way of life requires financial security, Rousseau began to develop the
"rich store of talents" that he hoped would allow him to make his
way in the world and repay Madame de Warens. This marks a crucial
turning point in his life, for he was immersed henceforth in the cares
and concerns of the social struggle, which intensified dramatically
once he launched his career as an author. He could no longer depend
on having a stable, confident sense of another's recognition; he had
to win it again and again, repeatedly losing the tranquillity and
happiness of solitude as he became preoccupied with what others
thought about him.

How can one cultivate solitude in the modern world, when establishing the conditions of fruitful solitude necessarily involves a person in the world of money, power, and ambition? Rousseau never
answered this question, yet the *Reveries* holds out the promise that
times of aloneness are the key to the fullest human happiness. In
Rousseau's myth of solitude, aloneness is not simply an interlude or
episode but rather the defining moment, the opportunity to choose
one's identity, to transcend the distorting and corrupting influence
of other people. This ideal functions as both a nostalgic memory and
a utopian dream, making intolerable any actual present condition
involving social anxiety and strife. Given Rousseau's failure to find a
practically realizable state of solitude in the world, autobiographical
writing becomes his only way to achieve the pleasures and spiritual
benefits of aloneness.

5

THOREAU AT WALDEN

"SOLILOQUIZING AND TALKING TO ALL THE UNIVERSE AT THE SAME TIME"

IN A CHAPTER of *Walden* on "Winter Animals," Thoreau describes his amusement at the antics of a red squirrel. The squirrel darts about with tremendous speed, then pauses "with a ludicrous expression and a gratuitous somerset, as if all the eyes of the universe were fixed on him—for all the motions of a squirrel, even in the most solitary recesses of the forest, imply spectators as much as those of a dancing girl."[1] After much starting and stopping and expense of time and energy, the squirrel suddenly appeared at the top of a tree, "winding up his clock and chiding all imaginary spectators, soliloquizing and talking to all the universe at the same time,—for no reason that I could ever detect, or he himself was aware of, I suspect." This anecdote suggests two ways in which *Walden* represents a significant new understanding of solitude. Thoreau's humorous but closely observed account of the squirrel (which goes on for more than a page) indicates the central purpose to which he devoted his solitude: intimate knowledge of the natural world. Furthermore, I take Thoreau's description of the red squirrel—"a singularly frivolous and whimsical fellow"—to represent his own complex mixture of needs for solitude and for society. Thoreau, too, was "soliloquizing and talking to all the universe at the same time," both getting away from others in order to discern new aspects of the world and proclaiming to others the significance of what he discovered in his "experiment" at Walden Pond. He recognized that his life at the pond, even in its most reclusive and private moments, "implied spectators," an imagined audience that influenced the character of his solitude. *Walden* explores with great insight the ways in which solitude and various modes of social engagement are intertwined and the ethical implications of this fact.

Henry David Thoreau lived at Walden Pond, about a mile south of Concord, Massachusetts, from July 4, 1845, until September 6, 1847. He had several motives for this sojourn in the woods. In the eight years since he had graduated from Harvard University he had briefly taught school, begun to write a journal, published a few short articles, and gotten to know Ralph Waldo Emerson. He had lived in Emerson's house in Concord, looking after the garden and woodpile of the increasingly famous poet and essayist. During the spring of 1845 Thoreau constructed a little house on Emerson's land near Walden Pond. Living at Walden was partly motivated by economic reasons. Having no money or steady employment, Thoreau wanted to have as much time as possible for his own pursuits. Reducing expenses to the minimum was the easiest way to do this. "Economy," the opening chapter of *Walden*, recommends a more austere life to his readers, and the book's recurring theme of simple living is frequently linked to solitude. Beyond financial expediency, Thoreau wanted to be independent, to put into practice Emerson's ideal of self-reliance. He had always lived with others: at home with his family in Concord, at college, and with the Emersons. Building his own cabin, growing vegetables to feed himself and beans for a little extra income, and trying to survive by his own efforts realized his ideals of manly independence and emancipation from the charity of others.

Thoreau also wanted a time and place to concentrate on two writing projects that would eventually be published as *A Week on the Concord and Merrimack Rivers* (1849) and *Walden*, which after extensive reworking was published in 1854. He could have sequestered himself in an attic, but he was increasingly drawn to study and write about the natural world. Just how much his sojourn at Walden Pond and his life's work were to focus on attending to nature became clear to him only gradually. The reader's experience of *Walden* recapitulates Thoreau's own discoveries within the natural world, for as the book unfolds, its emphasis shifts from social criticism to environmental consciousness. Solitude helped Thoreau pursue his goals of economic frugality, self-reliance, concentrated writing, and attention to the natural world.

There were at least three public contexts for Thoreau's private withdrawal, according to biographer Robert Richardson. Having recently tried to buy a farm, Thoreau was attracted to the Jeffersonian ideal of subsistance farming and interested in new organizations, such as the National Reform Association, that proposed laws to protect small farmers. Thoreau's experiment was, in a second context, "the self-reliant individual's answer to the challenge posed by the utopian communes such as Brook Farm, Hopedale, and Fruitlands."[2] Like the members of thirty-three utopian communities established in the two years before he went to Walden, Thoreau questioned the competition, consumerism, and modes of production of America's emerging industrial society by emphasizing the basic foundations of society—or, in his case, what is essential in a single individual's life. Finally, Thoreau's experiment coincided with the Mexican War, growing political conflict between northern and southern states, and the emergence of the abolitionist movement. *The Narrative of Frederick Douglass* was published in June 1845, the month before Thoreau began his own project of self-liberation. In the midst of intense controversy about the meaning and conditions of freedom in the United States, Thoreau's experiment at Walden Pond was a private version of the national debate about freedom, an attempt to choose his own destiny rather than allowing it to be determined for him.

In *Walden* Thoreau asserts as his primary motivation a desire to confront fundamental truths. He sought direct encounter with "the essential facts of life" and expressed a fervent faith in the value of his own experience, whether it confirmed or challenged religious tradition. Thoreau's distinctive spiritual stance is articulated in the most famous paragraph in *Walden:*

> I went to the woods because I wished to live deliberately, to front only the essential facts of life, and see if I could not learn what it had to teach, and not, when I came to die, discover that I had not lived. I did not wish to live what was not life, living is so dear; nor did I wish to practise resignation, unless it was quite necessary. I wanted to live deep and suck out all the marrow of life, to live so sturdily and Spartan-like as to put to rout all that was not life, to cut a broad swath and shave close, to drive life into a corner, and reduce it to its lowest terms, and, if it proved to be mean, why then to get the whole and genuine meanness of it, and publish its meanness to the world; or if it were sublime, to know it by experience, and be able to give a true account of it in my next excursion. For most men, it appears to me, are in a strange uncertainty about it, whether it is of the devil or of God, and have *somewhat hastily* concluded that it is the chief end of man here to "glorify God and enjoy him forever." (61)

This elevated goal—a direct experience of what was most central and important in life—had to be discovered for oneself, not received from others. The meaning of life had to be wrested from a potentially "mean" world, pondered, and published without too much concern about whether it would accord with conventional religious beliefs. If the term "spirituality" has any central meaning today, it is the emphasis on seeking wisdom in an individualized way that does not accept any single religious tradition as definitively normative. Thoreau and Emerson are the classic representatives of this impulse in American history, and Thoreau's writings are the fountainhead of the literature that links spiritual searching to solitude.

Immersion in the Natural World

If this is what Thoreau sought in solitude, what, according to *Walden*, did he actually find? The chapter "Solitude" answers that question by describing the value of attunement to the natural world. Thoreau describes his immersion in the natural world in terms both intensely sensual and deeply spiritual. "This is a delicious evening, when the whole body is one sense, and imbibes delight through every pore" (87). Solitude makes possible greater attentiveness to the physical world, and alert openness to all the ways it reaches the senses: hearing, vision, smell, and touch. This kind of experience is not possible for Thoreau, and probably for most people, when they are engaged with others. It is not simply sense experience but contact with "the essential facts of life" that Thoreau sought at Walden Pond. He sets this off against living in human society as if one must choose between them: "What do we want most to dwell near to? Not to many men surely, the depot, the post-office, the bar-room, the meeting-house, the school-house, the grocery, Beacon Hill, or the Five Points, where men most congregate, but to the perennial source of our life, whence in all our experience we have found that to issue, as the willow stands near the water and sends out its roots in that direction" (90). Thoreau frequently describes this process of attunement in pantheistic terms, as a matter of seeing the presence of the divine in the natural world. Sometimes he uses theistic metaphors, although usually without explicit Christian reference: "Nearest to all things is that power which fashions their being. *Next* to us the grandest laws are continually being executed. *Next* to us is not the workman whom we have hired, with whom we love so well to talk, but the workman whose work we are" (90). This passage is immediately followed by four quotations from Confucius, as Thoreau suggests that there is a common spiritual reality about which all religions speak, and that solitude helps us to know. There is a divine presence in the world that is accessible apart from human conventions and traditions, and encountering this presence is easier when a person is removed from the institutions and social forms that claim to mediate the sacred.

Being alone is conducive to immersion in nature, to realizing how we participate in its processes, and to sensing the presence of the divine. Solitude also facilitates the kind of contemplative detachment that Thoreau admired in Eastern religious traditions. "By a conscious effort of the mind we can stand aloof from actions and their consequences; and all things, good and bad, go by us like a torrent. We are not wholly involved in Nature. I may be either the driftwood in the stream, or Indra in the sky looking down on it" (91). He describes "a certain doubleness" in human consciousness that allows him to be a spectator of his life. Even in the most intense experience, part of the mind remains uninvolved, remote, aloof. Thoreau cultivated this detachment and realized that his capacity for it did not endear him to other people: "This doubleness may easily make us poor neighbors and friends sometimes." It is nonetheless an essential aspect of a spiritual view of the world to be able stand back from one's involvements and simply observe.

Thoreau says that solitude was only difficult for him at one time, for a moment early in his stay at Walden:

> I have never felt lonesome, or in the least oppressed by a sense of solitude, but once, and that was a few weeks after I came to the woods, when, for an hour, I doubted if the near neighborhood of man was not essential to a serene and healthy life. To be alone was something unpleasant. But I was at the same time conscious of a slight insanity in my mood, and seemed to foresee my recovery. In the midst of a gentle rain while these thoughts prevailed, I was suddenly sensible of such sweet and beneficent society in Nature, in the very pattering of the drops, and in every sound and sight around my house, an infinite and unacccountable friendliness all at once like an atmosphere sustaining me, as made the fancied advantages of human neighborhood insignificant, and I have never thought of them since. Every little pine needle expanded and swelled with sympathy and befriended me. (89)

Walden is full of descriptions of the beauty and beneficence of the natural world, and of moments when Thoreau experiences a sense of intimacy or companionship with some creature or natural force, sun or snow, winter wind or spring blooming. The narrator of these passages is always alone but never feels lonely. Rather, he imagines others yearning for what he has; he is like a hawk soaring and tumbling in the sky, who "was not lonely, but made all the earth lonely beneath it" (211). An absence of human companionship seems necessary for Thoreau to experience communion with nature, to which he attributes feelings of sympathy, tenderness, and friendly good will. Companionship may be found in any natural force, or in the cosmos itself: "Why should I feel lonely? Is not our planet in the Milky Way?" (90). We are never alone, he holds, if we will notice what is present around us. The bond between a solitary individual and nature should heal all human hurts: "There can be no very black melancholy to him who lives in the midst of Nature and has his senses still" (88). Solitude was crucial to Thoreau's experience of nature; in this he foreshadows a host of later American writers such as Edward Abbey and Annie Dillard, whose work I discuss in the next chapter.

Solitude and Community

The second aspect of Thoreau's originality is his distinctive insight into his life's rhythms of solitude and desire for community. These are not simply successive episodes, but influence each other in many ways. In several ways Thoreau discerns in his solitude ethical implications for understanding human society. In the opening paragraph of *Walden* he says that "at present I am a sojourner in civilized life again" (1), implying that his life has alternated between periods of more and less engagement with other people, and that this pattern will continue. The chapter "Solitude" is immediately followed by "Visitors," and the rest of *Walden* depicts Thoreau's frequent contact with other people. Given his reputation as a hermit, it is surprising to learn how involved with others he was on a regular basis. The railroad track was just across the pond, and the road to Concord close. Noticing the passage of other people does not destroy his sense of aloneness but intensifies it. So, for instance, he follows one of his many reflections on the railroad with a sudden awareness of solitude: "Now that the cars are gone by and all the restless world with them, and the fishes in the pond no longer feel their rumbling, I am more alone than ever" (83). Visitors came often to his cabin, and one night he entertained a party of twenty. He visited his mother in Concord once a week, dined with friends, and went for rambling walks in the neighborhood. He encountered fishermen, hunters, ice cutters, travelers, railroad workers, children playing, and an impoverished Irish family. Since wood was the primary fuel for every house in Concord, the forest around his hut rang with the sound of axes. He spent a night in the Concord jail (the origin of his essay *Resistance to Civil Government*) and traveled to Maine for two weeks. He took an active part in political and literary discussions at the Concord Lyceum and gave several lectures.

Like most solitaries, Thoreau claims that he is not a misanthrope and appreciates other people. But when he describes his relationship to other people there is often a defensive edge, a part of himself held in reserve, or a tone of sarcastic disdain: "I think that I love society as much as most, and am ready enough to fasten myself like a blood-sucker for the time to any full-blooded man that comes in my way. I am naturally no hermit, but might possibly sit out the sturdiest frequenter of the bar-room, if my business called me thither" (94). This remark suggests that those who love society are leeches who drain others of their life or drunks stupified with small talk. Thoreau's wish for distance from others sometimes expresses a misanthropic side of his temperament and a bristling superiority that impel him to withdraw from what irritates or angers him. Nevertheless, he has a certain wisdom about the need for detachment in human relationships. We need other people, he implies, but we need them less desperately than we often believe. We can appreciate others for who they actually are if we do not use them to satisfy our needs.

Even in the closest relationships we need to respect each other's independence and reserve. In a revealing aside, Thoreau says that when he received a visitor, he often experienced "the difficulty of getting to a sufficient distance from my guest when we began to utter the big thoughts in big words. . . . Individuals, like nations, must have suitable broad and natural boundaries, even a considerable neutral ground, between them. I have found it a singular luxury to talk across the pond to a companion on the opposite side" (94–95). This passage goes on to describe the ideal conditions of social interaction. In order to communicate about the deepest matters, Thoreau had to have a certain distance from the other person's physical presence and emotional needs: "If we are merely loquacious and loud talkers, then we can afford to stand very near together, cheek by jowl, and feel each other's breath; but if we speak reservedly and thoughtfully, we want to be farther apart, that all animal heat and moisture may have a chance to evaporate. If we would enjoy the most intimate society with that in each of us which is without, or above, being spoken to, we must not only be silent, but commonly so far apart bodily that we cannot possibly hear each other's voice in any case" (95). These

reflections reveal both the limitations of Thoreau's capacity for intimacy and his insight about the conditions that best allowed him to
relax, commune in silence, or speak honestly. Thoreau desires real
communion rather than simply passing time together: "Society is
commonly too cheap. We meet at very short intervals, not having
had time to acquire any new value for each other. We meet at meals
three times a day, and give each other a new taste of that old musty
cheese that we are" (92). For Thoreau, periods of solitude were not
antithetical to enjoyment of others but increased his appreciation of
them, as if a decrease in quantity led to an increase in quality of
interaction: "Fewer came to see me upon trivial business. In this
respect, my company was winnowed by my mere distance from
town. I had withdrawn so far within the great ocean of solitude, into
which the rivers of society empty, that for the most part, so far as my
needs were concerned, only the finest sediment was deposited
around me" (97). *Walden* reflects Thoreau's struggle to reconcile his
fierce desire for independence, his need for others, and his hatred of
the insincere or trivial. Thoreau's pessimistic statements about human
relationships also reflect his disappointed reaction to his frustrated
hope for friendship.[3]

From the vantage point of his partial withdrawal from society,
Thoreau casts a discerning eye on the social instincts and projects of
his neighbors. Their reaction to his solitude reveals a great deal
about them. For instance, "men of business, even farmers, thought
only of solitude and employment, and of the great distance at which
I dwelt from something or other; and though they said that they
loved a ramble in the woods occasionally, it was obvious that they
did not." These "restless committed men, whose time was all taken
up in getting a living or keeping it," cannot imagine interrupting
their frenetic moneymaking for so unproductive a practice as living
alone in the woods. Thoreau describes, with equal disdain, those
whose response to his experiment is the comment that a person can
not do much good to others in such a situation. "The self-styled
reformers, the greatest bores of all," can only evaluate any mode of
living as a scheme for improving society. "The old and infirm and
the timid" imagine the danger of accidents, and huddle together for
mutual defense. Reactions to a hermit reveal the various obsessions,
fears, and fixed purposes that motivate people to come together (103).

In contrast, the visitors whom Thoreau welcomes are open to encounter based on mutual choice and appreciation rather than manipu-
lative control or hidden agendas. They share his love of something not
found in Concord. Thoreau's "cheering visitors"—children looking

for berries, hunters and fishermen, poets and philosophers and Sunday walkers—were "all honest pilgrims, who came out to the woods for freedom's sake, and really left the village behind" (104). Thoreau endorses disinterested enjoyment of others and the shared pursuit of common values, but he is deeply suspicious of anyone who proposes an ideal of community and tries to enlist or organize others in its name. His politics are basically anarchist, imagining a perfect community that will arise effortlessly when conventional rules and institutions are eliminated, and criticizing every actually existing community as repressive of individual freedom and self-expression.[4] For Thoreau, the test of whether a community encourages individuality is its acceptance of solitude. Those of his visitors who appreciate and practice aloneness are the ones fit to be members of his ideal society.

When Thoreau situated himself one mile from Concord, "it was just far enough to be seen clearly."[5] His highly visible, semi-withdrawn residence at the pond was a political statement to his neighbors, taking the form of a conspicuous voluntary exile. Many of his reflections on solitude occur at the point of transition, as he joins or leaves the presence of others. Thoreau wanted not undiluted solitude but the repeated ritual of withdrawal from society, an act which by separating him from the evils he deplored affirmed his moral integrity and implicitly criticized the corruptions of American culture. Praise of solitude in *Walden* alternates with criticism of a wide range of political and social practices, and these two themes are related to each other in many ways. In "The Bean Field," the meditative state induced by hoeing ("It was no longer beans that I hoed, nor I that hoed beans") is interrupted by the firing of guns during the town's patriotic festivities. Thoreau describes with heavy irony the effect upon him of martial music: "I felt as if I could spit a Mexican with a good relish,—for why should we always stand for trifles?—and looked round for a woodchuck or a skunk to exercise my chivalry upon" (108).

In "The Village," Thoreau portrays what Concord offers with scant affection and a good deal of sarcasm. The village is a place of trivial gossip—although he admits he wants a "homeopathic dose" of it every day or two! More ominously, the arrangement of houses along the Concord lanes requires a visitor "to run the gantlet, and every man, woman, and child might get a lick at him" (113). Underlying all an individual's interactions with society is the state's power of compulsion. Thoreau describes with bitterness and resentment the night he spent in jail because he hadn't paid his poll tax: "Wherever a man goes, men will pursue and paw him with their dirty institu-tions, and, if they can, constrain him to belong to their desperate odd-fellow society" (115). Nearly as romantic and idealistic as was Rousseau about human nature, Thoreau sees the roots of violence in the coercive underpinnings of communal organization. He also avows that if all persons lived as simply as he did at Walden, theft and rob-bery would be eliminated, since these crimes are based on inequality of wealth. Thoreau thus represents his solitude as a radical moral alternative to the triviality, violence, and acquisitiveness that he thought were fostered by collective living arrangements. Although he expresses contempt for most social institutions, he weighs in on many political, economic, religious, and educational issues as he explains the meaning of his experiment in simplicity and solitude.

Thoreau needed regular contact with particular individuals to confirm his sense of identity and to remind himself of the value of being alone. *Walden* is interspersed with descriptions of his encoun-ters with various characters who help him to know his own mind and who by contrast justify his choice of life. In "Baker Farm" he tries to tell an impoverished Irish family, the Fields, that if they would simplify their lives they would not be trapped in degrading surroundings and habits. Don't work so hard and you won't have to eat so much, he informs them. But as he leaves the hut of the Irish family, his plan to catch fish that day "appeared for an instant trivial to me who had been sent to school and college" (139). This moment of self-doubt quickly dissipates as his "good genius" tells him that there are "no worthier games" than hunting and fishing, and that he should let himself roam and be wild. Rather than spend our lives buying and selling and working like the Field family, "we should come home from far, from adventures, and perils, and discoveries every day, with new experience and character" (140). Here solitary life is linked with mobility and adventure, while John Field's family ties him down geographically, economically, and imaginatively. This passage shows Thoreau at his least sympathetic; he is completely blind to the love and loyalty that bind this family together, and sees their "poor starveling brat" as but a burden, a ball and chain. He re-turns with relief and renewed appreciation to his solitary mode of life, never recognizing that he might be giving up something valu-able in order to live alone.

The book's most extended account of another person is intriguing because the woodchopper Alex Therien is more isolated from others than Thoreau himself. Simple, natural, and good-humored, Therien "interested me because he was so quiet and solitary and so happy withal" (98). While Thoreau praises Therien's humility and honesty, he is disturbed by his lack of spiritual and intellectual development and his uncritical Catholic piety: "His thinking was so primitive and immersed in his animal life, that, though more promising than a merely learned man's, it rarely ripened to any thing which can be reported" (101). Therien's unique outlook, his enigmatic wisdom or ignorance, appeals to Thoreau as a refreshing contrast to the tired clichés he hears from most of his fellows. Yet a disturbing undercurrent troubles his musings: could it be that too much solitude produces inarticulate contentment with merely physical existence? Thoreau seems obscurely worried that Therien embodies the most likely outcome of the way of life Thoreau recomends: solitary, simple, attuned to sense experience, and dull. He is at once drawn to and troubled by the woodcutter, whose life suggests that greater involvement with other people is necessary for the development of critical intellect and spiritual awareness.

Solitude could be taken too far, and the opportunities it offered could be squandered. At one point in *Walden*, Thoreau presents this recognition in humorous form, after an imaginary dialogue between "Poet" (probably representing his friend Ellery Channing) and "Hermit." When the hermit is alone again, we overhear his soliloquy as he tries to recreate his contemplative state before being interrupted:

> Let me see; where was I? Methinks I was nearly in this frame of mind; the world lay about at this angle. Shall I go to heaven or a-fishing? If I should soon bring this meditation to an end, would another so sweet occasion be likely to offer? I was as near being resolved into the essence of things as ever I was in my life. I fear my thoughts will not come back to me. If it would do any good, I would whistle for them. When they make us an offer, is it wise to say, We will think of it? My thoughts have left no track, and I cannot find the path again. What was it that I was thinking of? It was a very hazy day. I will just try these three sentences of Con-fut-see; they may fetch that state about again. I know not whether it was the dumps or a budding ecstasy. (150)

Thoreau can chuckle at the hermit's fussy preoccupation with his moods and fuzzy apprehension of spiritual realities. Soon the poet recalls the hermit to their immediate project of catching fish. This chapter, "Brute Neighbors," goes on to consider why a person has "just these species of animals for his neighbors, as if nothing but a mouse could have filled this crevice" (150–51). Thoreau considers the creatures with whom he shares the woods—mice, partridge, red and black ants, loons and ducks—and describes their habits and characteristics. Solitude may nurture this kind of attentive observation—or it may fix one's mind on oneself. Thoreau shows that there are many kinds of hermit and many uses of solitude, not all of equivalent value.

The consciousness of animals as "neighbors" that emerges from Thoreau's experience of solitude suggests an intriguing paradox. When Thoreau projects human attributes on animals, is he still solitary? He describes a war between red and black ants as a heroic struggle fought for a matter of principle. He plays a game of hide and seek with a loon which disappears beneath the surface of the pond. He wonders why ducks tack and veer, fly in circles and sail in the middle of the pond "unless they love the water for the same reason that I do" (158). As he interprets his fellow creatures, Thoreau suggests human motivations and finds companionship with them. He also describes inanimate objects and natural processes in anthropomorphic terms: "My house was not empty though I was gone. It was as if I had left a cheerful housekeeper behind. It was I and Fire that lived there" (169). When he installs a stove, it conceals the fire, "and I felt as if I had lost a companion. You can always see a face in the fire" (170). Thoreau feels more intimacy and connectedness with animals and elemental things than he does with living people. It is partly because of his detachment from other people that he perceives the nonhuman world in so intimate and personal a way.

Similarly, he is highly conscious of "former inhabitants" of the area, as one chapter is titled. Thoreau is not only unprecedented but almost unique in his linking of solitude to awareness of one's predecessors in a place.[6] "For human society I was obliged to conjure up the former occupants of these woods" (171). Again we may wonder whether this should be called solitude: is a vivid imagination of the dead a significant outcome of solitude or an escape from it? Ruined cottages and overgrown lots bring to mind what he knows of those who used to live in the vicinity, many of whom were people of color or impoverished laborers: a slave named Cato; Zilpha, a colored woman; Brister, "a handy Negro"; a family ruined by alcoholism; and a tragic Irish ditchdigger. Although he knows little about these folk, curiosity and solitude stimulate his desire to understand and imagine their hard lives. Thoreau allows himself to pity long-dead individuals in a way he seldom feels for living sufferers.

The melancholy reminders of these people are somewhat oppressive. Most of the former inhabitants of the area lived alone. As Thoreau broods over the gloomy ruins of their dwellings, he expresses indirectly his fear that his own experiment will also fail, his knowledge of the finitude of all human endeavors, and his sense of mortality. "Now only a dent in the earth marks the site of these dwellings. . . . These cellar dents, like deserted fox burrows, old holes, are all that is left where once were the stir and bustle of human life, and 'fate, free-will, foreknowledge absolute,' in some form and dialect or other were by turns discussed" (175). In the tone of elegy and mourning for unremembered lives, Thoreau hints at the lonely and painful side of his own solitude. His predominant attitude to solitude in *Walden* is celebration, and he claims that he "never felt lonesome, or in the least oppressed by a sense of solitude, but once" (89). Yet passages that linger over the traces of earlier residents of rural Concord reveal Thoreau's sympathy for the sad lives of other solitary figures and, in displaced form, express painful dimensions of his own experience of aloneness. Stories about former inhabitants provide him with an unusual kind of company, and "with such reminiscences I repeopled the woods and lulled myself asleep" (176).

Thoreau is keenly aware, even haunted by, the knowledge that Native Americans once dwelled on this ground. He discerns faint paths worn by the aboriginal hunters of the region, remembers legends associated with them, and sees in the Indians' relationship with the natural world much to emulate.[7] Thoreau's "savagist" view of Native Americans idealized a solitary, self-reliant hunter—not a member of a tribal community—who was doomed by encroaching Anglo-Saxon "civilization." This is in many ways a projection of Thoreau's hopes and fears about solitary life. Thoreau's example shows several ways in which solitude can orient a person to the past, at once inciting him to romanticize across the mists of time, stimulating historical consciousness, and nurturing imaginative empathy with those of another age.

Another way in which solitude has a social and ethical significance emerges in the way Thoreau considers his intellectual and manual work. The concentrated effort and focused purpose of engrossing intellectual labor separate a thinker from others, even when they are nearby: "A man thinking or working is always alone, let him be where he will. Solitude is not measured by the miles of space that intervene between a man and his fellows" (91). Living alone, a person must learn to do most practical things for himself. The self-reliance thus fostered by solitude is an alternative to the division of labor that characterizes modern industrial societies. Since Thoreau would minimize his involvement in the endless buying and selling that so often becomes the central activity of life, the purpose of working must be found elsewhere. Reading, writing, or hoeing beans must be done for its own sake rather than for utilitarian reasons. And not only its fruits, but work itself needs to be forgotten sometimes. The relentless American work-ethic, the incessant busy doing of this and that, is called into question by experiences of serene contentment. Thoreau finds that the value of his times of aloneness cannot always be understood in terms of what they produce. One of his most memorable descriptions of solitude celebrates a morning revery when he simply sits in the sun:

> There were times when I could not afford to sacrifice the bloom of the present moment to any work, whether of the head or hands. I love a broad margin to my life. Sometimes, in a summer morning, having taken my accustomed bath, I sat in my sunny doorway from sunrise till noon, rapt in a revery, amidst the pines and hickories and sumachs, in undisturbed solitude and stillness, while the birds sang around or flitted noiseless through the house, until by the sun falling in at my west window, or the noise of some traveller's wagon on the distant highway, I was reminded of the lapse of time. I grew in those seasons like corn in the night, and they were far better than any work of the hands would have been. They were not time subtracted from my life, but so much over and above my usual allowance. I realized what the Orientals mean by contemplation and the forsaking of works. (75)

Nothing tangible or productive is accomplished during such times of idleness, but something important happens nonetheless. The metaphor of ripening and organic growth ("like corn in the night") suggests the need for intervals when rest and inner changes can go on undisturbed, and natural processes take their course.

As in the claim that he realized "what the Orientals mean by contemplation and the forsaking of works," Thoreau's view of solitude is deeply influenced by extensive reading of Indian and Chinese philosophy and religious thought. He liked to think of himself as an American version of an Indian yogi, purifying himself of materialistic and egoistic desires. He quotes Hindu scripture to interpret the solitary practice of patient waiting as a duty of hospitality and openness to the divine: "I sometimes expected the Visitor who never comes. The Vishnu Purana says, 'The house-holder is to remain at eventide in his court-yard as long as it takes to milk a cow, or longer if he pleases, to await the arrival of a guest.' I often performed this duty of hospitality, waited long enough to milk a whole herd of cows, but did not see the man approaching from the town" (180). Here removing oneself from the presence of others is a prerequisite for the disciplines of serenity, attentiveness, and receptiveness—not to visitors from the town, but to the sacred. Thoreau frequently quotes Confucius and Chinese sages, who, although stressing more emphatically than does he the need for civic virtues, share his view that social harmony comes about through the cultivation of individual character.

Thoreau's depiction of solitude reflects and integrates many different strands of Western thought. Solitude promotes simplicity, the reduction of one's needs to a minimum. This ideal reflects American ideas of practical efficiency and echoes criticisms leveled by various reform movements against American economic practices. Thoreau's admiration for Greek and Latin Stoics shapes the ideals of independence and equanimity that he sought in solitude. His use of withdrawal for reading and writing resembles the classical ideal of pastoral retreat and the use of leisure to cultivate one's character through liberal studies.[8] The chapter "Reading" asserts that literary pursuits were one of his chief activities at Walden, and ideally should always be undertaken in solitude: "Books must be read as deliberately and reservedly as they were written" (68). He devotes his best hours to reading "Classics" and "Scriptures," contrasting these demanding studies with "easy reading" of contemporary works: "This only is reading, in a high sense, not that which lulls us as a luxury and suffers the nobler faculties to sleep the while, but what we have to stand on tiptoe to read and devote our most alert and wakeful hours to" (71). Thus Thoreau continues the humanistic tradition of solitary study of Petrarch, Montaigne, and Gibbon. Yet Thoreau was far more interested than they in scientific studies and in the natural world, and his constant concern to integrate his studies in relation to these interests represents a new departure.

Another tradition reflected in *Walden* is the pastoral literary genre. Leo Marx describes how this form of writing contrasts two ways of life that exemplify different conceptions of the relationship between humanity and nature.[9] The pastoral tradition idealizes a harmonious relation to nature and sees rural living as conducive to more honest dealings between individuals. Thoreau, too, aspired to these virtues and believed that solitude helped one attain them.

While he does not appeal to Christian tradition for either examples or justification of solitude, Thoreau attributes to solitude and to divinity many traits in common. "God is alone,—but the devil, he is far from being alone; he sees a great deal of company; he is legion" (92). Here the divine is interpreted as detached, transcendent, and serenely unaffected by the triviality and transience of finite affairs—

just as a hermit should be. (In other passages Thoreau conceives of ultimate spiritual reality in pantheistic and immanent terms, as pervading and related to all of the cosmos—just as a hermit should be!) Another passage compares Walden Pond, which has no visible inlet or outlet, to a hermit's purity, in contrast with Flints' Pond: "If by living thus reserved and austere, like a hermit in the woods, so long, it has acquired such wonderful purity, who would not regret that the comparatively impure waters of Flints' Pond should be mingled with it, or itself should ever go to waste its sweetness in the ocean wave?" (131).

Solitude is one of the austerities that Thoreau recommends in "Higher Laws" to overcome merely animal and sensual life (although these, too, are essential parts of our experience). Transcendentalist faith in a spiritual realm merges with his ascetic leanings when Thoreau recommends self-denial as the path to spiritual awakening. The "Higher Laws" or principles to which we should conform our lives will lead us eventually to chastity and vegetarianism, both of which are more easily practiced without the distractions and entertainments of other people. Thoreau never worries about the dangers of solitude or notes religious or ethical duties that would limit one's practice of it. Solitude is always a good thing that he associates with diverse religious traditions and values and affirms as both intrinsically valuable and leading to spiritual blessings and moral virtues.

From the very beginning, Thoreau has aroused strong criticism for his praise and practice of solitude. Emerson's funeral eulogy in 1862 presents Thoreau as a "hermit and ascetic" whose "endless walks" removed him from responsible social life. Emerson suggests that Thoreau's renunciation of social involvements wasted his talents. He implies that Thoreau's literary promise was unfulfilled, not even mentioning the publication of *Walden*. Thoreau's reclusive tendency led him to squander his potential to affect his society: "Had his genius been only contemplative, he had been fitted to his life, but with his energy and practical ability he seemed born for great enterprise and for command: and I so much regret the loss of his rare powers of action, that I cannot help counting it a fault in him that he had no ambition. Wanting this, instead of engineering for all America, he was the captain of a huckleberry party. Pounding beans is good to the end of pounding empires one of these days, but if, at the end of years, it is still only beans!"[10] This view, which reflects tensions that developed between Thoreau and Emerson after the Walden period, has been echoed by many critics. For Theodore Baird, he is "an impossible egotist" and "the judge of all the rest of the universe," whose lack of compassion for other people is a fatal flaw in his sensibility.[11] While this critic tempers his harsh judgment with appreciation of Thoreau's extraordinary use of language in his accounts of the natural world, he holds that Thoreau failed to integrate his concerns in a social vision that could be sustained. Similarly, Wright Morris attacks Thoreau's "principle of turning one's back on unpleasant facts" and sees this as a typically American tendency: "Somewhere between Walden Pond and Boston—at some point of tension, where these dreams cross—the schizoid soul of the American is polarized. On the one hand we are builders of bridges and cities, we are makers of things and believers in the future. On the other we have a powerful *private* urge to take to the woods."[12] Morris, writing in 1957, articulates what has become a common view of Thoreau as the epitome of individualism in American literature. In so much American writing, the hero finally abandons a corrupt society and withdraws into a private wilderness, deciding, like Huck Finn, to "light out for the territory." Thoreau's solitude is said to typify this selfish and usually male tendency, which needs to be challenged and, like an errant schoolboy, brought back to class.

Other readings of Thoreau, however, discern in his writing important social concerns, some of which I have described here. Robert Richardson traces ethical themes in Thoreau's work such as his shift of attention from the gross wealth of nations to the well-being of individuals as the criterion of economic thought, his interest in generativity and renewal on many levels, and the need to accept limits on our restless striving.[13] It should be clear from the argument of this chapter that I share the view that Thoreau was intensely interested in and addressed many of the political and social issues of his day, and that his thought remains significant today. What I would add to this debate is the insight that to see Thoreau's ethical significance does not mean that we must reject or ignore his experience of solitude. It was precisely through his practice of and reflections on solitude that Thoreau came to many of his most central and signficant ethical insights. Thoreau's example challenges both the individualist who claims solitude as an absolute and unqualified right and any ethical theory or community that does not make a place for solitude.

Thoreau's view of solitude may be contrasted with Rousseau's.[14] These two figures are alike in many ways, including their shared love of the natural world, their wish to escape from society's artificial roles and hypocrisies, and their anarchistic and utopian view that political and social life will flourish if individuals simply follow their spontaneous inclinations and impulses. When they discuss solitude, too, there are notable similarities, such as their mutual interest in the states of mind induced by walking or floating in a boat (compare Rousseau's account of the Lake of Bienne in his fifth Reverie with Thoreau's description of being "dreaming awake" in a drifting boat in "The Ponds" [129]). Yet these two writers diverge in the ways in which they understand solitude. Rousseau yearns for solitude as a permanent state of bliss, while Thoreau describes and envisions a rhythmic alternation of periods of solitude and times of engagement. Rousseau presents his love of solitude as a mark of his singularity and part of his claim to be utterly unique. Thoreau, along with his interest in the particularities of his own experience, discerns universal truths and lessons for others.

Thoreau's ethical concerns are reflected in his "rhetoric of commonality," the ways he uses the first-person plural to express his conclusions and call his readers to action. According to Richardson, "the very language of *Walden* creates the impression that while the experience at the pond is Thoreau's own, the conclusions and lessons to be drawn from it are common property, not just his but ours. The social ethic functions in *Walden* even—perhaps especially—at the all-important but nearly invisible level of grammar."[15] Thoreau's appreciation of solitude is not based on a desire for complete autonomy or a wish to be insulated from the demands of others, although he sometimes expresses these impulses. Far more than Rousseau, Thoreau also recognizes and affirms his inescapable dependence on continuing social involvements, and, in the ways that we have seen, he reflects on how solitude affects his relationships. In these ways, then, Thoreau's view of solitude differs from Rousseau's: he holds that solitude should be temporary, that it is not the grounds for a claim of uniqueness but a general if unrecognized need of all human beings, and that it should not be simply an escape from social responsibilities but offer a new perspective on them.

This defense of Thoreau's view of solitude sounds utilitarian, as if the value of aloneness is only a means to collectively approved ends. It would be paradoxical to defend solitude only as instrumental to better communal life, for this would undermine the value of solitude as an end in itself and the "useless" but significant discoveries that it may bring. Yet we should examine the insights that come from solitude for what is helpful for others. The insights of solitude are something like the experience of getting lost in the woods that Thoreau describes as offering a new vista: "Not till we are completely lost, or turned round,—for a man needs only to be turned round once with his eyes shut in this world to be lost,—do we appreciate the vastness and strangeness of Nature. . . . Not till we have lost the world, do we begin to find ourselves, and realize where we are and the infinite extent of our relations" (115). In this passage, being lost seems to be the precondition for reorientation and a new, more complex sense of where we are. Similarly, in solitude one may lose track of the immediate social context and discover a wider world that can later be reported to others. In solitude one may forget one's neighbors, only to find a new meaning of "neighbor" and insights that affect one's human relationships.

Solitude and Ecological Consciousness

At the start of *Walden*, the appeal of solitude is inseparably linked to the criticism of society. As the book unfolds, however, descriptions of the natural world take over as the narrator's primary focus.[16] Two "plots" give *Walden* a sense of development: the annual succession of seasons that concludes in the penultimate chapter "Spring," and the narrator's gradual mental disengagement from society so that its problems cease to preoccupy him. In the second half of *Walden*, Thoreau is primarily focused on understanding patterns in the natural world. He uses imagery of rebirth, awakening, regeneration, and dawn to describe both the coming of spring and the changes he desires in human consciousness.[17] Self-referential statements and social criticisms decrease as the author's mind becomes primarily attuned to the natural world.

The development in the perspective of *Walden*'s narrator is an important milestone in the emergence of an ecological consciousness in American culture.[18] It is equally significant in understanding Thoreau's view of solitude. As he dramatizes the transformation of the narrator's consciousness, Thoreau shows that merely physical isolation is not enough to achieve the true purposes of solitude; a disciplining of consciousness and a receptiveness to new influences are also necessary. If solitude is to be more than an excuse for narcissism or solipsism, the mind must be turned to something beyond itself. Thoreau portrays himself as initially drawn into solitude by reaction against the negative features of his social context. Only with time, attentiveness, and self-discipline does he discern positive reasons for seeking to be alone. By the end of the book, Thoreau's bitterness toward society has largely dissipated (although the Conclusion returns, in a more affirmative tone, to his vision of the right relationship between individual and society in America). As he reflected on the significance of his stay at Walden and made it the central event of his life, Thoreau tried to show that the most important outgrowth of his solitude was the transformation of his consciousness through attunement to nature. The spiritual journey he depicted was essentially a process of joyful self-renewal in harmony with the natural world's cycles of growth.

Appreciating the value of the natural world is closely linked to another value that Thoreau associates with solitude: wildness. He feels a strange and sudden desire to eat a woodchuck, "not that I was hungry then, except for that wildness which he represented" (140). Wildness should be respected both in the natural world and in humanity. He honors equally his yearnings for the good and for the wild: "I found in myself, and still find, an instinct toward a higher, or, as it is named, spiritual life, as do most men, and another toward a primitive rank and savage one, and I reverence them both. I love the wild not less than the good" (140–41). Just as the individual needs to acknowledge the part of him that will not conform to "higher laws," so society needs to respect the "wild men, who instinctively follow other fashions and trust other authorities than their townsmen, and by their goings and comings stitch towns together in parts where else they would be ripped" (188–89). Thoreau associates wildness not only with animals and sublime natural forces but also with those solitary persons who make their homes in the lonely places between villages. The wildness of these individuals is expressed in their independence, freedom, and solitude.

The climactic chapter "Spring" culminates in a celebration of nature's inexhaustible vitality, which we experience most powerfully in its capacity to exceed our efforts to control or even understand it:

> Our village life would stagnate if it were not for the unexplored forests and meadows which surround it. We need the tonic of wildness—to wade sometimes in marshes where the bittern and the meadow-hen lurk, and hear the booming of the snipe; to smell the whispering sedge where only some wilder and more solitary fowl builds her nest, and the mink crawls with its belly close to the ground. At the same time that we are earnest to explore and learn all things, we require that all things be mysterious and unexplorable, that land and sea be infinitely wild, unsurveyed and unfathomed by us because unfathomable. We can never have enough of Nature. . . . We need to witness our own limits transgressed, and some life pasturing freely where we never wander. (211–12)

In this passage, appreciating nature's wildness is an experience that must be undergone alone.[19] Contact with a wild and solitary fowl makes the human creature more wild and solitary. Life in community would stagnate without not only the surrounding natural environment, but also the wild individuals who live there, who by transgressing or ignoring society's rules and regulations show the rest of us their proper place, their necessary but limited validity. For Thoreau, the wildness and spiritual vitality of both the natural world and human nature are closely associated with solitude.

We need to be reminded, begins the "Conclusion" of *Walden*, that there is more to life than what our village, nation, or religion commends. "Thank Heaven, here is not all the world" (213). Thoreau's final chapter connects solitude with most of his central values. If one seeks simplicity, "the laws of the universe will appear less complex, and solitude will not be solitude, nor poverty poverty, nor weakness weakness" (216). Solitude will not be solitude? Here I think Thoreau implies the distinction between solitude and loneliness: one's time alone should be welcome and meaningful rather than emptiness aching for other people. Something valuable will fill what might seem a void: "God will see that you do not want society" (219). A love of solitude is bound up with Thoreau's praise of nonconformity, stepping to one's own music, hearing a different drummer, and expressing one's individuality. Experiences of aloneness help one to perceive the world in a singular way that others may not understand: "Why level downward to our dullest perception always, and praise that as common sense? The commonest sense is the sense of men asleep, which they express by snoring" (217). Cultivating solitude is an antidote to anxious concern with trivialities and dissipation of one's time and energies, and a discipline necessary to discern the lasting truths. It would be best "not to live in this restless, nervous, bustling, trivial Nineteenth Century, but stand or sit thoughtfully while it goes by" (220). The "solid bottom" of reality, the firm foundation of truth, is not to be found in "the bogs and quicksands of society" (221). Wake up! The images of awakening with which Thoreau concludes *Walden* call his reader to disengage from habitual social assumptions and to recognize the incessant flow of novelty into the world. The praise and practice of solitude are deeply connected to these exhortations to nurture one's individuality and perceive life's vitality and self-renewal.

Leaving Walden

As he looked back on his time at the pond, the Walden experiment became the key to Thoreau's self-understanding, what Georges Gusdorf calls the "mythic tale" that expresses a person's interpretation of the meaning of his life.[20] Solitude was a crucial part of Thoreau's mythic tale, as it was in a different way for Rousseau. This period was the time when Thoreau realized his vocation (along with the other discoveries I have described). During his two years at the pond he completed *A Week on the Concord and Merrimack Rivers* and the first draft of *Walden*. The Walden period was a rite of initiation into a new identity as a writer. When he left the pond, now age thirty, he knew, in spite of minimal success in publishing his works, that writing would be at the center of his life. The two-year experiment in solitude was a crucial time of disengagement from the world's expectations, the kind of delay and protracted uncertainty characteristic of adolescents that Erik Erikson discerns in the "late blooming" of many creative individuals.[21] Solitude was crucial to the formation of Thoreau's identity and to his discovery of a vocation.

"I left the woods for as good a reason as I went there. Perhaps it seemed to me that I had several more lives to live, and could not spare any more time for that one" (215). One limitation of *Walden* is that Thoreau does not show how his period of relative seclusion was integrated into the rest of his life, or how solitude was part of his life after the Walden experiment. He says little about why he ended his solitude, except that he felt himself slipping into a rut. The path he wore from his door to the pond was still visible when he returned six years later, symbolizing how easy it is to become a creature of habit, "how deep the ruts of tradition and conformity" (216). This remark only hints at the problems of boredom, apathy, and restless craving for novelty that disrupt most extended periods of solitude.

Two other factors that may have made it easier for him to leave the pond occurred in the summer of 1846, in the middle of his two-year sojourn. Someone—probably his Aunt Maria—paid his poll tax for him, and thereby freed him from jail after one night. Refusing to pay the poll tax was Thoreau's protest against the Mexican War, an attempt to assert his integrity in a corrupt society. One of Thoreau's biographers, Richard Lebeaux, speculates that "it was no doubt deeply embarrassing for him, the supposedly heroic and self-sufficient rebel and sojourner at Walden, to have underscored for all the community and himself to see the extent to which he remained linked to, and indebted to, his family (particularly the women) and civilized society."[22] Lebeaux argues, as well, that Thoreau's trip to Maine, where he encountered a harsh and forbidding side of nature that challenged his benign view of wildness, "dramatized to him just how much a member of human society he really was, led him further to ponder the viability of his Walden life, and forced him to face the fact that

the next developmental phase had to be lived out in civilized society."[23] Having proved to himself that he could be independent and
self-sufficient by his strategic withdrawal to the Pond, Thoreau was
ready to recognize and accept the ways in which he was still linked
to family, friends, and the pleasures of communal living.

The immediate occasion for leaving Walden Pond was that Emerson's wife Lidian asked Thoreau to live with their family and help
out while Emerson was lecturing in Europe. Thoreau did not know
what the future held, and wondered, writing in his journal five years
later, why he left Walden: "Why I left the woods I do not think I can
tell. I have often wished myself back. I do not know any better how I
ever came to go there. Perhaps it is none of my business, even if it is
yours. Perhaps I wanted a change. There was a little stagnation, it
may be. . . . Perhaps if I lived there much longer, I might live there
forever. One would think twice before he accepted heaven on such
terms."[24] In *Walden* solitude is described as a self-contained episode,
and the growth of the narrator's consciousness during this period
displaces the more traditional autobiographical plot of the course of
a life. Although *Walden* highlights the experience of solitude during
this pivotal time, we can wish that Thoreau had reflected on how
solitude was a part of his life after 1847. For this one must turn to his
journals.[25] Still, the presentation of solitude in *Walden* shows Thoreau's
basic understanding of the proper place of solitude in human life.
Walden portrays solitude as an interlude in the author's life, and as
interspersed even during this time with various forms of social engagement. Thoreau implies that periods of solitude should alternate with
times of involvement with others, and that solitude and engagement
constantly influence each other, each affecting the way the other is
experienced.

The final image in *Walden* epitomizes Thoreau's conviction that
one person's solitude may be significant for others. He tells a story
about "a strong and beautiful bug which came out of the dry leaf of
an old table of apple-tree wood, which had stood in a farmer's kitchen
for sixty years . . . which was heard gnawing out for several weeks,
hatched perchance by the heat of an urn" (222). This insect has had
solitude! What does it bring to society? "Who does not feel his faith
in a resurrection and immortality strengthened by hearing of this?
Who knows what beautiful and winged life, whose egg has been buried for ages under many concentric layers of woodenness in the dead
dry life of society, deposited at first in the alburnum of the green and
living tree, which has been gradually converted into the semblance
of its well-seasoned tomb,—heard perchance gnawing out now for

years by the astonished family of man, as they sat round the festive board,—may unexpectedly come forth from amidst society's most trivial and handselled furniture, to enjoy its perfect summer life at last!" (222–23). This anecdote expresses Thoreau's faith in individuality and nonconformity, and in the potential significance of what approaches a civilized community from beyond its boundaries. The insect comes to society from the natural world, from what was once a green and living tree, having spent years in the dead dry wood of human furniture. The bug has been sequestered for sixty years, removed from the ongoing social life of the family that owns the table. It emerges again, like Thoreau from his sojourn in the woods, with a message, though at first all that one might hear is the sound of gnawing (an apt metaphor for some of Thoreau's diatribes!). There is a lesson here for those who will heed it. A hermit comes from seclusion to express a perspective that, although it may seem strange to conventional notions, may be full of meaning. Like the image of the red squirrel with which I began, a creature "soliloquizing and talking to all the universe at the same time," the final parable in *Walden* expresses in symbolic form Thoreau's faith in the significance for others of the ethical and spiritual wisdom that can come from solitude.

6

TWENTIETH-CENTURY VARIETIES OF SOLITARY EXPERIENCE

As AUTOBIOGRAPHY has flourished in the nineteenth and twentieth centuries, many writers have explored the role of solitude in their lives. In this chapter, rather than making a close study of particular texts, I will explore some basic ways in which solitude is linked to ethics and spirituality in twentieth-century autobiographical narratives. I focus on experience because autobiography does not usually argue about solitude in abstract or theoretical terms, but explores its significance and problems in the process of offering an account of the author's life. The allusion to William James's work in the title of this chapter emphasizes variety; there are many kinds of solitude and many ways in which it has been found to be conducive to a spiritual value.

I will discuss five basic values that are sought in solitude: attunement to nature, healing, adventure, creative work, and self-formation. These values are closely linked to the ethical justification and spiritual meaning of solitude; they are purposes and concerns that some individuals think they can best pursue during periods of aloneness. Sometimes these values are explicitly linked to a conception of the divine, but most of the works I examine are by secular solitaries who are somewhat distanced from Christian tradition, even though they are influenced by it. As with any typology, this framework has its limits, generalizing where distinctions can be made and highlighting certain features at the expense of others. Many autobiographers are interested in more than one of these values. We have already seen some of these concerns in texts examined earlier. For instance, Thoreau and Rousseau are interested in how attunement to nature affects consciousness; nearly all life-writers find solitude conducive to the creative work of literary composition; Rousseau turns to solitude to heal the psychic wounds he believes a cruel society has inflicted. As I reflect on the basic values that autobiographers find in aloneness, I will indicate several works in which each value seems central and describe in more detail one or two representative texts.

Attunement to Nature

One of the main values sought in solitude is a sense of deeper connection with the natural world. According to eighteenth-century theories of the sublime, such as those of Burke and Kant, feelings of enthusiasm, admiration, and transport are evoked by awesome natural spectacles. A sublime landscape witnessed by a solitary observer offers not only insight into the human place in a vast and powerful universe but awe, emotional transport, and the desire to worship that which transcends humanity. Solitude seems to be necessary to apprehend fully the power of the natural world and, according to Kant, for the human soul's responsive recognition of its own freedom. Experiences of aloneness in the natural world became an important part of the Christian tradition in American history. A study of Jonathan Edwards shows that by the mid-eighteenth century, the natural world had become the preferred site of Christian solitude, replacing the Puritan home's "closet of prayer." As the American wilderness became a safer place, the out-of-doors became the favored location in which Edwards could practice his devotional disciplines, including prayer, Bible reading, singing or chanting, and cathartic weeping.[1]

Sensitivity to nature is a central theme of the Romantic movement and its spiritual offspring. William Wordsworth perceived nature's spiritual meaning in solitary excursions, referring in "I Wandered Lonely as a Cloud" to "that inward eye / which is the bliss of solitude." In *The Prelude* he composed an autobiographical epic in verse that described powerful experiences of healing in the natural world, usually when he was alone:

> When from our better selves we have too long
> Been parted by the hurrying world, and droop,
> Sick of its business, of its pleasures tired,
> How gracious, how benign, is Solitude. (4, 354–57)

The Romantic poets frequently rhapsodized about the effects of natural beauty on the human soul, even as they also worried about the effect of too much solitude. Autobiographers such as Rousseau and Thoreau describe the changes in consciousness wrought by prolonged immersion in the natural world, although Rousseau's frantic mind never seems to dwell outside itself for long. By the mid-nineteenth century, several distinct intellectual traditions converged on the questions of how solitary experiences of nature affect human consciousness and make possible apprehension of the divine.

The phrase "attunement to nature" derives from Philip Koch, who delineates this as one of five "virtues of solitude."[2] Koch helpfully distinguishes three ways in which solitary experience of nature is valuable: for facilitating clear perception, symbolic perception (or, I would say, interpretation), and the sense of fusion with nature. The concentrated attention that is possible when a person is alone facilitates clear, undistracted observation of the details of the natural world. For instance, think of Thoreau's nuanced descriptions of the intricacy and richly textured patterns of plant and animal life at Walden Pond. Second, nature is valued as a source of symbolic perception or interpretation, that is, insights into the meaning of other things, including oneself, human society, and the divine. For Thoreau the hooting of owls represents "the stark twilight and unsatisfied thoughts which all have" (85).[3] The thawing of sand and clay oozing down a railway bank, minutely observed, evokes insights into human nature and the world: "What is man but a mass of thawing clay? . . . Thus it seemed that this one hillside illustrated the principle of all the operations of Nature. . . . There is nothing inorganic" (205–6). Thoreau's role is to "decipher this hieroglyphic for us, that we may turn over a new leaf at last" (205).

According to Koch, the third sort of experience of nature that solitaries celebrate is fusion, "the loss of the sense of barriers between oneself and nature, the sense of flowing out into it as it simultaneously flows through oneself."[4] Thoreau's spell of sitting on his doorstep in the sun for a long afternoon or Rousseau's reveries drifting in a boat on the Lake of Bienne exemplify this kind of serenity and mental absorption into one's environment. Later writers describe how the awareness of boundaries between oneself and the world can dissolve when one is lost in contemplation of flowing water, expansive prairie, or desert vista. Such moments of identification, merging, or communion with the world are, at least for persons inclined to solitude, much more difficult to attain when one is attending to other people's reactions.

The American tradition of "nature writing" is often autobiographical, as Thoreau's example influenced later authors to explore various ways that the natural environment shapes consciousness and identity.[5] Solitude is usually a crucial condition for attunement to nature in the works of John Muir, Aldo Leopold, Loren Eiseley, Wendell Berry, Annie Dillard, Edward Abbey, and Barry Lopez. I will consider how Abbey's *Desert Solitaire* and Dillard's *Pilgrim at Tinker Creek* show crucial links between solitude and attunement to nature, and the contrasting ethical and spiritual values that grow out of their experiences.

Edward Abbey's *Desert Solitaire* (1968) recounts a season he spent as a ranger in Arches National Park, near Moab, Utah. The harsh and beautiful desert landscape was about to be "developed" so that large numbers of visitors could drive around it in automobiles, and Abbey voices his vehement protest against the imminent destruction of a place he loves: Arches will not be the same when it is crowded with noisy tourists. The qualities of the unpopulated desert shape both human and other forms of life within it:

> It seems to me that the strangeness and wonder of existence are emphasized here, in the desert, by the comparative sparsity of the flora and fauna: life not crowded upon life as in other places but scattered abroad in spareness and simplicity, with a generous gift of space for each herb and bush and tree, each stem of grass, so that the living organism stands out bold and brave and vivid against the lifeless sand and barren rock. The extreme clarity of the desert light is equaled by the extreme individuation of desert life-forms. Love flowers best in openness and freedom.[6]

Living in this sparse and open landscape shapes an ethos of freedom and individuality.

The bleakness, indifference, and "uselessness" of the desert are threatening to human beings, and our fear compels us to try to tame or domesticate it. Abbey shows how solitude, like the desert, is incomprehensible in a well-ordered society, as passers-by puzzle over why he lives alone and what he does in the desert. The relative lack of contact with other people makes possible contemplation of the natural environment, and Abbey conveys powerful moments of vivid perception and feelings of oneness with his surroundings. He sees no need for a God to justify or explain his love for this land: "Who the hell is He? There is nothing here, at the moment, but me and the desert. And that's the truth. Why confuse the issue by dragging in a superfluous entity? Occam's razor. Beyond atheism, nontheism. I am not an atheist but an earthiest. Be true to the earth" (208). Abbey's spirituality focuses on appreciating the intrinsic qualities of the desert for what they are.

He often introduces and rejects theological categories as interpretive tools. Exploring a side canyon off the Colorado River, Abbey wonders "Is this at last the *locus Dei?*" (200). He says that "there are enough cathedrals and temples and altars here for a Hindu pantheon of divinities." Then he tries to divest himself of religious categories and simply see the natural world unadorned, rejecting the need to interpret a strikingly beautiful place in religious terms: "If a man's imagination were not so weak, so easily tired, if his capacity for wonder not so limited, he would abandon forever such fantasies of the supernal. He would learn to perceive in water, leaves and silence more than sufficient of the absolute and marvelous, more than enough to console him for the loss of the ancient dreams" (200). Abbey constantly juxtaposes theological categories and religious symbols (mysticism, the sublime, a burning bush, baptismal water) with the ideal of a more spartan, ascetic, and ultimately truthful apprehension of the world. In Abbey's *via negativa*, the solitary desert explorer must leave behind not only people, but inherited religious presuppositions to discover bedrock, the fundamental reality. Yet of course a solitary continues to interpret the world using his society's basic concepts and categories, including religious ones. Thus in Abbey's work the theme of solitude in nature is linked to a basic theological question about the ability of human thought to comprehend the divine. Abbey proposes an impossible endeavor: to transcend his own humanness and his embeddedness in culture in order to know the world and the divine directly:

The personification of the natural is exactly the tendency I wish to suppress in myself, to eliminate for good. I am here not only to evade for a while the clamor and filth and confusion of the cultural apparatus but also to confront, immediately and directly if possible, the bare bones of existence, the elemental and fundamental, the bedrock which sustains us. I want to be able look at and into a juniper tree, a piece of quartz, a vulture, a spider, and see it as it is in itself, devoid of all humanly ascribed qualities, anti-Kantian, even the categories of scientific description. To meet God or Medusa face to face, even if it means risking everything human in myself. I dream of a hard and brutal mysticism in which the naked self merges with a non-human world and yet somehow survives still intact, individual, separate. Paradox and bedrock. (6)

Abbey draws strong ethical conclusions from his months of solitude in Utah. Like John Muir and Aldo Leopold, he writes in order to arouse readers to save a threatened wilderness environment. Yet Abbey has little interest in specific political remedies; his primary concern is to celebrate the freedom and wildness that the desert makes possible. His creed is not environmentalism but individualism and anarchism, although he would surely reject any attempt to formulate a consistent doctrine, an "ism" of any sort. He writes with cheerful contempt about the mass of complacent Americans who put up with domestic routines, boring jobs, destructive violence, arrogant elected officials, and hideously crowded cities. Floating down the Colorado River in "dual solitude" with a friend, Abbey feels deliriously exuberant as he leaves behind the organized clutter of civilization:

> Such are my—you wouldn't call them thoughts would you?—such are my feelings, a mixture of revulsion and delight, as we float away on the river, leaving behind for a while all that we most heartily and joyfully detest. That's what the first taste of the wild does to a man, after having been too long penned up in the city. No wonder the Authorities are so anxious to smother the wilderness under asphalt and resevoirs. They know what they're doing; their lives depend on it, and all their rotten institutions. Play safe. Ski only in clockwise direction. Let's all have fun together. (178)

The exhilarating freedom of being in the wilderness is precious to him, and his ornery animadversions against contemporary life show him trying to carry over what he learns in the natural world to his life in society. Abbey's quirky, provocative, and arrogant style asserts his originality and idiosyncratic value as an individual. His motto could be Thoreau's epigraph for *Walden:* "I do not propose to write an ode to dejection, but to brag as lustily as chanticleer in the morning, standing on the roost, if only to wake my neighbors up" (1). For Abbey, aloneness in the desert provides experiences of attunement to nature that are valuable in themselves. From his desert solitaire he also derives spiritual insights and an ethical perspective that is critical of his society's conventional banality, and that unabashedly affirms and celebrates the value of individuality.

If Abbey celebrates the self nurtured by periods of aloneness in the desert, Annie Dillard effaces her personal identity, losing herself in close observations and wide-ranging speculation. *Pilgrim at Tinker Creek* (1974) is a collection of thematic essays inspired by Dillard's perceptions of the land around her farm in southwestern Virginia. She provides very little personal information about herself, at least in terms of the usual biographical details. Unlike Abbey, she is not much interested in the ethics of aloneness, in defending solitude or deriving from it insights that might challenge prevailing social norms. She appropriates a different side of Thoreau than Abbey: "I propose to keep here what Thoreau called 'a meteorological journal of the mind,' telling some tales and describing some of the sights of this rather tamed valley, and exploring, in fear and trembling, some of the unmapped dim reaches and unholy fastnesses to which those tales and sights so dizzyingly lead."[7] The sights she sees and the emotions and thoughts they evoke are always described by a narrator who is alone. Dillard places herself in the tradition of medieval anchoresses, those women who secluded themselves for religious reasons in a permanently enclosed room attached to a church:

> I live by a creek, Tinker Creek, in a valley in Virginia's Blue Ridge. An anchorite's hermitage is called an anchor-hold; some anchor-holds were simple sheds clamped to the side of a church like a barnacle to a rock. I think of this house clamped to the side of Tinker Creek as an anchorhold. It holds me at anchor to the rock bottom of the creek itself and it keeps me steadied in the current, as a sea anchor does, facing the stream of light pouring down. It's a good place to live; there's a lot to think about. The creeks—Tinker's and Carvin's—are an active mystery, fresh every minute. Theirs is the mystery of the continuous creation and all that providence implies: the uncertainty of vision, the horror of the fixed, the dissolution of the present, the intricacy of beauty, the pressure of fecundity, the elusiveness of the free, and the flawed nature of perfection. (2–3)

There are two primary spiritual dimensions of *Pilgrim at Tinker Creek*. First, theological reflections: Dillard is a pilgrim on a journey both physical and spiritual, geographical and religious, as her wanderings around the creeks, mountains, and valleys prompt reflections on the power that made and sustains this world. Like a tinker, this power is itinerant, elusive, unpredictable; it fixes or mends things eventually but often in a somewhat haphazard way, by an experimental, trial-and-error process. Dillard writes a poetic natural theology, always trying to draw conclusions about the divine from the natural world. Although she is constantly in dialogue with the history of Jewish and Christian thought, she is less concerned with being orthodox than she is in showing the plausibility of a bewildering array of theological views that all seem to find some degree of support in the natural world.

A second spiritual dimension is Dillard's interest in what these sights and reflections do to the human spirit: "I watch the running sheets of light raised on the creek's surface. The sight has the appeal of the purely passive, like the racing of light under clouds on a field, the beautiful dream at the moment of being dreamed. The breeze is the merest puff, but you yourself sail headlong and breathless under the gale force of the spirit" (14). She depicts the ways that her solitary rambles through the natural environment heighten her awareness and influence her consciousness. One of the most powerful chapters is on "Seeing," that is, on learning to see what we usually glance at. In the central epiphany in the book, Dillard sees "the tree with the lights in it" described by a once-blind girl who recovered her sight. Dillard writes:

> One day I was walking along Tinker Creek thinking of nothing at all and I saw the tree with the lights in it. I saw the backyard cedar where the mourning doves roost charged and transfigured, each cell buzzing with flame. I stood on the grass with the lights in it, grass that was wholly fire, utterly focused and utterly dreamed. It was less like seeing than like being for the first time seen, knocked breathless by a powerful glance. The flood of fire abated, but I'm still spending the power. . . . I have since only very rarely seen the tree with the lights in it. The vision comes and goes, mostly goes, but I live for it, for the moment when the mountains open and a new light roars in spate through the crack, and the mountains slam. (35)

A crucial condition for such moments of seeing, for discerning the fire within all things, is a kind of receptivity and attentiveness that are usually impossible when one is with others. In a long chapter on "The Present," Dillard explores how self-consciousness changes one's experience of the present moment, diverting attention from whatever one was focused on. In contrast, what she calls innocence is "the spirit's unself-conscious state at any moment of pure devotion to any object. It is at once a receptiveness and total concentration" (83). The presence of other people seems to inhibit unselfconscious attentiveness and receptivity. With this sort of meditative reflection, interwoven with a kaleidoscope of allusions to biblical, philosophical, and theological texts, Dillard explores the psychology of solitary religious experience.

Dillard's spirituality, the adventures of the mind and spirit made possible by observation and interpretation of nature's mysteries, is deeply rooted in her solitary explorations of rural Virginia. Her religious experience seems to pull her away from other people and not to reorient her view of them. In *Pilgrim at Tinker Creek* she shows little interest in what the solitary brings back to society, ethical implications of solitude, or the rhythms of aloneness and engagement. One would never know from Dillard's account that southwestern Virginia is a well-populated agricultural area or that her life was shared in any way with other human beings. She cultivates the role of solitary, saying that her ecstatic responses to nature's blood, guts, and beauty make her "no longer quite fit for company" (274). She places herself in the tradition of the fifth-century Egyptian desert hermits, quoting one who tells a disciple, "Go and sit in your cell, and your cell will teach you everything" (264). Dillard doesn't sit in a cell, but she practices attentive aloneness and self-disciplined alertness, the stilling of the ego that makes possible moments of direct perception and a sense of unity or fusion with the world: "The death of the self of which the great writers speak is no violent act. It is merely the joining of the great rock heart of the earth in its roll. It is merely the slow cessation of the will's sprints and the intellect's chatter: it is waiting like a hollow bell with stilled tongue. *Fuge, tace, quiesce.* The waiting itself is the thing" (265). Like Edward Abbey, Dillard constructs an autobiographical narrative that uses solitude in nature as the occasion and inspiration for distinctive spiritual concerns.

Healing

A second form of solitude related to spirituality has its origin in periods of aloneness in response to loss, trauma, or suffering, when a person sequesters himself in order to heal physical or psychic wounds. Solitude is an important part of the mourning process in many religions and cultures. Coming to terms with bereavement often requires not only the support of relatives and friends but solitary immersion in the emotions of grief and sorrow and confrontation with the reality of loss, separation, and ending. Solitude offers retreat from the pressures of ordinary social engagement, a refuge or respite from interaction that allows the healing powers within the self and in the natural environment to restore well-being. Probably the impetus for a great deal of human solitude arises from the feeling of being drained and depleted by the interactions of normal social life, such as "the wretchedness of the busy man" that Petrarch describes at the beginning of *De Vita Solitaria.* Rousseau's *Reveries* show his withdrawal from others to lick his psychic wounds and indulge in consoling fantasies. Paul Auster's *The Invention of Solitude*, which I examine in a subsequent chapter, was written soon after his father's death and his own divorce, during a period of despondency about his prospects as a poet and fiction writer.

Philip Koch rightly cautions that emphasizing the restorative virtues of solitude, its power to strengthen a person for renewed social activity, "can lead one to think of this profound experience as a mere instrumentality of relationship."[8] Such a view would see solitude's value merely as equipping a person for further involvement in society. But the experience of being healed by solitude can involve much more than this, and can be interpreted as a significant life event and spiritual experience. A person may understand her healing as caused by beneficent powers that are fundamental to the world. Healing is such an essentially and self-evidently good thing that few writers spend much energy justifying periods of aloneness devoted to recuperating their powers. An ethical argument for solitude for the purpose of healing might be instrumental—that is, appealing to the need to have the inner resources to give anything to others—or it might justify health as an intrinsic good or a right of every individual.

Solitude is linked to healing in a distinctive group of American works of nature writing that are also grief narratives. In such works as Terry Tempest Williams's *Refuge*, Sue Hubbel's *A Country Year*, Bill Barich's *Laughing in the Hills*, William Least Heat-Moon's *Blue Highways*, Peter Matthiesen's *The Snow Leopard*, and Gretel Ehrlich's *The Solace of Open Spaces*, the author mourns a recent loss, usually a death or divorce. Mark Allister traces the ways these writers work though their grief by focusing on some natural object, animal, or landscape that absorbs them and helps them to reinterpret their own past lives.[9] Often the author is able to see that sickness or death is part of the natural cycle, and this larger perspective contributes to the process of mourning. In each of these books, the author forms bonds with the landscape or animals that help in coming to terms with a human loss. The authors may use their time alone to care for and nurture a house, garden, or animals. When one has lost a loved one, it is hard for a person to move beyond numbness and vulnerability and to reestablish emotional bonds with the world. Taking care of something that is not a person may allow a grieving individual eventually to establish new human relationships. In any case, caring for the nonhuman world is an intrinsically valuable experience, and the capacity to form bonds of attachment is itself a sign of healing. Disengagement from habitual social routines and close attention to nature are crucial aspects of these authors' mourning and healing, and periods of solitude seem essential to the process. The healing that comes about in solitude may be interpreted as a crucial spiritual experience, involving discernment of a pattern and meaning in life, connection with the ultimate powers, and reintegration of self into the cycles of nature.

A somewhat different picture of solitude as a healing experience emerges in May Sarton's *Journal of a Solitude,* a diary of a year the author spent living by herself in a farmhouse in New Hampshire. What causes the author's suffering is not an obvious traumatic event, and only gradually does the reader understand why Sarton is depressed, insomniac, and "close to suicide more than once."[10] At the end of the work, which culminates in Sarton's decision to end a long-term relationship with "X," we realize that this unsatisfactory emotional entanglement was the major factor in the author's wish to live alone: "This journal began in September nearly a year ago and has recorded, whatever I may have wished not to speak of, a steady decline in my relationship with X" (183). At the outset, Sarton confesses that "every meeting with another human being has been a collision. I feel too much, am exhausted by the reverberations after even the simplest conversation" (12). She cannot simply blame her unhappiness on other people, or specifically on X. For she knows that it is her own volatile and demanding character that makes relationships with other people so problematic. Sarton admits that her commitment to demanding creative work, writing novels and poems, makes her a difficult person with whom to live. (I will return to her thoughts about the necessity of solitude for creativity later in this chapter.) Solitude is important to Sarton for its regenerative power, its capacity to replenish her energy, ability to work, and desire for encounter with other persons.

Being alone is not always easy for Sarton: "boredom and panic are the two devils the solitary must combat" (94). But she finally accepts that her need for solitude is essential, and, in the last journal entry in the book, Sarton seems to have undergone healing simply by accepting this fact about herself: "I begin to have intimations, now, of a return to some deep self that has been too absorbed and too battered to function for a long time. That self tells me that I was meant to live alone, meant to write the poems for others—poems that seldom in my life have reached the one person for whom they were intended" (207). Her account of aloneness moves toward an act of self-acceptance, culminating in the grateful recognition that there is nothing wrong with wanting to be sequestered, and an affirmation that solitude will play a large role in the author's future life. The book's final line: "Once more the house and I are alone" (208).

Another way in which solitude may be healing is through the activity of writing an autobiography. Many psychologically oriented theories of autobiography stress the therapeutic benefits of life writing. Writing about one's life has been interpreted as a way to cope with trauma, overcome shame, or work through grief related to bereavement or loss.[11] According to these theories, healing is accomplished by the process of writing, the activity of ordering and narrating one's life that is usually (although not always, as in collaborative works) a solitary process. In the case of theories of shame, healing is said to come from being able to confront what has been concealed, such aspects of identity as illegitimacy, illness, race, alcoholism, sexual orientation, or being the victim of violence.

The dynamics of shame in relation to solitude are complex, because one of shame's characteristics is that the person suffering from it wants to withdraw and hide from others. The feeling of being isolated or estranged from others is part of the stigma of shame, part of the suffering it causes, while a crucial part of healing is breaking out of one's isolation and reestablishing contact with others. Simply being alone is no cure for shame and may keep a person trapped in its destructive effects. Yet the psychological self-understanding that is sometimes fostered by life writing may play a crucial role in an author's movement toward greater well-being. Shame can be confronted and evaluated, and sometimes its harmful effects can be mitigated. Moreover, the assessment of shame involves significant ethical reflection; it may be a matter for the scrutiny of conscience. I think that overcoming shame is not simply a matter of breaking out of isolating solitude but often requires psychological and ethical self-scrutiny that must be done alone, and is sometimes central to life writing. I have argued elsewhere that a crucial aspect of Mary McCarthy's depiction of shame in her autobiographies is her struggle to evaluate shame ethically. That is, McCarthy distinguishes between those actions that she still feels ashamed of and those things that as a girl she experienced as shameful but can be reassessed according to her mature sense of self-worth.[12]

The therapeutic value of autobiography is highly debatable, and to do justice to the psychological dimensions of composition and confession would be a major project in itself. Many life writers and theorists of this genre attest to the psychological healing that can attend the writing process. I do not think that such healing can only happen in solitude and cannot also occur through interaction with other people.

But for certain people, healing does in fact take place when they are alone. Solitude as an occasion for healing, both as recalled in the past and in the writing process itself, is for many autobiographers a spiritual experience, whether the source of healing is understood in terms of God's grace, the restorative power of the natural world, the mysterious recuperative capacities of the human psyche, or the writer's conscious attempt to reevaluate the proper basis of self-worth.

Solo Adventure

A third variety of solitude is that of those who seek a challenging adventure, setting out alone on an expedition to a remote location. There are many first-person accounts of "solo" travels by authors who have kayaked around Lake Superior, hiked through the Grand Canyon, sailed around the world, crossed the Sahara Desert, climbed a formidable mountain, wandered through a jungle, or survived on an open lifeboat.[13] Unlike most of the other solitaries discussed in this book, these authors are not stay-at-home hermits but travelers in search of a test that will bring out their resourcefulness and strength of character. Any form of aloneness is potentially dangerous because no one will rescue a solitary from mishap. Solitary adventurers embrace the dangerous aspects of solitude along with the inherently risky aspects of wilderness travel. The additional danger of their circumstances enhances their awareness and enjoyment of their journey in several ways. The concentrated attention involved in taking calculated risks can be an exhilarating experience. The author may take pride in the self-reliance, self-knowledge, and technical knowledge involved in a harrowing journey. Lucid observations of nature sometimes come to an adventurer when, his utmost concentration momentarily relaxed, he witnesses a rainbow, waterfall, or the Northern Lights. A sense of immense gratitude simply to be alive may flow from relief at having survived an ordeal. Adventurers seek a test partly to find out what sort of person they are, and they believe that facing the challenge alone will best reveal what they want to know. They believe that what is discovered in an ordeal of body, mind, and spirit justifies this form of solitude and its risks. What these authors learn in their travels seems to them of ultimate importance, the deepest truth they know. Two early examples of the genre of the solitary adventure tale show the kind of spiritual insight that characterizes the best of this kind of writing.

Joshua Slocum's *Sailing Alone around the World* (1900) recounts the voyage of the first person to accomplish this feat. Slocum set out from Boston in April 1895 and completed his voyage in June 1898, covering some 46,000 miles in thirty-eight months. Slocum crossed the Atlantic to Gibraltar and, changing his route, recrossed this ocean to Brazil and fought his way around Cape Horn. He crossed the Pacific and Indian Oceans, rounded the Cape of Good Hope, and crossed the Atlantic a third time. He made this extraordinary voyage on a rebuilt, one-hundred-year-old thirty-six-foot sloop, the *Spray*. Like most sailors of his era, he did not know how to swim. The key to Slocum's exploit was the amazing ability of the *Spray* to hold a course with the helm lashed. Slocum claims to have sailed 2,700 miles in the Indian Ocean in twenty-three days with only a few hours at the wheel. He was free to read, muse, and watch the waves and weather while his sloop apparently made its own way, like the Ancient Mariner's ship. In spite of the immense dangers of his journey, Slocum's tone in *Sailing Alone around the World* is understated and ironic and he minimizes the risks he took. "The sea has been much maligned," he says, and it was never as perilous as the human predators he encountered in ports and on coastlines along his way. Compared with earlier explorers, he says, "for me is left to tell only of pleasant experiences, till finally my adventures are prosy and tame."[14]

At the outset of his voyage, Slocum has a few days of painful loneliness, as he feels himself "an insect on a straw in the midst of the elements" (25). Solitary immersion in the ocean's vastness releases powerful memories: "During these days a feeling of awe crept over me. My memory worked with startling power. The ominous, the insignificant, the great, the small, the wonderful, the commonplace— all appeared before my mental vision in magical succession. Pages of my history were recalled which had been so long forgotten that they seemed to belong to a previous existence. I heard all the voices of the past laughing, crying, telling what I had heard them tell in many corners of the earth" (25). His feeling of loneliness dissipates as soon as he must respond to challenging weather and does not recur. Thereafter, Slocum alternates between practical tasks and moments of heightened consciousness that recall Transcendentalist thinkers.[15] Like most solitaries, he personalizes nonhuman objects and creatures and finds himself absorbed in activity: "There was no end of companionship; the very coral reefs kept me company, or gave me no time to feel lonely, which is the same thing, and there were many of them now in my course to Samoa" (132).

Amazingly, Slocum navigated much of his voyage by dead reckoning. He leaves his marine chronometer at home and instead brings a one-dollar tin clock which he needs to boil to keep it going. Making difficult lunar calculations, he discovers errors in the navigation tables that would allow him to know his longitude. His uncanny ability to navigate alone makes him the epitome of self-reliance: "The tables being corrected, I sailed on with self-reliance unshaken, and with my tin clock fast asleep" (130). When the blades of his patent log, used for measuring distance traveled, are chewed by a shark, Slocum discards this device. As he is approaching dangerous reefs off the West Indies, a goat eats his chart, so he lacks even a map for orientation. By the end of the voyage, he seems to find his way by pure instinct, or to be guided by supernatural forces.

His nautical progress gives Slocum a deep sense of harmony with the ocean and an intuition of the Creator: "I was *en rapport* now with my surroundings, and was carried on a vast stream where I felt the buoyancy of His hand who made all the worlds" (130). He has a profound sense of intimacy with the *Spray*, arguing with her and urging her on as he feels her subtle responses to wind and water current. Slocum is eccentric but not misanthropic; his lengthy stays in ports along the way bring welcome social encounters, and he heartily appreciates good hospitality. Solitude has a good effect on his moral character, he asserts: "a spirit of charity and even benevolence grew stronger in my nature through the meditations of these supreme hours on the sea" (224). He even attributes his growing inclination to vegetarianism to solitary living and an unpopulated landscape: "In the loneliness of the dreary country about Cape Horn I found myself in no mood to make one life less in the world, except in self-defense, and as I sailed this trait of the hermit character grew till the mention of killing food-animals was revolting to me" (224–25).

Slocum sailed with a library of more than five hundred volumes and spent a great deal of his time reading, sometimes "day and night": "I read on, oblivious of hunger or wind or sea, thinking that all was going well, when suddenly a comber rolled over the stern and slopped saucily into the cabin, wetting the very book I was reading" (218–19). Like Don Quixote, this self-educated man constantly interprets his life in terms of the books he loves, many of which are about solitude. Slocum was especially fond of Coleridge's "Rime of the Ancient Mariner," and we can discern its influence in his way of alluding to the weight of past regrets and griefs (such as the death of his first wife, who accompanied him on many ill-fated voyages), in the moments when he discerns and blesses natural beauty, and in the feelings of communion with the world that grow out of a time of aloneness. *Sailing Alone* is so full of allusions to Thoreau's *Walden* that one commentator dubs it "Walden-on-Sea."[16] Slocum visits the island of

Juan Fernandez, the place where Alexander Selkirk, the historical source for *Robinson Crusoe*, was stranded alone for over four years. He makes a "pilgrimage" to Selkirk's lookout and constructs a memorial to this involuntary solitary, then returns to spend the "pleasantest" day on his voyage playing with children. Leaving the island, he returns to his constant friends, his books: "I sat and read my books, mended my clothes, or cooked my meals and ate them in peace. I had already found that it was not good to be alone, and so I made companionship with what there was around me, sometimes with the universe and sometimes with my own insignificant self; but my books were always my friends, let all else fail" (127).

Knowing that "it is not good to be alone," Slocum sets forth to cross the Pacific Ocean by himself! But like most hermits, he finds that disengagement from the immediate presence of other people makes possible other kinds of intimacy: with books, the weather, the spiders that accompany him from Boston, and the miraculously self-steering *Spray*. At the end of his narrative, Slocum says that his adventure rejuvenated him: "As for aging, why, the dial of my life was turned back till my friends all said, 'Slocum is young again.' And so I was, at least ten years younger than the day I felled the first tree for the construction of the *Spray*" (242–43). He has reversed time, undone the disastrous decade that preceded the voyage of the *Spray*, and come back to bless the world. When the *Spray* arrives back in her home port, like a hermit rejoining a human community, she has effected not only a geographical withdrawal and return but also Slocum's symbolic death and rebirth, a renewal of the spirit.

If Slocum's solitude was for the most part an idyll, Richard Byrd's turned into an excruciating ordeal, which he describes in *Alone* (1938). In 1934 Byrd decided to spend six months by himself in the Antarctic winter operating Bolling Advance Weather Base. Although the ostensible purpose of this sojourn was to collect scientific data, Byrd admits that he really wanted to go "for the experience's sake," to satisfy "one man's desire to know that kind of experience to the full, to be by himself for a while and to taste peace and quiet and solitude long enough to find out how good they really are."[17] Byrd sought to escape the busy organizing and fund-raising for polar expeditions that had dominated his life for fourteen years. He wanted to find a "replenishing philosophy" that would give him a new sense of direction and meaning: "Out there on the South Polar barrier, in cold and darkness as complete as that of the Pleistocene, I should have time to catch up, to study and think and listen to the phonograph; and, for maybe seven months, remote from all but the simplest distractions,

I should be able to live exactly as I chose, obedient to no necessities but those imposed by wind and night and cold, and to no man's laws but my own" (7). Four hundred miles away from his base camp at Little America, during the polar night at temperatures that dropped to −80 degrees F, Byrd was completely cut off from help: "Whoever should elect to inhabit such a spot must reconcile themselves to enduring the bitterest temperatures in nature, a long night as black as that on the dark side of the moon, and an isolation which no power on earth could lift for at least six months" (14). He believed that the isolation, lack of change, and indistinguishable days and nights would drive him deep inside himself to "hidden levels of self-replenishment" (15). The ordeal would be a test of character: "The ones who survive with a measure of happiness are those who can live profoundly off their intellectual resources, as hibernating animals live off their fat" (17). He ordered that no rescue efforts be made on his behalf in the event of radio failure.

At the same time that Byrd sought solitude, however, he arranged for maximum public recognition of his feat. Spending the winter at the weather station was in part a publicity stunt to help the expedition's constant fund-raising efforts. Byrd, who was already skilled in what he called "the hero business," maintained radio contact with his men at Little America, who relayed his messages to the press. The Chicago World's Fair paused to listen to Byrd tap out a greeting. We are fascinated by solitaries, perhaps especially the ones, like Byrd or Saint Simon Stylites on his pillar, who learn how to exploit their solitude and make it a spectacle. Sometimes all the world loves a hermit.

For two months Byrd enjoyed his isolation, awed by the turning of the constellations, thinking that he had thrown off the superfluities of civilization: "All this was mine: the stars, the constellations, even the earth as it turned on its axis. If great inward peace and exhilaration can exist together, then this, I decided my first night alone, was what should possess the senses" (57). Byrd rhapsodizes about the harmony of cosmic forces and asserts his belief in man's oneness with the universe. A feeling transcending reason tells him that the universe is "a cosmos, not a chaos" (85). His enjoyment of fantastic displays of the aurora australis is enhanced by the feeling that he witnesses scenes denied to all other men. Byrd formulates a philosophy to capture his mystical sense of unity with the world and his feeling of being more alive than at any other time in his life. During this, his "grand period," Byrd has moments of tranquillity and bliss that continue to sustain him: "A man's moments of serenity are few, but a few will sustain him a lifetime. I found my measure of inward peace then; the stately echoes lasted a long time. For the world then was like poetry—that poetry which is 'emotion remembered in tranquility'" (144). With Wordsworth, he shares the conviction that times of solitude in the natural world provide a storehouse of memories and emotions from which a person can draw for the rest of his life.

Unfortunately, Byrd began to suffer inexplicable symptoms of physical and mental illness. He finally realized that carbon monoxide from a defective stovepipe was slowly poisoning him, and he began a horrific struggle to survive: without his stove's heat he would freeze to death, but too much combustion would kill him. Byrd's agony and delirium during the next three months made him realize how much he needed others: "To some men sickness brings a desire to be left alone; animal-like, their one instinct is to crawl into a hole and lick the hurt. It used to be so with me. But that night, as never before, I discovered how alone I was; and the realization evoked an indescribable desire to have about me those who knew me best" (171). He reevaluates his whole life and decides that all that really matters is family and friends. The rest of *Alone* recounts Byrd's desperate struggle to stay alive while keeping his team at Little America from knowing how badly off he was, which would endanger their lives on a rescue mission. He lies to them, and they, coming to suspect that something is wrong with their leader, deceive him, too, and finally rescue him. What had been blissful aloneness turns into an involuntary isolation that Byrd longs to escape. The character of his solitude changes completely; physically isolated, he becomes preoccupied with maintaining radio contact with Little America and calculating how his team is interpreting his erratic messages.

His Antarctic ordeal teaches Byrd important lessons. He discovers within himself deep wells of strength never drawn on. Struggling desperately to stay alive, he learns a new meaning of self-reliance, at the same time that he hungers for familiar voices and recognizes how much he depends upon other people. When he is finally rescued, after 204 days in a tiny shack buried under ice and snow, he feels indescribable joy. The return of human company is a symbolic rebirth: "In that miraculous instant all the despair and suffering of June and July fell away, and I felt as if I had just been born again" (291). When solitude goes bad, when it turns into loneliness or life-threatening isolation, it may still teach the most vital truths. Byrd claims that his experience taught him "appreciation of the sheer beauty and miracle of being alive, and a humble set of values" (295). He asserts that in consequence he lives more simply and with greater serenity. Like

Slocum's voyage, Byrd's polar ordeal leads to ethical and spiritual insights that have become familiar in the genre of the solo adventure tale, although rarely are they so eloquently expressed as by Slocum and Byrd.

Creativity

For certain creative individuals, solitude is necessary to do their work. In a psychological study of solitude, Anthony Storr studies the importance of solitude for thinkers and writers including Descartes, Newton, Locke, Pascal, Spinoza, Kant, Leibniz, Schopenhauer, Nietzsche, Kierkegaard, Wittgenstein, Kafka, Trollope, Kipling, Henry James, Rilke, and Jung. Storr's central thesis is that psychological health should be defined not only in terms of a person's relationships with other people but also as the ability to do meaningful work. The individuals Storr discusses all needed to be alone to do their creative work. The origins of their capacity to make productive use of solitude usually reach back to childhood, when they learned to turn inward for the primary meanings of life. Building on Donald Winnicot's work, Storr describes "the capacity to be alone" as a crucial basis of creativity: "The capacity to be alone thus becomes linked with self-discovery and self-realization; with becoming aware of one's deepest needs, feelings, and impulses."[18] In many creative individuals, the development of complex imaginative worlds of thought is a reaction to being cut off from ordinary emotional fulfillment with parents. Although imagination and invention may have their origins in the absence of intimate attachments, the creative activities of these individuals are not a poor, second-best substitute for love: "What began as compensation for deprivation became a rewarding way of life. All these writers were successful, in spite of the emotional scars they bore. . . . What began as compensation ended as a way of life which is as valid as any other, and more interesting than most. Even if their intimate attachments were not the hub around which their lives revolved, there is no reason to suppose that these lives were unfulfilled."[19] Storr provides a psychological analysis of the origins of creativity in the childhoods of many artistic geniuses and philosophers, and he argues that solitude is also an important and often unrecognized need in ordinary people.

Many writers attest to the importance of solitude for their work, for interestingly different reasons. Kafka writes to his fiancée, Felice: "You once said that you would like to sit beside me while I write. Listen, in that case I could not write at all. For writing means revealing oneself to excess; that utmost of self-revelation and surrender, in which a human being, when involved with others, would feel he was losing himself, and from which, therefore, he will always shrink as long as he is in his right mind. . . . That is why one can never be alone enough when one writes, why there can never be enough silence around one when one writes, why even night is not night enough."[20] For Kafka, to expose one's secrets and vulnerability in writing requires the feeling of being safe, hidden, protected by privacy.

According to a study of autobiographical accounts of childhood, there is a deep connection between experiences of solitude and a focus on the subject matter of childhood: "Almost without exception, the man or woman who, later in life, returns in imagination to re-visit and re-create a past childhood was, in that childhood, a solitary, an alienated, an exceptional child. Not necessarily lonely, but, in all essential ways, conscious of being alone."[21] Rainer Maria Rilke links the solitary's perspective to that of the child and the poet. Rilke advises a young poet to cultivate a "vast inner solitude," because this creates a detachment from other people that allows an artist to see them as strangely different:

> What is necessary, after all, is only this: solitude, vast inner solitude. To walk inside yourself and meet no one for hours—that is what you must be able to attain. To be solitary as you were when you were a child, when the grownups walked around involved with matters that seemed large and important because *they* looked so busy and because you didn't understand a thing about what they were doing. And when you realize that their activities are shabby, that their vocations are petrified and no longer connected with life, why not then continue to look upon it all as a child would, as if you were looking at something unfamiliar, out of the depths of your own world, from the vastness of your own solitude, which is itself work and status and vocation?[22]

Rilke locates the capacity for detached observation in the child's—or artist's—perspective as an outsider.

Many factors contribute to the common view that artists are solitary beings: popular images of the starving artist in his garret, the existentialist emphasis on alienation and estrangement as signs of authenticity, and the economic marginality of much modern art, given the demanding and difficult nature of groundbreaking work and the constraints imposed by what sells in the marketplace. Since the modern ideal of artistic creativity celebrates originality above all aesthetic values, many artists and writers have felt the need to isolate themselves from the influence of other artists and relationships, as if the sources of creativity come only from within. When an artist writes his memoirs, he may present himself as having been a solitary genius whose ideas are entirely self-generated. In the next section I will discuss how Friedrich Nietzsche and Carl Jung portray themselves in terms of the myth of solitary genius, which sees both creative work and the nature of the self as *sui genesis*. In his memoir *The Invention of Solitude,* to be discussed in a later chapter, Paul Auster examines cultural myths about "invention" or creative imagination and their links to solitude.

May Sarton's *Journal of a Solitude,* discussed above as an example of healing in solitude, also reflects extensively about the aloneness of her life as a creative writer. Like Anthony Storr, Sarton is influenced by Carl Jung's psychology, especially his view of the sources of creativity in the unconscious: "There has been a long hiatus in this journal because I have had no days here alone, no days when time opened out before me. I find that when I have any appointment, even an afternoon one, it changes the whole quality of time. I feel overcharged. There is no space for what wells up from the subconscious; those dreams and images live in deep still water and simply submerge when the day gets scattered" (145). According to this view, the symbols and metaphors of poetry emerge from a deep spring within the self, and they are elusive, fleeting, easily dispersed. Attending to other people prevents Sarton from retrieving the psyche's images.

Sarton also articulates an important theme in the work of many women artists, asserting that solitude is necessary for a woman to be fully commited to her creative work. Sarton hears from former students that the constant demands of marriage and motherhood have squeezed poetry out of their lives. Inevitably, gender differences mean that marriage affects a woman far differently than a man: "The fact remains that, in marrying, the wife has suffered an earthquake and the husband has not. . . . What is really at stake is unbelief in the woman as artist, as creator. K. no longer sees her talent as relevant or valid, language itself as a masculine invention" (71–72). Like Virginia Woolf's *A Room of One's Own* and Tillie Olson's *Silences,* Sarton's journal shows the need for a private space and uninterrupted time when a woman can be free of family demands and express herself. Her own life as a single woman and a lesbian (although the significance of the latter identity is not developed in this book) allows Sarton to focus on poetry, fiction, and journal writing. But given the socialization of women to be primarily caretakers, the mental disengagement necessary for her work is still a struggle for her: "It may be outwardly silent here but in the back of my mind is a clamor of human voices, too many needs, hopes, fears. I hardly ever sit still without being haunted by the 'undone' and the 'unsent.' I often feel exhausted, but it is not my work that tires (work is a rest); it is the effort of pushing away the lives and needs of others before I can come to the work with any freshness and zest" (12–13).

May Sarton's *Journal* presents solitude as both a constant challenge and an opportunity and condition for certain forms of creativity. The imperative Sarton feels to produce imaginative writing is for her tantamount to a religious vocation, a spiritual calling. Like many intellectuals and artists, including most of the life-writers in this study, Sarton presents the fruits of her creativity as the ethical justification for spending so much time alone. The process of creating this work, with its struggles, demands, and exhilaration, is for her a spiritual practice, a discipline of attention, focus, and self-transcendence in the service of a vision of truth and beauty.

Self-Formation

Solitude is presented by certain autobiographers as a crucial condition for the formation of a distinct self, a coherent personal identity. Such individuals feel other people's demands, expectations, and constraints as inhibiting the discovery of their own deepest needs and desires. For some persons, self-formation is conceived of as a matter of discovery, as coming about through recognition of thoughts, emotions, and hopes that may conflict with social norms. For others, forming a personal identity is more a matter of creation than discovery, involving the integration of discordant elements, the willing of some chosen purpose, or the invention and realization of an ideal version of the self. Creating an autobiography is often a crucial stage in self-formation. It involves at once an author's discernment of an evolving identity in the past and a continuing process of self-invention through the activity of writing. Autobiography is at once a story about the past formation of the author's sense of personal identity and a part of that ongoing process. This kind of writing individualizes or, in John Sturrock's words, "singularizes" the author: "If autobiography starts in the writer's sense of his singularity, it also singularizes as it goes: it is the story of a singularization, or of how the autobiographer came to acquire the conviction of uniqueness that has impelled him to write."[23] If Sturrock's assertion too closely ties autobiography to individualism, eliding the ways that personal identity also incorporates collective meanings and shared values, he formulates concisely the crucial desire of autobiographers to delineate a unique and distinctive character. Autobiography describes and performs the processes of singularization, individuation, and self-formation: the ways persons come to understand and represent who they are.

One of the reasons why self-formation is sometimes linked to withdrawal from society is clarified by studies of the ideal of authenticity by Lionel Trilling and Charles Taylor. The concept of authenticity powerfully shapes the sort of self that Western individuals have strived to become. For Trilling, authenticity is an ideal of personal being that necessarily involves opposition to what is socially expected and approved of. Being true to oneself seems to require rebellion, a break with conformity, freedom from established moral standards. Trilling sees the sources of the ideal of authenticity in the late eighteenth century, especially Rousseau's thought: "From Rousseau we learned that what destroys our authenticity is society—our sentiment of being depends upon the opinion of other people. . . . Authenticity is implicitly a polemical concept, fulfilling its nature by dealing aggressively with received and habitual opinion."[24] Authenticity is linked to the Romantic ideals of subjectivity, feeling, and self-determining freedom.

Charles Taylor describes how authenticity means a moral ideal of being true to oneself, understood as turning inward rather than shaping one's life according to models from outside:

> It accords crucial moral importance to a kind of contact with myself, with my own inner nature, which it sees as in danger of being lost, partly through the pressures towards outward conformity, but also because in taking an instrumental stance to myself, I may have lost the capacity to listen to this inner voice. And then it greatly increases the importance of this self-contact by introducing the principle of originality: each of our voices has something of its own to say. Not only should I not fit my life to the demands of external conformity; I can't even find the model to live by outside myself. I can find it only within.[25]

If one's truest self is neglected because of one's dependence on others, then turning away from them and recovering contact with what Taylor calls "the sources of the self" within one is necessary for anyone who desires to live an authentic life. In addition to authenticity, many related ideals such as autonomy, inwardness, liberty of conscience, emotional expressivity, and self-reliance suggest a crucial role for solitude in the formation of individual identity. Of many autobiographical works that would illustrate the role of solitude in self-formation, I will discuss those of two well-known figures, Friedrich Nietzsche and Carl Jung, and the more recent work of Alice Koller.

In one of Nietzsche's last letters, he writes: "I am *solitude* become man—That no word ever reached me, forced me to reach myself."[26] In *Ecce Homo*, written in 1888 as he descended into madness, Nietzsche explains "Why I Am So Wise" in terms of his "energy to choose solitude and leave the life to which I had become accustomed" (224). In the context of the task of "constant self-overcoming," by which he means transcending his revulsion toward human nature, he describes his need for solitude, "which is to say, recovery, return to myself, the breath of a free, light, playful air" (233). *Ecce Homo* focuses on the conditions that made it possible for him to write his books. Like many other modern writers, Nietzsche is deeply invested in the myth or ideology of the solitary genius, the idea that a worthwhile life is bound up with creativity and originality, and that heroic creators stand apart from all influences or at least outgrow them.[27] In writing one's life story, the challenge to a would-be genius is at once to describe one's historical development and to demonstrate originality. *Ecce Homo* tries to establish its author's genius in several ways ("Why I Am So Clever," "Why I Write Such Good Books"). Central to Nietzsche's claim of genius is his assertion of his utter aloneness during his years of literary productivity.

Nietzsche calls his masterpiece, *Thus Spoke Zarathustra*, "a dithyramb on solitude" (234). A dithyramb is a Greek choric hymn celebrating Dionysus, the god of fertility and wine. Nietzsche suggests that this work celebrates solitude as the source of human creativity and the will to power. Zarathustra is the exemplar and exponent of a life of solitude. According to one interpreter, "Zarathustra's experiences of and meditations upon solitude provide the dramatic framework of the first three parts of the text."[28] Nietzsche's ideal of solitude combines asceticism and passionate feeling, and is "the spiritual discipline of godless creators."[29] Nietzsche's loneliness and pride in his capacity to endure isolation emerge in his descriptions of Zarathustra's lofty remoteness from others, including his disciples. In *Ecce Homo*, Nietzsche quotes his earlier work, as Zarathustra tells his disciples to henceforth find their own way: "Now I go alone, my disciples, You, too, go now, alone. Thus I want it" (220). Solitude is necessary for those who would choose an authentic life.

For Nietzsche, solitude means rejecting God, one's society, and all values outside of oneself. Living alone requires imposing a law on oneself, willing new values and virtues. A worthwhile life, which

Nietzsche thinks only a few great spirits like himself are capable of, means isolation, creativity, contempt for compromise and cooperation, and the assertion of one's own will. Nietzsche is probably as extreme an example as can be found of the ideal of self-formation by means of solitude, for he sees any sustained contact with others as weakening his resolution to transvalue all prior values and become a new Dionysus and Antichrist. His example illustrates starkly the claim that solitude is necessary for the formation of an authentic self and a worthwhile life. For Nietzsche, commitment to this task is the highest ethical and spiritual calling.

From almost any point of view, Nietzsche's *Übermensch*, who finds little value in his social world and must create his own morality, seems hopelessly solipsistic, either a frightening or pathetic example of what happens when solitude is asserted to be self-sufficient, unrelated to a context of human relationships and community. The isolation and moral solipsism of the Nietzschean great man seem sterile and self-destructive, and Nietzsche rather clearly reveals his own deep longing for the recognition by others that he says a creative spirit should despise. Like Rousseau, much of what he says about solitude seems like wishful thinking. Still, to dismiss Nietzsche's advocacy of solitude as necessary for self-formation would be to underestimate his powerful appeal and influence on countless intellectuals and artists of the past century. After Nietzsche, the call to choose one's own values—alone, in rebellion against a morally bankrupt bourgeois society—has seemed to many intellectuals the highest ethical demand and the noblest spiritual path. As have many hermits through the ages, this would-be solitary has evoked a fascinated response in others and influenced their understandings of self and society. Nietzsche's advocacy of solitude is not, then, sterile or solipsistic, yet it is unbalanced in its refusal to consider how solitude can be integrated with social concerns.

Self-formation is also closely connected with experiences of solitude in Carl Jung's work. Jung's central contribution to psychology was his theory of individuation, the process by which an adult discovers and expresses a unique personality. His *Memories, Dreams, Reflections,* a complex work that is partly autobiographical, shows the process of individuation in Jung's own life.[30] A particular period of solitude was crucial in his personal development and in the formulation of his ideas about the human pysche. After his break from a close relationship with Freud in 1913, Jung went through a period of disorientation that he said was close to a psychosis. For the next eight years he published very little, focusing on recording dreams, fantasies, and visions as they spontaneously came to consciousness. In the chapter "Confrontation with the Unconscious," he describes how he sequestered himself and cultivated childhood memories, playing as he had as a child, building with blocks and gathering stones. Jung believed that his own psychic disturbances mirrored the tensions that erupted in the First World War, and that understanding his own mind was the key to a better psychology and an understanding of history: "On August 1 the world war broke out. Now my task was clear: I had to try to understand what had happened and to what extent my own experience coincided with that of mankind in general. Therefore my first obligation was to probe the depths of my own psyche. I made a beginning by writing down the fantasies which had come to me during my building game. This work took precedence over everything else."[31] From 1913 to 1919 Jung practiced self-induced trances in order to discover the images that he believed were produced by the "collective unconscious," the part of the unconscious mind that all humans have in common. During this period of intense introspection, he gathered the psychological material on which he would base his theory of the archetypes, or recurrent images, of the collective unconscious.

Jung uncharitably omitted or distorted the actual influences on his ideas by his contemporaries as he tried to show his originality and unique genius. He says that the period of solitude he underwent at this time in his life allowed him to formulate his own psychological theory. He portrays himself as a misunderstood and isolated figure, abandoned by nearly all of his friends and colleagues. Yet he insists that his solitude was not self-destructive isolation, and he contrasts himself with Nietzsche in that his family and professional work with patients kept him grounded in reality:

> It was most essential for me to have a normal life in the real world as a counterpoise to that strange inner world. My family and my profession remained the base to which I could always return, assuring me that I was an actually existing, ordinary person. . . . I was not a blank page whirling about in the winds of the spirit, like Nietzsche. Nietzsche had lost the ground under his feet because he possessed nothing more than the inner world of his thoughts—which incidentally possessed him more than he it. . . . For me, such irreality was the quintessence of horror, for I aimed, after all, at *this* world and *this* life. (189)

In the Prologue of *Memories,* Jung describes his life as "a story of the self-realization of the unconscious" (3). He says that he will tell his "personal myth," and that outward circumstances, objective documentation, and external verification are irrelevant to this aim: "Whether or not the stories are 'true' is not the problem. The only question is whether what I tell is *my* fable, *my* truth" (3). The important thing about his life, he thinks, is his process of "discovering my own myth" (175). Central to Jung's personal myth is the image of himself as a solitary genius. Even as a twelve-year-old boy, his "blasphemous" vision of God made him feel set apart: "My entire youth can be understood in terms of this secret. It induced in me an almost unendurable loneliness. My one great achievement during those years was that I resisted the temptation to talk about it with anyone. Thus the pattern of my relationship to the world was already prefigured: today as then I am a solitary, because I know things and must hint at things which other people do not know, and usually do not even want to know" (41–42). Jung pitied his father, who he thought had not developed his intellect or searched for experiential knowledge of God, but instead relied on Christian tradition and orthodoxy. For Jung, authentic experience of the divine requires abandoning the safety of shared beliefs: "For God's sake I now found myself cut off from the Church and from my father's and everybody else's faith. Insofar as they all represented the Christian religion, I was an outsider" (56).

Again and again in *Memories,* Jung describes himself as unwelcome, forlorn, and cut off from others by his insights and his compulsion to say things that disturb others' complacency. Like Nietzsche's *Ecce Homo,* Jung's self-representation is decisively shaped by ideas about the nature of solitary genius. Jung associates his destiny with mythic solitaries (or figures whose significance he interprets as their solitary destiny) including Jesus, Buddha, Faust, Goethe, Nietzsche, Elijah, Salome, Philemon, and Siegfried. Most of these figures enact a heroic journey of withdrawal and return to society with a new perspective or message: "There are dozens of allusions and echoes in *Memories, Dreams, Reflections* that make it abundantly clear that Jung wished to depict himself in heroic terms, in terms of chosenness and separateness, and to align himself with the gifted, solitary, visionary, often romantic and heterodox questers of the mythology, literature, and religion in which Jung steeped himself from childhood to old age."[32] Jung places himself in the company of these figures and links their religious and creative power to solitude, which represents a ritualized social death and rebirth. Jung's personal myth as expressed in *Memories, Dreams, Reflections* reveals his view that the capacity for solitude is the key to both his original psychological ideas and his own individuation, his development into a unique self.

The link between solitude and the formation of self is also an important and contested issue in the writings of many women.[33] In Western culture, solitude has usually been denied to women by social custom, law, and powerful male authorities. Even when women have had the opportunity for solitude, it has been difficult for them for two reasons. Because women are more vulnerable to violence than men, their solitude is often marked by a sense of apprehensiveness and guardedness that detracts from the positive qualities of aloneness. And because women have been seen, and often see themselves, primarily as caretakers of others, they have been prevented from enjoying solitude by their own internalized sense of value, their belief that they are being selfish when they enjoy time alone.

Some contemporary feminist writers challenge the desirability of solitude because they associate it with the supposedly male values of self-reliance and independence. If the traditional or critically reinterpreted female values of caring, connection, and relationality are seen as most important, a desire for solitude may be viewed as either an unimportant interest or a negative trait that should be overcome. Furthermore, solitude is associated by some feminist writers with the enforced separateness, isolation, or exclusion of women from the public domains of society. I agree that if women's solitude does not represent a choice but involuntary marginalization from public life, it should be challenged. For men and women alike, solitude should be chosen, not a coerced condition or an inescapable destiny. I take seriously feminist criticisms of solitude as often reflecting a male sense of privilege and patriarchal values. Most of the male writers discussed in this book seem rather unreflective about how their aloneness depends upon others who provide for their basic needs. However, I think the opportunity for solitude is as valuable for women as it is for men in relation to all the spiritual and ethical values outlined in this chapter, including its role in the process of self-formation.

There have always been women who sought out periods of solitude, such as, in the Christian tradition, early "desert mothers," medieval anchorites, mystics such as Julian of Norwich and Saint Teresa of Avila, and such monastic leaders as Saint Scholastica and Saint Clare. These women's religious concerns and their practice of periods of solitude were closely linked to the development of a strong sense of personal identity. Autobiographical works by women that deal with solitude include the poetry of Emily Dickinson, Christianne Ritter's *Woman in the Polar Night* (1954), Virginia Woolf's *A Room of One's Own* (1929), Anne Morrow Lindbergh's *Gift from the Sea* (1955), May Sarton's *Journal of a Solitude* (1973), Doris Grumbach's

Fifty Days of Solitude (1994), and Alice Koller's *The Stations of Solitude* (1990). For these women, solitude is important for the same reasons for which it is important to male writers. In addition, its role in the process of self-formation is crucial because of the ways that women have so often been defined solely in terms of those they care for as wife, mother, daughter, teacher, nurse, social reformer, or in another kind of relationship or service.

In *The Stations of Solitude,* Alice Koller explores solitude as thoroughly as any recent writer, male or female. The stations or stopping places of solitude are the crucial choices every person must make to become an individual:

> In circuiting the stations of solitude, your destination is the kind of person you wish to become. The line of travel is the process of shaping a human being, and the stations are stopping places in the process: they are recurring circumstances in which a certain kind of decision, and then acting on it, are required of you. The decision you're called on to make will have far-reaching consequences for the person you are, the person you wish to become. It is the price of the journey: that at this stopping place you must make a choice. . . . At every station, therefore, you pay. But you also profit: you will learn, and will approach more closely, who you want to be.[34]

Koller, born in 1925, received a Ph.D. in philosophy from Harvard University but was unable to find permanent work as a professor. She has supported herself with various jobs, moved frequently, and lived alone, or rather with a series of beloved dogs. The chapter titles of *The Stations of Solitude* describe the stations and the basic life choices she thinks are required: unbinding, standing open, awakening, working, homing, loving, moneying, and singling. Koller's way of life reflects her commitment to three main values: her desire to live in a rural environment, her love for three German Shepherd dogs, and her determination to put as much time and energy as possible into her philosophical work, while minimizing "moneying," doing the jobs that pay the bills.

Koller's life of aloneness is definitely shaped by her gender. When she earns her Ph.D. in the late 1950s, her professors do nothing to help her find a teaching position. During this era, "professors could arrange teaching jobs for their male students as deliberately as they chose their dinner guests" (147). Koller's male classmates were hired to teach at major universities, sometimes five or seven years before they submitted their dissertations. Living alone in a rural area poses special challenges for a woman; Koller must learn all the practical tasks of country living, such as caring for a troublesome electric pump, building a stone fence, and interacting with testy neighbors. She must reckon with the cultural expectation that a woman's life is only complete if she has a long-term relationship with a man. She rejects marriage and relationships based on need: "Loving a man and his loving me would have to be of the same sort: having no purpose beyond our loving one another. . . . I would not need him, nor he me. We would only want one another: want to be part of one another's lives" (196). Since all the men she has met "are still at the level of needs," she asserts that she does not seek a relationship with a man, that erotic longing has vanished, and that she does not want anyone to rescue her from aloneness. Being single for her does not mean being unmarried, but being "individual, one only, unlike" (198). It means knowing who she is and consciously choosing her own values rather than trying to please someone else. In these ways gender shapes Koller's view of solitude.

At the same time, Koller clearly sees her ideas about solitude as applicable to all persons. The goal that orients her life is not becoming a woman but becoming a person, and she asserts that her readers should deliberately seize this opportunity: "Your life is entirely within your own hands: to shape to you, to make fit you, as only you know how best to do, how to do at all" (5). Given the way that Koller defines a person's singular purposes as contrasting with the expectations of others, choices made at the stations of solitude are indispensable: "To lone (I am inventing the verb) is to become oneself and *thereby* to be able to spend one's time pursuing one's purposes independently of the presence or absence of other human beings. You lone in the process of becoming able to be alone well, but also in the practice of being alone well" (5). Koller does not understand human agency as simply freedom from external demands. Following Kant, she views true freedom as self-determination, or "being self-governing according to laws of your own choosing" (12). One cannot choose one's own purposes and shape one's own life until one has ceased serving the purposes of others: "The question is only: whose shaping will you permit? Either you know your own purposes, or you will in your ignorance allow your life to be carved away, slice by fine slice, pursuing the purposes of others" (40). By writing about the role of solitude in her own self-formation, Koller practices the only kind of philosophy that truly matters to her; she uses her intellectual training and skills to understand her own life and its possible significance for others. She sees her choice of solitude as universally significant for anyone who desires a freely chosen life, which is finally what it means to be a person or self: "In a sense, this whole book is a philosophical inquiry into what it is to be a person: how one becomes a person, and what it is that one has become. I am teaching not by telling but by displaying the process. By writing of what it is for me to be solitary, I am sketching the outlines of the life of solitude everyone else lives. Can live, if you choose" (67).

For Koller, and for Nietzsche, Jung, and many other autobiographers who seek solitude, being alone is indispensable to their sense of identity. For these persons autobiographical writing recalls crucial times of aloneness in the past and, through the process of composition, nurtures the kind of insight and reflection involved in the ongoing process of self-formation. The last two varieties of solitary experience I have considered in this chapter—creativity and self-formation—are deeply connected for life-writers. They usually see both activities as taking place in solitude; the production of literary works often seems to their creators the most important deeds of their lives; and the construction of the self is seen as a work of art. For autobiographers, text-creation and self-creation are inextricably linked and take place largely in solitude. Interpreting the past is a crucial step toward further self-formation, as the order and unity created through life-writing is transferred to the writer's own sense of identity, and a new integration and coherence is achieved both in the literary work and in the psyche. Not only creativity but the other three values I traced in the varieties of solitary experience (attunement to nature, healing, and adventure) also contribute to self-formation, as a writer recalls past experiences of solitude to clarify and strengthen the ethical and spiritual values that will orient her in the future. The turn toward solitude represented by introspective life-writing is itself often a profoundly religious and moral action, a withdrawal from involvement with others to seek contact with deeper sources of the self, other dimensions of reality, and spiritual aspirations easily dissipated by normal social interactions.

7

THOMAS MERTON AND
SOLITUDE

"THE DOOR TO SOLITUDE OPENS ONLY
FROM THE INSIDE"

No one has made so compelling a case for the religious value of the
solitary life as Thomas Merton. Interpretation and advocacy of solitude are a constant theme in his roughly fifty books, three hundred
essays, one thousand pages of poetry, four thousand letters, and many
volumes of selections from his journals. Although some of Merton's
writing is historical or philosophical in its consideration of solitude, a
great deal of it is autobiographical. He wrote one traditional autobiography, *The Seven Storey Mountain,* published in 1948 when Merton
was thirty-three years old, after seven of his twenty-seven years of
monastic life. In the other forms of writing he did for the next twenty
years, he reflected continually on solitude. Since the meaning of
aloneness changed for him and he wrote about it in many different
genres and in connection with so many issues, it is difficult to interpret Merton's understanding of solitude economically. This chapter
moves through Merton's life and work in three stages, first discussing *The Seven Storey Mountain* and his *Sign of Jonas* to understand
his early view of solitude. I turn next to several central essays written
in the 1950s in which Merton defines an ideal of Christian solitude,
and finally to what Merton's journals reveal about his actual experience of solitude when at last, in the 1960s, he was able to enjoy the
solitude he had sought for many years.

Merton's Early View of Solitude

Given that Merton is the most prominent advocate and exemplar of the hermit's life in Christian history, solitude figures less significantly than one would expect in *The Seven Storey Mountain*. One sees the author's temperamental proclivity to enjoy being alone in his solitary travels in Europe, his love of walking in the natural world, and his absorption in reading. But Merton was also a gregarious person with many friends and a strong need to interact with others. Although solitude was not what drew him to Christian faith, it was a factor in his choice of a monastic vocation and shapes his conception of what that life means. After his conversion to Catholicism in 1938, Merton pondered for three years how to make a more total commitment to God. In 1941 he began to study the various Catholic religious orders, particularly the Carthusians, the Camaldolese, and the Trappists, a group of strict Cistercian monks. These orders, who formed stable monastic communities and were separated from the secular world, appealed more to Merton than the Jesuits, Dominicans, and Franciscans. Merton's attraction to a monastic order, like his conversion to Christianity, was largely a revulsion from the world's sinfulness. That he saw solitude as a withdrawal from sin is clear from his account of his reaction to an encyclopedia article about monastic orders:

> What I saw on those pages pierced me to the heart like a knife.
> What wonderful happiness there was, then, in the world! There were still men on this miserable, noisy, cruel earth, who tasted the marvelous joy of silence and solitude, who dwelt in forgotten mountain cells, in secluded monasteries, where the news and desires and appetites and conflicts of the world no longer reached them.
> They were free from the burden of the flesh's tyranny, and their clear vision, clean of the world's smoke and of its bitter sting, were raised to heaven and penetrated into the deeps of heaven's infinite and healing light. (*SSM*, 316)[1]

At this time in Merton's life, solitude meant primarily remoteness from the world, and was part of the appeal of a life of self-denial, purity, and "hiddenness" from other men that allows a monk to be utterly focused on God. These "hidden men had come so close to God in their hiddenness that they no longer saw anyone but Him" (*SSM*, 317). As he read about the monastic orders, "in an instant the desire of those solitudes was wide open within me like a wound" (*SSM*, 318). He was particularly drawn to the Carthusians because they were "the ones who had gone the farthest, climbed the highest on the mountain of isolation that lifted them above the world and concealed them in God" (*SSM*, 327). Conceived in this way in terms of the book's mountain imagery, solitude elevates a hermit to a realm of moral purity far beyond the conflicts and corruption of ordinary human existence. There was no Carthusian monastery in the United States, however, and the war made Europe inaccessible. The several reasons for Merton's entrance into the Trappist monastery of Gethsemani, in Kentucky, in December 1941 include his revulsion from his own past sins, his desire for a life of stability and order in contrast to his parents' and his own wandering, rootless lives, and the expectation that he would soon be drafted into military service in a war that he believed to be a terrible evil. These motivations have been well analysed by biographers and need not be repeated here, except to note that the desire for solitude is not a dominant or clearly articulated factor in Merton's own account of his decision to become a monk.[2]

Remarks toward the end of Merton's autobiography intimate both the attraction to solitude that would develop in coming years and ethical reservations about solitude that influence his mature views. He asserts that commitment to a community is a crucial test of the depth of one's faith and religious vocation: "The first and most elementary test of one's call to the religious life—whether as a Jesuit, Franciscan, Cistercian, or Carthusian—is the willingness to accept life in a community in which everybody is more or less imperfect" (*SSM*, 381). Many of the things Merton sought in solitude can be found in a communal monastic order. For instance, the silence of Trappist communal life and worship was even more powerful than being alone: "The silence with people moving in it was ten times more gripping than it had been in my own empty room" (*SSM*, 323). The central purpose of monastic life, according to Merton, is contemplation, the disinterested love of God. Contemplation may best be learned and practiced in a monastery, where "all the apparently meaningless little rules and observances and fasts and obediences and penances and humiliations and labors that go to make up the routine of existence in a contemplative monastery . . . serve to remind us of what we are and Who God is—that we may get sick of the sight of ourselves and turn to Him" (*SSM*, 372).

A hermit would be deprived of this salutary social discipline. Merton suspects that the desire for solitude often expresses selfishness. Admitted to the infirmary, he was secretly joyful that at last he would have some time alone. He censures this reaction: "I was fully convinced that I was going to indulge all the selfish appetites that I did not yet know how to recognize as selfish because they appeared so spiritual in their new disguise" (SSM, 387). Solitude is ambiguous, at once a temptation to self-indulgence that should be resisted and an expression of a monk's purity and unworldliness. Merton's scruples about solitude recur in his essays and journals, giving his view of solitude a judicious balance not found in most advocates of the hermit's life.

Already in The Seven Storey Mountain Merton links solitude to the work of writing that he knew would be an essential part of his life. In the epilogue, Merton describes a conflict between his contemplative vocation and his desire to write. The writer is a shadow, a double, and a Judas-figure who follows him into the cloister and diverts his times of solitude to the wrong ends: "He generates books in the silence that ought to be sweet with the infinitely productive darkness of contemplation" (SSM, 410). Merton fears that his identity as a writer will displace his monastic vocation: "Maybe in the end he will kill me, he will drink my blood. Nobody seems to understand that one of us has got to die" (SSM, 410). Both writing and contemplation depend on solitude, and Merton was torn between these two uses of it. In the final two pages of the book, he expresses his desire for a form of solitude that will allow him to transcend this conflict and all earthly attachments: "That is the only reason why I desire solitude—to be lost to all created things, to die to them and to the knowledge of them, for they remind me of my distance from You. They tell me something about You: that You are far from them, even though You are in them. You have made them and Your presence sustains their being, and they hide You from me. And I would live alone, and out of them. O beata solitudo!" (SSM, 421).

Merton concludes his autobiography with an italicized passage representing the words of God. God says He will lead Merton to solitude by turning all things against him so that he withdraws in pain: "And when you have been praised a little and loved a little I will take away all your gifts and all your love and all your praise and you will be utterly forgotten and abandoned and you will be nothing, a dead thing, a rejection. And in that day you shall begin to possess the solitude you have so long desired. And your solitude will bear immense fruit in the souls of men you will never see on earth" (SSM, 422). This ending resolves Merton's conflict about solitude, because he imagines an aloneness not selfishly chosen by him but forced on him by the world's rejection and affirmed by God. He gets the solitude he has always craved, with divine approval. This solitude is free of all self-indulgent tendencies and has a stark, ascetic, world-denying quality like the impulse that led him to conversion and into the monastery. The ambiguities of solitude for a person who is both writer and monk are resolved from without, as God transforms solitude from a selfish desire into an imposed condition and a form of penance that guarantees this Christian hermit's moral purity and permanent separation from the world. Furthermore, this kind of solitude will "bear immense fruit" in the lives of other people Merton will never see. The ending of *The Seven Storey Mountain* reveals the ethical scruples about solitude that were to preoccupy Merton all his life, particularly his awareness of a hermit's possible selfishness in terms of both motivation and the effects of his solitude on others. But whereas in his autobiography Merton imagines a divine fiat resolving his uncertainties, the meaning and value of solitude during the next years of his life were not so clear. He began to see the need for a theoretical understanding of solitude that would do justice to both the value and the dangers of this way of life.

For several years Merton tried to resist his growing desire for solitude, viewing his own wishes as almost necessarily opposed to God's will. *The Sign of Jonas,* Merton's published version of his journal between 1946 and 1952, reveals his identification with the biblical prophet: "Like the prophet Jonas, whom God ordered to go to Nineveh, I found myself with an almost uncontrollable desire to go in the opposite direction. God pointed one way and all my 'ideals' pointed in the other" (*SJ*, 10). When the success of *The Seven Storey Mountain* brought fame, his abbot, recognizing Merton's literary gifts, asked him to work on several writing projects that would help the Cisterician order. Even as he did this work and began his massive correspondence with publishers, enthusiastic readers, and other authors, Merton recorded in his journal his sense of being distracted from a monk's true purpose. *The Sign of Jonas* expresses nagging doubts about his writing commitments and confesses his temptation to seek greater solitude by joining the Carthusian order.

Merton attempts to resolve this conflict by discerning God's will, usually in the words of a retreat master, confessor, or his abbot reassuring him that he belonged at Gethsemani. Identifying with Jonas, Merton attempts to stifle his longing for solitude and to acquiesce in his superiors' wish that he remain with the Trappists. His commitment to stability in one monastic community overrides his desire to find another order that would allow a different balance of solitude and community. "Every man called to contemplation is called to some degree of solitude. God knows well enough how much each one needs. We need faith to let Him decide how much we are to obtain" (*SJ*, 10). And so, as in *The Seven Storey Mountain*, submission to God's will resolves a conflict about solitude. This time solitude is not granted by an imagined divine fiat but rationed by his religious superiors. Knowing what came later in his life, one could interpret Merton's attempts to talk himself out of his need for solitude as wishful thinking or even self-deception. Yet for this dedicated monk it was no easy matter to discern God's will when the needs of his own spirit pulled him in a different direction than the call of the community to which he had committed himself.

Essays on Solitude

Increasingly during the 1950s, Merton found that he could not deny his need for solitude. For many years he sought more information on other orders and seriously considered transfering to one. In 1953 and 1960 he petitioned to transfer to an eremetical order but was rejected by the Roman Congregation of Religious. At the same time, he tried to secure opportunities for solitude at Gethsemani. He needed it partly because of cramped conditions at the monastery, which by the early 1950s had more than two hundred people living in very close quarters. The daily schedule was extremely demanding and Merton had little free time. The monks rarely went beyond the walls of the monastery, even into the forested hills around it. When Merton speaks of the need for solitude during these years, he often means the privacy that he found to be necessary for concentration.[3] There were numerous construction projects during the 1950s, and the incessant noise disturbed him. As well as his difficulties with physical conditions in the monastery, he had a different view of the ideal balance of activity and contemplation in the monks' daily schedule. Already in *The Seven Storey Mountain* he had complained that there was too much activity and too little contemplation at the monastery. Now he began to assert the need for "exterior" solitude—privacy and silence—as well as "interior" solitude, the meditative and contemplative orientation to life that his superiors told him should be possible under any conditions.

Merton's abbot, Dom James Fox, began to grant him limited periods of solitude in 1953. An abandoned toolshed was converted to a day study and named Saint Anne's; Merton spent as much time there as he could. Still it was not enough for him, and for more than a decade he pursued greater solitude. Finally, in 1965, he was allowed to live permanently as a hermit. The years of intermittent periods of aloneness are the context for Merton's most substantial essays on solitude, in which he argues for its legitimacy as a form of Christian life and tries to define its meaning. His most significant theoretical accounts of solitude are *Thoughts in Solitude*, written in 1953–54 and published in 1958; "Notes for a Philosophy of Solitude" in *Disputed Questions* (published in 1960); and "The Solitary Life" (published in 1960).[4] These three essays, based on Merton's study of eremeticism in the history of the Church and on his own limited experience, present a normative conception of the hermit's life, including analysis of the dangers and temptations of solitude. They are part of Merton's campaign to make a place for solitude in the Cistercian order, which although it valued silence was strictly cenobitical and viewed solitude with suspicion.

While these essays have an important autobiographical dimension, Merton's primary purpose is not to describe his own life but to define an ideal. Although *Thoughts in Solitude* grows out of times of aloneness, Merton says that his reflections "are in no way intended as an account of spiritual adventures" but "are simply thoughts on the contemplative life" (*TS*, 11). He recognizes that there is something absurd about exhorting others to become solitary, for "those who are to become solitary are, as a rule, solitary already" (*DQ*, 178). Nonetheless, these essays are very compelling arguments for the value of the solitary life. Their rhetorical power and religious profundity are partly due to Merton's critical perspective on solitude, his belief that solitude needs to be understood in relation to many values, especially concern for community.

One of Merton's chief concerns is with the motivation for solitude. This concern lies behind the cryptic statement that serves as the subtitle for this chapter: "The door to solitude opens only from the inside" (*DQ*, 196). Merton criticizes those who seek solitude in order to assert themselves—those who, so to speak, push open from outside the door to solitude. In contrast to this are those persons who have "not so much chosen solitude as been chosen by it." Ideally, one both chooses solitude and is called to it as one's destiny. Solitude requires "a deep interior decision." But "no amount of deciding will do any good, if one has not first been invited to make the decision." One does not enter the desert of solitude by asserting one's will but rather by following God into emptiness and silence: "It should therefore be clear that one who seeks to enter into this kind of solitude by affirming himself, and separating himself from others, and intensifying his awareness of his own individual being, is only travelling further and further away from it. But the one who has been found by solitude, and invited to enter it, and has entered freely, falls into the desert the way a ripe fruit falls out of a tree" (DQ, 197). With these metaphors Merton tries to explain how solitude as a Christian spiritual path differs from the aloneness of a self-asserting individualist. This contrast is crucially important to Merton, but how it applied to his own life is not easy to see. How did he know when the impulse to be alone reflected egotistical striving and when it was a response to God? Merton's journals show him trying to discern God's calling in the details of his own life, and learning how difficult it is to understand one's own motives and to act according to the spiritual ideal he proposed.

Merton's religious superiors and spiritual advisors told him that he should not need physical isolation if he could attain "inner" solitude, that is, detachment and serenity even in the midst of company. He understood the insight in this claim and struggled to accept his limited periods of separation from others. Still, he asserted that genuine solitude requires physical isolation. He knew that "a merely subjective and inward solitude, the fruit of an effort at interiorisation, would never be enough. Solitude has to be objective and concrete" (TS, 85). Similarly, he argued that a sustained period of solitude has a different effect than the short intervals doled out to him: "The truly solitary life has a completely different character from the partial solitude which can be enjoyed from time to time in the intervals allowed by social living. When we receive our solitude by intervals, we taste its value by contrast with another value. When we really live alone, there is no contrast" (TS, 107–8). When solitude is but an interval in life with others, it is a halt, a stillness, a moment of concentration. In contrast, "where solitude is not an interval but a continuous whole, we may well renounce altogether the sense of concentration and the feeling of spiritual stillness. Our whole life may flow out to meet the Being and the Silence of the days in which we are immersed, and we can work out our salvation by quiet, continued action" (TS, 108). Merton defended the need for exterior as well as interior solitude, and idealized the sustained and fully solitary life that he had not yet actually experienced. At the same time, he recognized that more than simply isolation was necessary for what he was seeking. One can reproduce all the sins and triviality of social existence all by oneself.

Merton's awareness of the perils of solitude gives his essays of the 1950s a distinctive character as compared to *The Seven Storey Mountain* and the writings of his first years in the monastery. Solitude, like the mountain imagery he uses to depict monastic life, had earlier represented withdrawal from an evil society, renunciation of a corrupt world. The new convert's disdain and harsh rejection of the secular world contrast starkly with his praise for the purity of the monastery and solitude. But after another decade at Gethsemani, Merton asserts that the Christian solitary is as much a sinner as anyone, even in his seeking of aloneness: "Only the false solitary sees no danger in solitude" (DQ, 185). The pursuit of aloneness should not reject Christian community or express one's "special and exalted spirituality." Rather, "it may express the solitary's conviction that he is not good enough for most of the visible exercises of the community, that his own part is to carry out some hidden function, in the community's spiritual cellar" (TS, 103). Merton warns that withdrawal from the company of others ought not to express pride, condemnation, or despair about the world. The purpose of solitude is no longer to protect one's moral purity, but to love God and humans in a life of prayer and contemplation.

How can solitude express solidarity and love for others? Merton's most substantial essay, "Notes for a Philosophy of Solitude," focuses especially on this question, as he addresses the customary accusation that a hermit is being selfish when he abandons society. Merton tries to explain the possible social benefits of the hermit's way of life without absurdly making one person's solitude simply useful to others. He writes of the Christian hermit's specific contribution to monastic tradition and the Church, and also of a more general significance of a solitary who "may well be a layman, and of the sort most remote from cloistered life, like Thoreau or Emily Dickinson" (DQ, 177). Merton's central idea is that a hermit's distance from society allows him to criticize its myths and illusions. Therefore, his solitude has a prophetic character, providing a corrective to the social fictions that pervade any community. The Christian hermit warns his fellow believers about frenetic busyness and secularizing temptations: "The hermit remains to put us on our guard against our natural obsession with the visible, social and communal forms of Christian life which tend at times to be inordinately active, and often become deeply involved in the life of secular, non-Christian society" (DQ, 191).

His view of the hermit's significance in the modern world reflects Merton's reading during the 1950s about totalitarianism, the pressures of conformity, the growing power of the media, and American capitalism and consumerism. A hermit can reject these social fictions without rejecting humanity: "Withdrawal from other men can be a special form of love for them. It should never be a rejection of man or of his society. But it may well be a quiet and humble refusal to accept the myths and fictions with which social life cannot help but be full—especially today. To despair of the illusions and facades which man builds around himself is certainly not to despair of man. On the contrary, it may be a sign of love and of hope" (DQ, 192). The hermit shows that there is an alternative to social fictions. He provides a different perspective, although his primary purpose is not to protest or rebel. He is a "mute witness," and he should be critical, first of all, of himself: "Otherwise he will divert himself with a fiction worse than that of all the others, becoming a more insane and self-opinionated liar than the worst of them, cheating no one more than himself. Solitude is not for rebels like this, and it promptly rejects them" (DQ, 194). A hermit should not go into the desert to become a prophet or preach to others but to be healed. Nonetheless, others may find something of value in the hermit's perspective.

In his introduction to a collection of sayings by the first Christian hermits, *The Wisdom of the Desert*, also written at this time, Merton explains how others followed the desert fathers, seeking a "word" that would help them. These early hermits usually welcomed others, although there are amusing anecdotes about incidents when they hid or were cranky. Even though they were suspicious of too much talk, idle curiosity, and abstruse speculation, the desert fathers were masters at finding a concrete and precise message for every individual who approached them. The duties of charity and hospitality took precedence over ascetic routines, learning, prayer, or solitude. The desert fathers were for Merton models of how a hermit could be at once critical of prevailing social values and yet open to and compassionate toward others (WD, 16–17).

There is a basic tension in Merton's thought between his desire to defend solitude as an end in itself and his wish to discern its value for others. He tried to explain how a Christian hermit may indirectly offer something to others even though this is not his primary aim. Merton wrote that solitude "is neither an argument, an accusation, a reproach or a sermon. It is simply itself. It *is*" (DQ, 184). Yet he quickly goes on in this essay to develop an extended interpretation of the hermit's prophetic function for those with openness to his hidden meaning, his mute witness. William Shannon puts concisely the idea that the contemplative life is its own justification and yet ought also to be responsible to the world: "Mission can never be the goal of contemplation; yet it can be, and perhaps ought to be, its fruit."[5]

The hermit has a message for those who listen because he is not essentially different from them. Rather than stressing basic differences between a solitary and others, Merton holds that the hermit recognizes a level of humanity deeper than the usual social markers by which we define ourselves: "It is not that he is solitary while everybody else is social: but that everyone is solitary, in a solitude masked by that symbolism which they use to cheat and counteract their solitariness. What the solitary renounces is not his union with other men, but rather the deceptive fictions and inadequate symbols which tend to take the place of genuine social unity—to produce a facade of apparent unity without really uniting men on a deep level" (DQ, 188). We are all alike in our aloneness at the deepest level, asserts Merton; yet most of us try to distract ourselves from awareness of this in the ways Pascal called "divertissement," the "occupations and recreations, so mercifully provided by society, which enable a man to avoid his own company for twenty-four hours a day" (DQ, 178).

The hermit tries to avoid the temptation of distractedness and to recognize the fundamental aloneness of every individual. He may discover a level of personhood deeper than social identity. To value personhood is not the same as asserting one's individuality; there is a crucial difference between seeking one's "true self" and seeking one's "superficial, false social self" (DQ, 206). It is at the level of personhood, and not the selfhood that is achieved, not the "I" asserted by individualism, that solitude makes possible genuine love of others. "Notes" ends by contrasting "the shallow 'I' of individualism" that we try to cultivate and possess with a deeper "I" of which he says: "The deep 'I' of the spirit, of solitude and of love, cannot be 'had,' possessed, developed, perfected. It can only be, and act according to deep inner laws which are not of man's contriving, but which come from God. . . . It is only this inmost and solitary 'I' that truly loves with the love and the spirit of Christ. This 'I' is Christ Himself, living in us: and we, in Him, living in the Father" (DQ, 207). Thus Merton interprets in Christian terms a basic paradox: solitude helps one understand both the aloneness of every person and his connectedness to others.

Merton follows Saint Benedict's Rule in seeing the eremetical life as requiring long preparation in communal living: "Do not flee to solitude from the community. Find God first in the community, then he will lead you to solitude" (TS, 114). A hermit needs the continuing support of a community, both in material ways and for an occasional reality check, to prevent delusion, and to seek guidance. A community shows its integrity and respect for personhood when it values and nurtures solitaries. In this way, too, Merton developed a dialectic between solitude and community that showed them to be, at least in principle, mutually dependent rather than antagonistic.

For Merton, solitude is not only a spiritual practice but a theological concept and a symbol of God. Society often rejects the hermit because he represents certain qualities of God: "For that is what the world resents about God: His utter otherness, His absolute incapacity to be absorbed into the context of worldly and practical slogans, His mysterious transcendency which places Him infinitely beyond the reach of catchwords, advertisements and politics" (DQ, 204). A hermit reminds others of both "the dreaded solitude of God" and God's compassion and love. The solitary, like God, has a mysterious communion with other people even when they are not aware of it. At the same time, Merton sees loneliness as a divine attribute, and the hermit's life helps us understand this: "Man's loneliness is, in fact, the loneliness of God. That is why it is such a great thing for a man to discover his solitude and learn to live in it. For there he finds that he and God are one: that God is alone as he himself is alone. That God wills to be alone in him" (DQ, 190). This description of communion with God preserves the solitariness of both God and the human person. Unlike many accounts of mystical experience, Merton's view of the divine-human encounter does not overcome the sense of separateness and aloneness, but enhances it. The emptiness, poverty, and suffering of the solitary life also link the Christian hermit with the kenotic, or self-sacrificial aspect of Christ. Solitary life is an imitation of Christ. It is also modeled on the desert fathers, who were drawn into the wilderness "to be nourished by no other spiritual food than Jesus" (TS, 107). Merton interpreted solitude in terms of the most central Christian theological concepts: God's transcendence and hidden love and Christ's suffering and self-emptying compassion.

These essays represent a highly developed, insightful, and wise theory of solitude. Merton balances the hermit's continuing social responsibility with his pursuit of spiritual values that do not directly serve others. He sees the dangers of solitude as well as its potential benefits, the characteristic illusions of hermits as well as their abiding insights. He views the hermit as similar to other persons in essential ways, yet called to a distinctive way of life that should be honored and supported by his community. Merton's ideal of solitude was shaped by his own experience and yearnings as well as by extensive research into the history of Christian eremeticism. We see a somewhat different picture, however, when we turn to his explicitly autobiographical writings in the next years. For in the 1960s, as he was able to spend more time in his hermitage, he found discrepancies between his normative ideal of solitude and his actual life. As well, he discovered dimensions of aloneness that he had not anticipated or argued for in the essays he wrote during the 1950s. What do Merton's journals in these years reveal about his experience of solitude?

Journals of the 1960s

Starting in December 1960, Merton had the opportunity for a few hours of solitude every day at a retreat house on a small hill called Mount Olivet. In October 1964 he began to sleep occasionally at this hermitage, which he called Saint Mary of Carmel. In August 1965 he gave up his teaching responsibilities as Master of Novices, and from then until his final travels in 1968 he stayed at the hermitage all day and night, except for certain periods when he went to the monastery for Mass and one meal. His journals document the stages of his increasing solitude and his new appreciation of the dawn, eating on his porch, and celebrating Mass in a meadow. He felt that he moved to a different rhythm and that time had a different meaning connected to the seasons and the shifts of light during the day. He records his close observations of the natural world: the wind in the pines, crickets in the grass, deer running across an open field, a hawk flying overhead. When he sees "the *Mantu* or 'spirit' shown in the running of the deer," he calls this "a contemplative intuition! Yet perfectly ordinary, everyday seeing" (*IM*, 258).[6] Living at the hermitage was a "return to the world," direct contact with God's creation. Merton defined his task as getting rid of the division between sacred and secular by recognizing God's grace throughout the whole world. His theoretical essays on solitude had not stressed closeness to nature as a primary aspect of the hermit's life, but this was clearly an unexpected and continual source of joy. His journals' loving and attentive descriptions of his environment show that for him this was a central dimension of the religious meaning of his time alone. Like many American nature writers, he found it easier, or more meaningful, to appreciate the fresh power of the natural world without being distracted by other people.

Other aspects of solitary life proved to be surprisingly difficult, even though his essays had cautioned that the hermit's was not an easy way of life. Merton suffered from many ailments, including back problems, stomach trouble, dermatitis, an arthritic hip, sinusitis, "perpetual diarrhea and a bleeding anus; most of my teeth gone; most of my hair gone; a chewed-up vertebra in my neck, which causes my hands to go numb and my shoulder to ache and for which I sometimes need traction" (*IM*, 265). He experienced periods of boredom, restlessness, and distraction; he knew first-hand the *accidie* (spiritual torpor) that the desert fathers warn about. Seeing a group of monks gathering the potato harvest in the late summer, Merton "remembered the communal beauty of work in this season—the sense of brotherhood and joy. . . . I felt lonely, seeing them out there" (*IM*, 257–58). In a series of journal entries during the dark, rainy December of 1964, Merton wrote of the deceitfulness of the heart, his bitterness, and his fear of death: "Is this what solitude is for? Then it is good, but I must pray for the strength to bear it!" (*IM*, 228). He realized "how quickly one can fall apart" in a hermitage and "the nearness of disintegration." As he experienced solitude for longer periods, including sleeping at the hermitage, he learned how fragile were his confidence, sanity, and self-knowledge: "One can pretend in the solitude of an afternoon walk, but the night destroys all pretenses. One is reduced to nothing and compelled to begin laboriously the long return to truth" (*IM*, 229). Only reliance on God could pull him through these hard times: "In the hermitage one must pray or go to seed."

When he did lose his grip and felt terror or despair, he tried to discern what God was doing in his life. He remembered stories about the desert fathers' struggles with demons and in this light interpreted his own darker times: "The desert is given us to get the evil unnested from the crannies of our own hearts. Perhaps again my tendency to find this in solitude rather than in community is simply subjective. After twenty-three years all the nests are well established. But in solitude and open air they are revealed and the wind blows on them and I know they must go!" (*IM*, 229). Aloneness helped him "sweat out the nonsense," get rid of illusions, learn to depend on God rather than himself. In his fiftieth year, feeling the nearness of death, he interpreted solitude as preparation for dying: "To face my untruth in solitude in preparation for the awful experience of facing it irrevocably in death with no more hope in anything earthly, only in God (totally unseen!)" (*IM*, 251–52).

Merton never stopped thinking about how to reconcile his need for solitude with his need for other people and his sense of social responsibility. Frequently he longed for greater privacy. His solitude was constantly interrupted, even during his years in the hermitage, as friends and visitors came and went. Local hunters pursued game onto the monastery's land. The whine of saws and the rumble of trucks disturbed him as the monastery engaged in construction projects. Several times students or admirers of his writing arrived unannounced, having learned the location of the famous monk's dwelling. While many of these visitors were welcome, Merton complained in his journal in 1968 that "real solitude" (a phrase that recurs many times in his last years) had become impossible for him at Gethsemani:

"The problem of real solitude: I don't have it here. I am not really living as a hermit. I see too many people, have too much active work to do, the place is too noisy, too accessible. People are always coming up here. I have been too slack about granting visits, interviews, etc., going to town too often, socializing, drinking, all that. All I have is a certain privacy, but real solitude is less and less possible here. Everyone now knows where the hermitage is" (*IM*, 323).

He fantasized about the ever-elusive perfect place for solitude, mulling over the relative merits of the California coast, New Mexico, Alaska, Nicaragua, the Himalayas, and other locations. In spite of his love for the Kentucky hills and his commitment to stability at Gethsemani, he often imagined wistfully that the grass that nurtures solitude was greener elsewhere. His search for a more secluded place was one of the motivations for his travels during his last six months, including the trip to Asia. I think that Merton was referring to his uncertainty about where to live when he enigmatically refers to "the great affair" in a journal entry written as he flew over the Pacific Ocean on October 15, 1968: "May I not come back without having settled the great affair. And found also the great compassion, mahakaruna" (*AJ*, 4). That was always Merton's ideal and hope: to combine solitude and compassion.

It was a time in American history when it was not easy to withdraw one's thoughts from the world, no matter how much privacy one had. Merton was greatly concerned about the tumultuous events of the 1960s: the Viet Nam War, the sense of a generation in rebellion against all traditions, the civil rights movement and race riots, assassinations, poverty in the Third World, and controversies in the Catholic Church regarding reforms introduced during the Second Vatican Council. Many of his published writings address current political issues from his perspective as an outsider, sharing the "conjectures of a guilty bystander," as he titled one book. When a young man from the Catholic Worker organization committed suicide by burning himself in front of the United Nations building in November 1965, Merton was horrified, and withdrew from the Catholic Peace Fellowship. This terrible event made him agonize about how to be a contemplative and also involved in the world: "Sometimes I wish it was possible simply to be the kind of hermit who is so cut off that he knows *nothing* that goes on, but that is not right, either" (*IM*, 263). He did not want to hide from the world's problems, but what he had to offer was not direct participation in politics, for there is "a certain incompatibility between my solitary life and active involvement in a movement." What he could best do from his position was write, sharing his concerns and engaging in dialogue with other views. This stance and activity put in practice his earlier justification of the hermit as a marginal person whose detachment from society offers an outsider's valuable perspective.

Merton struggled constantly with how much and what kind of writing he should do. He received countless requests to write about a worthy cause or sign his name to a letter of concern, and it was hard to refuse. Yet the primary purpose of his vocation as Christian hermit was stillness and silence, and he determined again and again to write less. In June 1963 he wrote: "I don't want to turn off into desperation and negativism, but there has to be a far greater reserve and caution and *silence* in my looking at the world and my attempts to help us all survive" (*IM*, 209). Three years later he admonished himself to refuse to make "declarations and affirmations of what I do not fully and actually know, experience, believe *myself*" (*IM*, 303). He needed to learn how to say no, he told himself, and to avoid "diffuse benevolence" in favor of more focused and personal responses. Several times he made assessments of all that he had written, distinguishing between what was better and worse and resolving henceforth to write only what came from his heart and simply had to be shared.

He was bothered, too, by how easily in his writing he could play the role of a writer, a monk, or even a hermit, falling into the illusions from which he had hoped solitude would free him: a fixed and consistent identity, self-conscious pretension, or performing for others. If writing was one of the most important things he did with his solitude, and sometimes a spiritual process that helped him to discern God's will, being an author could also express egoism, pride, and preoccupation with himself: "I have got to face the fact that there is in me a desire for survival as pontiff, prophet, and writer, and this has to be renounced before I can be myself at last" (*IM*, 166). The difference between his writing that he affirmed and that which he devalued was whether it was done to try to influence people: "The bad writing I have done has all been authoritarian, the declaration of musts and the announcement of punishments. Bad because it implies a lack of love, good insofar as there may yet have been some in it. The best stuff has been more straight confession and witness" (*IM*, 266).

Even journal-writing was problematic, for he intended for his journals to be read by others, and he felt them looking over his shoulder. He was ambivalent about the Merton Room at Bellarmine College dedicated to his writings, calling it a place "in which a paper-self builds its nest to be visited by strangers in a strange land of unreal intimacy" (*IM*, 312). He worried that perhaps his writing was a secret and futile attempt to impress others, or "a last despairing childish effort at love for some unknown people in some unknown future." He hoped that the technique of free association in his poetry would help him escape from self-consciousness and introspection: "It may be my final liberation from all diaries. Maybe that is my one remaining task" (*IM*, 312). Merton saw his writerly persona, even as expressed in his journals, as at once drawn to solitude and subverting "real solitude" by trying to persuade future readers that he was a certain kind of writer, monk, or hermit. Surely no other hermit has so scrupulously probed the ways that first-person writing can hinder the solitary's ideal of detachment from concern with other people. No other solitary so closely examines the ways that autobiographical writing can either bring a person closer to God by discerning grace in daily life or narrow one's awareness to the self and its efforts to control its image.

A crisis in Merton's commitment to solitude was precipitated in 1966 when he fell in love with a young nurse. She cared for him after he had back surgery in a Louisville hospital. Before long they were involved in correspondence, telephone calls, and meetings at Gethsemani and in Louisville. Merton's relationship with "M." lasted for several months during the spring and summer of 1966 and is recorded in detail in several journals written at this time. He recognized his "deep emotional need for feminine companionship and love" (*IM*, 276). He was surprised at his own capacity for love, given his childhood as an orphan without many long-term bonds and several youthful sexual encounters that he regretted. Now, justifying his love for M., he emphasizes with a new intensity his long-term belief that solitude must be open to others: "One thing has suddenly hit me— that nothing counts except love and that a solitude that is not simply the wide-openness of love and freedom is nothing. Love and solitude are the one ground of true maturity and freedom. Solitude that is just solitude and nothing else (i.e., *excludes* everything else but solitude) is worthless. True solitude embraces everything, for it is the fullness of love that rejects nothing and no one, that is open to All in All" (*IM*, 276). At this point his insistence on openness all but negates the authentic meaning of solitude, and he even debates whether he should continue as a hermit. It was a tumultuous time of joy and happiness but he also suffered anxiety, depression, and shame.

For all the power of love, at some deep level he knew that he could not renounce his monastic vows and his solitary vocation. He reconceptualizes solitude "as act," a constantly renewed commitment, and says that it is usually misunderstood as a passive, inert condition.

"One has to work actively at solitude" (IM, 292). His journal entries during these months show how difficult it was for him to choose solitude every day and that on many days he would gladly have given it up. His resolve vacillated and he continually tried to renew contact with M. The need for secrecy was painful to him, and it may have been a wish to escape his intolerable situation that led him to reckless behavior that ended the relationship. He made telephone calls to her that were overheard by another monk, who reported it to the abbot. Merton realized that he was in "real spiritual danger" and was relieved that he had been caught: "It is providential that everything has been blocked at the moment. Perhaps it is saving me from a real wreck" (IM, 288). The abbot, Dom James, urged a complete break with M. and hinted that Merton's loneliness was responsible for his attraction to her and his very un-hermitlike behavior. The abbot saw better than did Merton at this point how vulnerable solitude can make a person. The need for human contact, when denied, can lead to impulsive attempts at intimacy at the expense of long-term commitments.

For months Merton agonized about how to integrate his love for M. and his need for solitude. His journal explores various imagined solutions to his dilemma, envisioning schemes to share a life with M. while continuing on a religious path. Expressions of wishful thinking, rationalization, and agonized self-doubt alternate with avowals that he could never leave the monastic life. He gave his most emotionally raw outpourings, a journal in June 1966 called "A Midsummer Diary for M," this subtitle: "Or the account of how I once again became untouchable." There is more than a hint of bitterness and resignation in this phrase, but also the self-knowledge that he was set apart from other people by a vow of celibacy and a commitment to solitude. Merton fully acknowledges and affirms both sides of the conflicts that divided him: the ideal of chastity against the demands of sexual love, and the values of solitude in tension with full and complete relationship with another person. But finally his deliberate and sacred commitments took priority and he ended the relationship with M. She subsequently married and had a family, and little is known of her perspective on these events.

In September, Merton signed "a commitment 'to live in solitude for the rest of my life so far as health may permit.' After that I was at peace and said Mass with great joy" (IM, 301). Although he continued to think of M. and believed that his love for her would forever stay with him, he rededicated himself to being a hermit monk, and his life slowly settled into a more tranquil routine. In November

1966 he compared the theme of the wilderness in the Bible to his own experience: "How evident it becomes now that this whole thing with M. was, in fact, an attempt to escape the demands of my vocation. Not consciously, certainly, but a substitution of human love (and erotic love after all) for a special covenant with loneliness and solitude, which is the very heart of my vocation. I did not stand the test at all but allowed the whole essence to be questioned and tried to change it. I could not see I was doing this. Fortunately God's grace protected me from the worst errors. My difficult return to my right way is a gift of His grace" (IM, 303). Merton speaks of grace but does not explicitly acknowledge the fact that God's providence had come through the institutional structures of monastic life that had prevented him from leaving his vocation and disciplined his impulsive nature. Perhaps the greatest spiritual challenge for a hermit is to recognize the ways in which God works through the institutional forms and social conventions the solitary rejects.

His relationship with M. shows how solitude was not always easy for Merton but at times an agonizing struggle, a choice he could not make whole-heartedly. The experience made him, I think, a wiser hermit than most advocates of solitude, especially those who present it as a test or proof of self-reliance and independence. Merton's relationship with M. showed him his vulnerability and the depths of his need to love and be loved. His journal reveals the capacities for erotic passion and personal intimacy that he sacrificed to be alone. Yet even as he renounced a continuing relationship with M., Merton asserted that a solitary does not renounce the human need for love. According to biographer Michael Mott, "he was overwhelmed by the experience and it changed him forever. . . Thomas Merton never again talked of his inability to love, or to be loved."[7]

It is significant that Merton did not destroy his journals describing his love for M. and wanted them to be published. He burned her correspondence shortly before he began his final travels: "I burned M.'s letters. Incredible stupidity in 1966! I did not even glance at any one of them. High hot flames of pine branches in the sun!" (IM, 336). But he intended his journals to be published twenty-five years after his death. He wished this record to reveal his weakness, inconsistency, and mistakes, destroying others' breathless admiration of him that bothered him during his life. He specifically wanted the journals, including "the M. business," to show the paradoxes of his solitude, as he noted in May 1967: "I have no intention of keeping the M. business entirely out of sight. I have always wanted to be completely open, both about my mistakes and about my effort to make sense out of

my life. The affair with M. is an important part of it—and shows my
limitations as well as a side of me that is—well, it needs to be known
too, for it is part of me. My need for love, my loneliness, my inner
division, the struggle in which solitude is at once a problem and a
'solution.' And perhaps not a perfect solution either" (LL, 234). By
this time in his life Merton no longer viewed solitude as the highest
religious calling, as he had portrayed it in The Seven Storey Mountain,
but as a form of human experience that reveals the typical struggles
and sin of human life and the ways that, in their midst, grace is
sometimes known.

Merton's Asian Journey

During the 1960s Merton became interested in Asian religions, especially Buddhism's monastic traditions and the Taoist hermits who
shared his love of contemplation, the natural world, and detachment
from society. His desire to understand solitude as a spiritual practice
led not to a narrower view of the world, but to an inquiring and
appreciative dialogue with other religious traditions. Merton's interest in Asia produced the essays collected in Mystics and Zen Masters
and Zen and the Birds of Appetite and to his editing a collection of
Taoist stories, The Way of Chuang Tzu. The motif of solitude runs
through all of Merton's thoughts about Asian religions, and Asian
views influenced his own understanding of solitude. For example, in
May 1965 his journal contains several Zen-inspired passages that show
him trying to practice an effortless and unselfconscious awareness of
ordinary living, as opposed to the striving, sense of moral duty, and
prescriptive self-definition of even a hermit's "spiritual life":

> This is not a hermitage—it is a house. ("Who was that hermitage I
> seen you with last night?") What I wear is pants. What I do is live.
> How I pray is breathe. Who said Zen? Wash out your mouth if you said
> Zen. If you see a meditation going by, shoot it. Who said "Love"? Love
> is in the movies. The spiritual life is something that people worry
> about when they are so busy with something else they think they
> ought to be spiritual. Spiritual life is guilt. Up here in the woods is
> seen the New Testament: that is to say, the wind comes through the
> trees and you breathe it. (IM, 244)

In an imaginary conversation, an interlocutor asks him whether he is
"practicing Zen in secret." Merton: "Pardon me, I don't speak English"
(IM, 245). The Zen masters and Taoist sages epitomized for Merton

the possibility of direct perception of reality and freedom from social posturing. Alone at his cabin, he felt surrounded and strengthened by "all the silent Tzu's and Fu's (men without office and without obligation)" (IM, 249). Their example shaped his interpretation of his own solitude; their wisdom enriched his understanding of aloneness.

His desire to better understand Asian traditions was the primary incentive for Merton's journey to Asia, a two-month trip to India, Sri Lanka, and Thailand that he spoke of as a pilgrimage. Pilgrimage had many meanings for Merton, which I have explored elsewhere.[8] A surprising dimension of his understanding of pilgrimage is that it can involve the practice of solitude. In his essay "From Pilgrimage to Crusade," Merton describes an ancient Christian understanding of travel as a form of solitude. The Celtic monks of Ireland practiced *peregrinatio,* or "going forth into strange countries," as a form of asceticism and exile. These pilgrims engaged in a period of home-lessness and wandering, not choosing a direction but trusting God's Providence. They let the wind and the sea's tides take them, "in the hope of being led to the place of solitude which God himself would pick for them" (MZM, 94). Although Merton's travel to Asia's crowded cities has seemed to many scholars like an escape from solitude, this journey was actually motivated partly by his continuing search for a place of greater solitude than he could find at Gethsemani. In his Asian journal he repeatedly ponders whether he should establish a more secluded retreat in California, New Mexico, Alaska, or a place he hoped to discover in Asia.

Furthermore, he felt that the journey itself could express some of the religious meaning of solitude. For instance, the "homelessness" of the traveler was another path to realize the ideal of availability to others that was central to the monastic vocation as practiced by a Christian hermit. The open-endedness of his journey is also signifi-cant. His Asian travels had a tentative and evolving itinerary, and when he died in Bangkok, on December 8, 1968, he was considering whether and when to visit Japan, Indonesia, Hong Kong, a Tibetan center in Scotland, and experts on Asian religions residing in Switzer-land and Wales. He was living out the pattern he described in the wandering Celtic monks, who had no fixed destination but under-took "a journey to a mysterious, unknown, but divinely appointed place, which was to be the place of the monk's ultimate meeting with God" (MZM, 98). For Merton, as for the Celtic monks, pilgrim-age was similar to the eremitical life, a vocation to "mystery and growth, to liberty and abandonment to God" (MZM, 97). Merton's journey to Asia was not a flight from solitude but an extension of the same religious concerns that motivated and shaped his life as a hermit: the hope for inner transformation, a belief in the perspective of "marginal" outsiders, and an attempt to be open to other people and to discern God's grace in the world.

During his travels Merton sought out hermits with whom he compared experiences of aloneness. In northern India he met the Dalai Lama and other rimpoches (spiritual leaders) of Tibetan Buddhism. As usual, Merton was thinking about his uncertain future life and the difficulty of finding real solitude, even in the Himalayas: "To have real solitude one would have to get very high up and far back!" (AJ, 103). The Tibetan teachers gave him some advice that echoed his own belief that solitude should be balanced with concern for others: "For solitude, Alaska really seems the very best place. But everyone I have talked to says I must also consider others and keep open to them to some extent. The rimpoches all advise against absolute solitude and stress 'compassion.' They seem to agree that being in solitude much of the year and coming 'out' for a while would be a good solution" (AJ, 103). The suggestion that there needs to be a rhythm of withdrawal and engagement, of solitude and sociality, seems wiser than Merton's preoccupation with finding the perfect setting for solitude.

Soon after he heard this view, Merton described how contemplation can nurture compassion through the experience of a certain kind of temporality that he calls "temps vierge," virgin time:

> The contemplative life must provide an area, a space of liberty, of silence, in which possibilities are allowed to surface and new choices—beyond routine choice—become manifest. It should create a new experience of time, not as stopgap, stillness, but as "temps vierge"—not a blank to be filled or an untouched space to be conquered and violated, but a space which can enjoy its own potentialities and hopes—and its own presence to itself. One's own time. But not dominated by one's own ego and its demands. Hence open to others—compassionate time, rooted in the sense of common illusion and in criticism of it. (AJ, 117)[9]

A time of solitude free from the demands of others and from one's egotistical striving to impress them should culminate in openness to others and in compassion. Merton was struck by the common Buddhist and Christian emphasis on the links between compassion and solitude. He noted that a book on Buddhism he was reading held that the ability to bear solitude in the pursuit of truth is one of the "elementary qualifications for those who aspire towards selfless love"

(*AJ*, 157). A hermit rimpoche taught that "the hermit's retreat is not for his own salvation but for that of all sentient beings" (*AJ*, 165).

Merton pursued "hermit questions" with several other rimpoches. One of them "said he had meditated in solitude for thirty years or more and had not attained to perfect emptiness and I said I hadn't either" (*AJ*, 143). Deeper than the doctrinal differences that separated them, Merton sensed a common commitment to an ultimate reality that transcends all religions, and he felt a fundamental kinship with others who had chosen a solitary path: "The unspoken or half-spoken message of the talk was our complete understanding of each other as people who were somehow *on the edge* of great realization and knew it and were trying, somehow or other, to go out and get lost in it—and that it was a grace for us to meet one another" (*AJ*, 143). Merton believed that monks and hermits stand outside the established institutions of society and thus have a unique potential both to understand something of God's transcendent mystery and to commune with the essential humanity of others that underlies cultural differences.

Another way that solitude may have a religious dimension is revealed in Merton's encounter with the enormous Buddhist statues at Polonnaruwa in Sri Lanka, six days before his death. Leaving behind the vicar general, who avoided what he saw as paganism, Merton was "able to approach the Buddhas barefoot and undisturbed, my feet in wet grass, wet sand. Then the silence of the extraordinary faces" (*AJ*, 233). He describes the powerful effect on him of these works of religious art: "Looking at these figures I was suddenly, almost forcibly, jerked clean out of the habitual, half-tied vision of things, and an inner clearness, clarity, as if exploding from the rocks themselves, became evident and obvious. . . . I don't know when in my life I have ever had such a sense of beauty and spiritual validity running together in one aesthetic illumination. Surely, with Mahabalipuram and Polonnaruwa my Asian pilgrimage has come clear and purified itself. I mean, I know and have seen what I was obscurely looking for" (*AJ*, 233–36). Exactly what Merton thought he saw remains enigmatic. His account of this experience shows how deeply aesthetic experience could move him, and how art can provide essentially religious insights into the nature of ultimate reality. Comparing the statues to a Zen garden, Merton perceived "a span of bareness and openness and evidence, and the great figures, motionless, yet with the lines in full movement, waves of vesture and bodily form, a beautiful and holy vision" (*AJ*, 236). Significantly, the meaning of his pilgrimage emerges when he is alone, in solitary communion with religious statuary. For all his love of dialogue with Asian monks and religious thinkers, Merton grasps the meaning of his pilgrimage in a moment of solitude. His encounter with the Buddhist statues demonstrates his life-long convictions about the religious value of art, as well as the fact that some forms of aesthetic response may be most moving and revelatory when a work of art is experienced alone.

THOMAS MERTON was a fascinating person because he combined a number of apparently contradictory characteristics. He desired contemplation yet hoped for engagement with the world. He appreciated such classic texts of his tradition as the works of the desert fathers and also contemporary artistic achievements and popular culture. He affirmed both his deep commitment to Christian tradition and his aspiration to learn from the widest possible range of religious and nonreligious worldviews. Merton's understanding of solitude was as central, complex, and paradoxical as any other theme in his life and thought. His ideal was not to be consistent at the expense of complexity but rather "to be conscious of both extremes in my solitary life. Consolation and desolation; understanding and obscurity; obedience and protest; freedom and imprisonment" (*IM*, 250). His contrasting opinions and shifting perspectives on solitude through decades of autobiographical writing offer the most profound understanding of aloneness that I know of. Unlike many advocates of solitude (including himself when he wrote *The Seven Storey Mountain*), the mature Merton does not present aloneness as a clearly superior spiritual path. Rather, he thought that his journals showed his struggle with solitude as at once a problem and a solution—"and perhaps not a perfect solution either" (*LL*, 234). Although Merton never claimed to have solved the problems raised by solitude as a way of life, the way he lives with and explores the tensions that are part of the hermit's life is a compelling example, as has been affirmed not only by countless fellow Christians but a variety of others, including Buddhists, atheists, and seekers of wisdom who are unattached to any tradition. Merton's reflections on solitude show a creative mind and a couragous and joyful spirit raising vital questions, taking risks, and keeping in mind considerations not easy to reconcile.

Above all, Merton wrestled with two issues. He tried to understand how solitude can be combined with openness to other people and compassion for their suffering. And he wrestled with the question of right motivation, that is, how to discern when the desire for solitude springs from egotistical impulses and when it represents an authentic response to God's call. "The door to solitude opens only from the inside." This enigmatic statement means, I think, that genuine solitude should respond to God's invitation, not assert one's individuality or antagonism to others. For Merton, only the right understanding of solitude—and ultimately, only God's grace—could save it from being simply a refined form of self-indulgence. For him, a Christian hermit's life meant prayer, contemplation, and dialogue by means of reading and writing.

In the end, these two issues—the balance of solitude and connection to others, and the question of the right motivation for solitude—are linked. As both the desert fathers and Tibetan rimpoches agreed, whether or not solitude leads to compassion for others is the best measure of its spiritual worth. Yet the ethical justification for solitude is not reducible to what a hermit does for other people; the hermit has a spiritual path with its own integrity and value apart from what he contributes to others. Merton does not explain away the ethical and spiritual paradoxes of solitude but helps us understand them. His autobiographical writings can guide and inspire others trying to understand the moral ambiguities and spiritual significance of solitude.

8

SOLITUDE, WRITING, AND FATHERS IN PAUL AUSTER'S *THE INVENTION OF SOLITUDE*

MUCH RECENT autobiographical theory has emphasized the ways in which life writing delineates the author's identity in relation to other persons. The earlier model of autobiography as a feat of autonomous self-determination has been replaced by a new model that understands narrative identity in terms of how relationships with other persons form the self. Paul John Eakin summarizes this tendency in recent critical theory in his discussion of "relational selves" and "relational lives."[1] This understanding of life writing is especially applicable in the case of family memoirs which explore the bonds and tensions between generations, for instance such powerful contemporary works as Mary Gordon's *The Shadow Man*, Adam Hochschild's *Half the Way Home*, Geoffrey Wolff's *The Duke of Deception*, John Edgar Wideman's *Fatheralong*, Frank McCourt's *Angela's Ashes*, Kim Chernin's *In My Mother's House*, Carolyn Steedman's *Landscape for a Good Woman*, and Art Spiegelman's *Maus: A Survivor's Tale*. In these works "unfinished business" between parents and children structures the narrative, as the author delineates personal identity largely in relation to a parent. Usually because of some suppressed, shameful, or hidden aspect of the parent's past life, the parent was absent or emotionally distant during the autobiographer's childhood. Writing a memoir helps the author come to terms with and redefine the problematic relationship to a mother or father.

Paul Auster's *The Invention of Solitude* is an example of this genre of family memoir centered on the author's relationship to a parent. Auster's narrative is unusual, however, in its focus on the role of solitude in the parent/child relationship. Solitude is both the cause of estrangement between Auster and his father and a common experience that links them. The theme of solitude links the two parts of the book: "Portrait of an Invisible Man," which describes his father's life and influence, and "The Book of Memory," which explores the psychology of the writer's work and asserts the necessary role of solitude in literary creation. In his memoir Auster tries to "invent" or redefine solitude in a more positive way than his father's example left him. He tries to redefine solitude by considering its connection to his creative work and by exploring its effect on his relationship with his own son. These two aspects of his life express his deepest values, and I will interpret them as forms of spirituality. Insofar as he invents a new meaning for solitude, Auster's work also involves a process of ethical assessment. He affirms certain dimensions of aloneness under specific conditions, while also criticizing alternative understandings of solitude and the destructive effects of solitude in particular circumstances.

In Part I, "Portrait of an Invisible Man," Auster presents his father as a man with no inner life and little ability to be intimate with others. Samuel Auster lacked self-knowledge and authenticity: "My father's capacity for evasion was almost limitless. Because the domain of the other was unreal to him, his incursions into that domain were made with a part of himself he considered to be equally unreal, another self he had trained as an actor to represent him in the empty comedy of the world-at-large."[2] Auster describes his father's remoteness from others in terms of negative images of solitude: "He himself remained invisible, a puppeteer working the strings of his alter-ego from a dark, solitary place behind the curtain" (16). For Auster, solitude means more than physical separation from others, for he uses this term to describe emotional disconnection and inaccessibility in the presence of others. Hinting at the way in which he will formulate a more positive view of solitude, Auster presents his father's aloneness as an attempt to hide from both himself and others: "Solitary. But not in the sense of being alone. Not solitary in the way Thoreau was, for example, exiling himself in order to find out where he was; not solitary in the way Jonah was, praying for deliverance in the belly of the whale. Solitary in the sense of retreat. In the sense of not having to see himself, of not having to see himself being seen by anyone else" (16–17). To be in the presence of such a person is confusing and exhausting; to have a parent like this is debilitating. His father's remoteness caused Auster a good deal of self-doubt, sadness, and anger: "You do not stop hungering for your father's love, even after you are grown up" (19). His earliest memories are of his father's absence, the father's distracted unawareness of the son's needs. Auster's portrait of his father shows the destructive effects of aloneness both on the quality of life of a person who seeks solitude only to escape from others, and on those who must interact with him, especially family members.

Auster's writing of the first section of *The Invention of Solitude* was prompted by his father's death. As he sorts through his father's belongings, he reconstructs Samuel Auster's mysterious past. He learns that at the age of nine, his father had witnessed his mother shoot and kill his father, Paul Auster's grandfather. This traumatic event and the sensational trial that followed explain a lot about Samuel: "A boy cannot live through this kind of thing without being affected by it as a man" (36). Auster believes that his father "learned never to trust anyone. Not even himself" (50). The scandalous murder and trial explain why Samuel worked hard all his life to make himself untouchable, inaccessible, invulnerable. He was always out of step with those around him; even the "clothes he wore seemed to be an expression of solitude, a concrete way of affirming his absence" (55). Auster understands how family trauma influenced his father's incapacity for intimacy, but this insight does not lessen his continuing sense of having been damaged by his father's remoteness. His unhappy relationship to his father motivates the two tasks he undertakes in the second part of the book: to establish a different understanding of his father and to define an alternative meaning of solitude. He interprets solitude in a more positive way by showing its potential role in fostering creativity and its very different place in Auster's relationship to his own young son.

Auster's attempt to explore the links between solitude and creativity may be compared to British psychoanalyst Anthony Storr's *Solitude: A Return to the Self*, which I discussed in chapter 6. Focusing on the psychological links between solitude and creativity and building on Donald Winnicot's essay "The Capacity to Be Alone," Storr argues that an adult's capacity for solitude "originates with the infant's experience of being alone in the presence of the mother."[3] According to this theory, the capacity to be alone depends on a child's secure attachment to the mother, so that the child is not anxious about her possible departure. Moreover, the capacity to be alone is linked to an individual's ability to understand and express his inner feelings and impulses. A basic assurance that one is loved frees one from having to produce an expected or acceptable response, so that one can explore what one really wants or thinks. In this way Storr links solitude to imagination and creativity, and in a series of brief portraits tries to demonstrate how the capacity to be alone shaped the work of creative artists. More than a theory of solitude, Storr's work represents a fundamental reconsideration of psychological health. He proposes that the way psychoanalytic theory has defined emotional maturity overemphasizes the significance of human relationships. The ability to form attachments is indeed important, he recognizes, but equally significant is the capacity to do meaningful work, and for some people solitude seems to be necessary for such work.

Auster's memoir seems consistent with some of Storr's ideas, yet contrasts in certain ways. In an interview in 1991, Auster refers to Jacques Lacan's idea of the "mirror-stage" of human development, when an infant learns that he is separate from his mother: "It's no longer the mother who is looking at us then—we're looking at ourselves. But we can only see ourselves because someone else has seen us first. In other words, we learn our solitude from others."[4] Auster sees self-consciousness, and presumably the solitary introspection of autobiographical writing, as an extension of this early experience. Although in this interview Auster does not make the connection between solitude and creativity, in The Invention of Solitude he does, and I will explore his reasons for thinking that aloneness is necessary for artistic creativity. The Invention of Solitude also diverges from Storr's theory, for it does not portray a secure bond with a parent but rather a son's troubled sense of disconnection and uneasy wariness. Storr might interpret Auster's difficulties in enduring solitude as illustrating the point that only secure attachment to a parent can make aloneness enjoyable and productive. Perhaps Auster's mother, whose role in his life remains sketchy in the memoir, provided a more reassuring presence that compensated for the father's absence, and his ambivalence about solitude reflects these conflicting parental influences. Or perhaps, like many of the artists Storr discusses, Auster learned to compensate for the lack of family intimacy by turning to creative activities.

Auster's portrayal of the painful aspects of his lonely life as a writer seems to me to show a more balanced view of solitude than does Storr; Auster shows the dark side of solitude as well as its value, while Storr is almost entirely positive, enthusiastically advocating solitude. Another contrast with Storr's view is that, while psychoanalytic theory tends to see the capacity for solitude as largely determined by childhood experience, Auster's memoir suggests that an adult can change his view of solitude, at least to some extent. Auster tries to reinvent what solitude means for him, giving it a positive value that he did not see in his father's version of aloneness. He recognizes the continuing effect of his childhood relationship to his father and, like a patient in therapy, hopes to become more free from the past by understanding it. He tries, as well, to provide the conditions for his own son to develop the capacity to be alone, providing a kind of companionship that involves, paradoxically, a sharing of certain experiences of aloneness.

In the second part of the book, "The Book of Memory," Auster writes about himself in the third person, referring to himself as A. He makes explicit his autobiographical and confessional meaning: "A. realizes, as he sits in his room writing The Book of Memory, he speaks of himself as another in order to tell the story of himself. He must make himself absent in order to find himself there. And so he says A., even as he means to say I" (154). The anecdotes in this section of the book explore several interrelated themes, returning again and again to the role of solitude in creative work. Auster quotes Pascal: "All the unhappiness of man stems from one thing only: that he is incapable of staying quietly in his room" (76). Staying in one's room and using this time productively are surprisingly difficult, yet indispensable for creative work such as writing. Auster describes his life as a young author in New York City, living in cold apartments, struggling with the blank page on his desk, pacing, smoking, brooding. It is winter, the darkest time of the year, "a hermetic season, a long moment of inwardness" (78). He seems to have chosen to reenact the twentieth-century myth of the alienated artist, suffering miserably while devoting himself to work that only he can understand. Sitting in his tiny chamber, recently divorced, cut off from others, Auster's situation is eerily reminiscent of his father's isolation: "He feels himself sliding through events, hovering like a ghost around his own presence, as if he were living somewhere to the side of himself—not really here, but not anywhere else either" (78). His ambition to be a writer—or his desire to live out the role of misunderstood genius—seems to condemn him to repeat his father's negative experience of solitude.

To simply stay in his room and write requires "real spiritual work" (77). Auster describes the challenges of literary creation as a spiritual ordeal, a form of asceticism, and a dark night of the soul. It is a time to "dig more and more deeply into himself" (79), to concentrate and focus his powers. Only if he can find peace in his dreary room will he be able to do the same in the world: "The world has shrunk to the size of this room for him, and for as long as it takes him to understand it, he must stay where he is. Only one thing is certain: he cannot be anywhere until he is here" (79). This commitment to finding contentment in a fixed abode recalls the meaning of the vow of stability taken by monks and Christian hermits. Avoiding social interaction is a form of asceticism, an austere self-denial in the name of a spiritual discipline. According to one critic, in Auster's world the self must die "in order to live; there is a redemptive sense to annulment; hence Auster's heroes push themselves to the limit of hunger and physical deprivation. This self-destructive passion . . . transforms this confinement in one's room into a sort of secular asceticism without transcendence, without God."[5] The way in which his own name suggests austerity is one of many meaningful coincidences in which Auster delights. Austerity characterizes Auster's literary style and his vision of life; sometimes less is more, as simplicity and deprivation suggest longing, yearning, or hidden meaning. One interpreter argues for the specifically Jewish character of the theme of hunger in Auster's work.[6] Asceticism, austerity, and "hunger" in various forms, including the yearning created by lack of contact with others, are crucial parts of the artistic search for meaning for Auster.

Auster meditates at length on the spaces of solitude, especially artists' and writers' rooms. An artist's room is a "dream space," a place where contracted space frees the mind to roam and encourages the imagination to explore vast and distant worlds. The artist's room is tomb and womb, a place where one form of the self dies and another is born. Of the tiny room occupied by a composer he calls S., Auster writes: "This was the womb, the belly of the whale, the original site of the imagination. By placing himself in that darkness, S. had invented a way of dreaming with open eyes" (89). S.'s room in Paris reveals "the infinite possibilities of a limited space" (89). S. uses solitude creatively, yet welcomes A. warmly. A. is drawn to him as a father-figure; with S. he can "experience, for the first time, what it felt like to have a father" (92). Auster imagines other solitary writers working in a tiny enclosed space, such as Friedrich Hölderlin, Emily Dickinson, and Anne Frank. The situation of these artists recalls the medieval anchorites who were walled into a cell attached to a cathedral, tying the meaning of solitude to immobility, enclosure, and spiritual work.

Solitude is necessary for creative work, and for Auster it shows the seriousness of an artist's search for spiritual meaning. An artist's indifference to worldly success demonstrates a commitment to ends more elusive, yet important. In S.'s commitment to music that would probably never be finished or performed, A. sees an acceptance of failure "almost as a theological premise," a necessary falling-short whose purpose is humility in relation to God: "For only in the mind of God were such dreams as S.'s possible. But by dreaming in the way he did, S. had found a way of participating in all that was beyond him, of drawing himself several inches closer to the heart of the infinite" (91–92). S. is a recluse who equates his life with his work, has no audience, and asserts that "everything is miraculous" (90). This characterization demonstrates Auster's view of the spiritual significance of an artist's work and its connection to solitude. New vision comes when one is alone, as in the case of Pascal's famous mystical experience one night in 1654, which he described in the Memorial sewed into the lining of his clothes.[7] Auster describes this experience as "the moment of illumination that burns across the sky of solitude" (137). He compares Pascal's experience to a crucial moment in his own life, on Christmas Eve, 1979, when he realized "that even alone, in the deepest solitude of his room, he was not alone, or more precisely, that the moment he began to try to speak of that solitude, he had become more than just himself" (139). S., Pascal, and A. all find in solitude an intense if fleeting awareness of the presence of something beyond the self, although Auster does not draw the theological conclusion that what he has sensed is Pascal's "God of Abraham, God of Isaac, God of Jacob."

Auster explores the meanings of aloneness in religious and literary exemplars such as Jonah. The biblical prophet's story symbolizes several aspects of the artist's situation in modern culture, for like Jonah the artist tells unpleasant, harsh truths to an audience that may not want to listen. An artist may find himself alone in a room like Jonah in the belly of the whale, enduring solitude that is painful but prepares him to speak by giving him a radically different perspective on his society. The whale saves Jonah from drowning in the sea and enables him to deliver his message:

> Jonah is given back to life, as if the death he had found in the belly of the fish were a preparation for new life, a life that has passed through death, and therefore a life that can at last speak. For death has frightened him into opening his mouth. "I cried by reason of mine affliction unto the Lord, and he heard me; out of the belly of hell cried I, and thou heardest my voice." In the darkness of the solitude that is death, the tongue is finally loosened, and at the moment it begins to speak, there is an answer. And even if there is no answer, the man has begun to speak. (125–26)

The anguish of aloneness drives the prophet to speak, and A. to write. The third person mode of narration in the Book of Jonah is for Auster an instructive example of how to render the insights of solitude. His description of the biblical book applies as well to "The Book of Memory": "This brief work, the only one to be written in the third person, is more dramatically a story of solitude than anything else in the Bible, and yet it is told as if from outside that solitude, as if, by plunging into the darkness of that solitude, the 'I' has vanished from itself. It cannot speak about itself, therefore, except as another. As in Rimbaud's phrase: 'Je est un autre'" (124). The suggestion that the "I" can vanish from itself states Auster's hope that by means of solitude he can transcend self-consciousness and discover the world anew. Writing in the third person, viewing A. as if from outside, is intended to bring a new kind of objectivity or detachment from himself, a perspective on himself as other.

Auster ponders other mythic solitaries, such as Cassandra, who speaks from her prison cell, and Robinson Crusoe, alone on his island. He quotes lines from Billie Holliday's song "Solitude": "In my solitude you haunt me / with reveries of days gone by. / In my solitude you taunt me / With memories that never die" (123). These lines, expressing how persistent memories of a lover torment the singer, suggest the continuing presence of Auster's father in his life, and the way that a person may experience solitude not as a time of isolation, but as accompanied by—haunted by—vivid memories of others. A. contrasts paintings of rooms by Vermeer and van Gogh, discerning in them very different visions of solitude. The utter stillness of a solitary woman in one of Vermeer's rooms, with bright light pouring through an open window, conveys "the fullness and self-sufficiency of the present moment" (140), and openness to the world. Vincent van Gogh's *The Bedroom*, in contrast, suggests a prison cell and a mind unwillingly trapped. The man who painted this room "has been alone too much, has struggled too much in the depths of solitude. The world ends at that barricaded door. For the room is not a representation of solitude, it is the substance of solitude" (143). These literary and visual images of solitude portray positive and negative aspects of aloneness in the Western cultural imagination and the diverse meanings solitude holds for creative artists.

The story that most fascinates Auster is the tale of Pinocchio. What apparently led him to associate this children's tale with the meaning of solitude is the image of Gepetto, Pinocchio's father, in the belly of the whale. Because Pinocchio rescues his father from being trapped in the whale, the story symbolizes Auster's desire to

save his own father from a deadly isolation, the wrong kind of solitude. *Pinocchio* is about a wooden toy who "becomes a real boy";
this idea expresses Auster's feelings of deadness and unreality in
relation to his father, and his sense that, like Pinocchio, he will not
"become a real boy . . . until he is reunited with his father" (132). The
image of Pinocchio saving Gepetto has great power: "For this same
incompetent little marionette, who is not even a real boy, to become
a figure of redemption, the very being who saves his father from the
grip of death, is a sublime moment of revelation. The son saves the
father. This must be fully imagined from the perspective of the little
boy. And this, in the mind of the father who was once a little boy, a
son, that is, to his own father, must be fully imagined" (134). How
does the son save the father? In *Pinocchio*, by rescuing him from the
whale. But Auster's father is dead; a reunion can come about only in
a symbolic form. Auster's memoir represents a symbolic rescue of and
reunion with the author's father. In it he explores a bond he shares
with his father: their common experience of solitude. Auster knows
the pain of solitude, and this gives him, if not forgiveness, at least
empathy for his father's isolation. Moreover, he "saves" not only his
father but himself as well by giving solitude a new and positive meaning. He "becomes real" as he discerns in solitude not soul-destroying
isolation, but an experience that can foster imagination, creativity,
and even intimacy with his own son. Auster saves his father and
himself by inventing a new meaning of solitude.

The Invention of Solitude redefines solitude in two ways, both of
which involve the paradoxical idea that solitude can be shared with
others. First, Auster interprets solitude as necessary for a writer's
creativity. "Every book is an image of solitude" (136), the outcome of
a great deal of time spent alone in a room. Literature is at once the
product of an author's solitude and the means by which a reader reaches
through his own and the author's solitude. In reading, an isolated
individual becomes absorbed in something beyond his own preoccupations and communes with another mind. A. discovers when he
translates French works into English that "it is as though he were
entering that man's solitude and making it his own. . . . Therefore, he
tells himself, it is possible to be alone and not alone at the same
moment" (136). Reading literature creates a kind of companionship
that preserves the solitariness of writing and reading.

Auster presents the sharing of stories as a life-saving act, comparing
it to the storytelling of the heroine of *The Thousand and One Nights*.
As long as Shehrzad goes on narrating, she will be saved from death. Her
fictions delight the king, turning him away from his preoccupation

with death: "An obsession of this sort walls one up in solitude. One sees nothing but one's own thoughts. A story, however, in that it is not a logical argument, breaks down those walls. For it posits the existence of others and allows the listener to come into contact with them—if only in his thoughts" (152). Auster interprets the act of reading as a form of companionship based on the shared solitude of author and reader. The oxymoron "shared solitude" represents an idealized fusion of aloneness and communion. It is a union of opposites that may be logically absurd, but expresses a spiritual yearning for synthesis or reconciliation of the tensions of human existence. Auster's way of describing the writing and reading of literature strives to reconcile solitude and relationship to others. He tries to reconceive solitude as not solipsistic isolation but the necessary condition for a more meaningful form of connection with others than is possible in normal social interaction.

Writing is a redemptive act and a way out of solitude for Auster not only because it ultimately aims at communication with others, but also because the writer's exploration of language is a mode of discovery of the world. Writing is "a search for the world as it appears in language" (161). Playing with words, as he did as a schoolboy, A. discovers networks of connection among words, for example in rhymes (such as room/tomb/womb). The hidden relationships among words offer a new perspective on the world: "It is only at those rare moments when one happens to glimpse a rhyme in the world that the mind can leap out of itself and serve as a bridge for things across time and space, across seeing and memory" (161). The writer's mind connects the things of the world, constructing metaphors that link the objects of the world to each other and to himself: "Wherever his eye or mind seems to stop, he discovers another connection, another bridge to carry him to yet another place, and even in the solitude of his room, the world has been rushing in on him at a dizzying speed, as if it were all suddenly converging in him and happening to him at once" (162).

Memoir, the particular form of writing in which Auster engages, gives solitude another kind of redemptive meaning: "It is only in the darkness of solitude that the work of memory begins" (164). When one turns away from the present and from immediate contact with others, one can recover the past and save it from oblivion and meaninglessness. In the recollection of the past, especially childhood, the memoir writer finds a world that would otherwise be lost. He finds that memories are linked to particular places, that places evoke word associations, and that the past is evoked by natural objects, so that in exploring memory one discovers a web of connections both in the world and to oneself: "To wander about in the world, then, is also to wander about in ourselves. That is to say, the moment we step into the space of memory, we walk into the world" (166). Memory links A. to the past and to the world. More than simply a means of recovery, it is a way of being fully present, a mode of self-transcendence: "Memory, then, not so much as the past contained within us, but as proof of our life in the present. If a man is to be truly present among his surroundings, he must be thinking not of himself, but of what he sees. He must forget himself in order to be there. And from that forgetfulness arises the power of memory. It is a way of living one's life so that nothing is ever lost" (138).

Solitude makes possible the self-forgetfulness necessary for full attention to the world as revealed in memory. It is not just what turns up in memory that is important but attaining this spiritual state, when one is utterly present, receptive, and attentive. In his conception of memory, Auster interprets solitude as a way out of isolation and a mode of access to the world, including other people. He realizes that "even alone, in the deepest solitude of his room, he was not alone, or, more precisely, that the moment he began to try to speak of that solitude, he had become more than just himself. Memory, therefore, not simply as the resurrection of one's private past, but an immersion in the past of others, which is to say: history" (139). By interpreting writing as a process of communication and a way of exploring the world, language, and memory, Auster gives solitude a very different meaning than it had in his father's life.

In these several ways Auster presents writing done in solitude as a special way of knowing what is beyond the self. In an interview he explains how the insights that can come in solitude do not lead to some core or essential self but to understanding of language, memory, and other people:

> What is so startling to me, finally, is that you don't begin to understand your connection to others until you are alone. And the more intensely you are alone, the more deeply you plunge into a state of solitude, the more deeply you feel the connection. It isn't possible for a person to isolate himself from other people. No matter how apart you might find yourself in a physical sense—whether you've been marooned on a desert island or locked up in solitary confinement—you discover that you are inhabited by others. Your language, your memories, even your sense of isolation—every thought in your head has been born from your connection with others. This is what I was trying to explore in "The Book of Memory," to examine both sides of the word "solitude."

> I felt as though I were looking down to the bottom of myself, and what
> I found there was more than just myself—I found the world. That's
> why the book is filled with so many references and quotations, in order
> to pay homage to all the others inside me. On the one hand, it's a work
> about being alone; on the other hand, it's about community.[8]

Introspection ("looking down to the bottom of myself") is facilitated
by solitude, but what Auster discovers is that the self is made out of
the world. In an eerie way, the search for his own selfhood in "The
Book of Memory" proves as futile as that for his father in "Portrait of
an Invisible Man"; in both cases the detective work of locating a miss-
ing identity produces fragmentary and inconclusive results. Yet there
is an enormous difference in the ways Auster constructs his father's
and his own identity, because of the contrast between a form of solitude
that tries to seal itself off from the world and solitude that is understood to contain within itself innumerable connections to the world.

If solitude was a shell that enclosed Auster's father and undermined
his relationship to his son, can Paul Auster pass on a different understanding of solitude to Daniel, his own young son? Is the positive,
productive meaning of solitude that he invents in this book capable
of being transmitted to the next generation? Auster's memoir does not
clearly answer this question, but it shows him attempting to redefine
solitude in a second way, as the basis for a bond between father and
son. Already at three years old, Daniel takes great pleasure in imaginative experience and enjoys time alone. "I have to be alone to
think," says the boy. In several scenes Auster portrays himself reading to Daniel. They gravitate toward the story of Pinocchio, both of
them relishing the story of the separation and reunion of Gepetto
and the boy who becomes real by saving his father. Children need
stories, imaginative play, and the leap into fantasy. Following a
fictional story is at once a movement into a private inner world and
a shared experience that bonds father and son. When Daniel says,
"Tell me a story, daddy," his father lies down in the darkness and
makes up a tale that takes his son into an imaginary world and into
the aloneness of sleep. But the boy takes his father's voice with him:
"And even as the boy closes his eyes and goes to sleep, his father's
voice goes on speaking in the dark" (154). Auster's description of
bedtime storytelling represents another attempt to reconcile togeth-
erness and aloneness, intimacy and solitude. He depicts himself
nourishing Daniel's capacity for solitude by sharing bedtime stories,
transporting him into an imaginary world and into sleep with the
assurance of his father's love.

For Auster, being Daniel's father has the deepest spiritual significance, as is clear from many passages invoking religious language. A.
translates the fragmentary poems Mallarmé wrote for his dying son.
This project helps A. come to terms with his own terror during Daniel's
illness, and he realizes that his son's life means more to him than
does his own, more than anything. Recognizing his willingness to
die to save his son, A. understands fatherhood in a new way. Trans-
lating these poems is "the equivalent of offering a prayer of thanks
for the life of his son. A prayer to what? To nothing perhaps. To his
sense of life. To *the modern nothingness*" (110). This unusual prayer
expresses Auster's sense of what is ultimate for him and his gratitude for his son's precious and fragile life. In reflections on the suffering of children in Nazi Germany, 1970s Cambodia, and *The Brothers
Karamazov*, A. asserts that the world is monstrous and can lead one
to despair. His only consolation and antidote to despair is the image
of his son, or that of any child. Because of his responsibility for the
next generation, he knows that he must not despair. Behind these
reflections on the problem of evil we sense Auster's own childhood
suffering, his anger at his father's failures to reach out to him, and
his determination to do better as a father. A. asserts that there is
nothing more important to him than his son. Among the gifts of love
that he wants to pass on to Daniel are intimacy and a capacity for
solitude. These are not antithetical but deeply connected.

Part I, "Portrait of an Invisible Man," ends with the image of Daniel
asleep in his crib, as Auster wonders "what he will make of these pages
when he is old enough to read them" (69). One of the last passages in
"The Book of Memory" similarly envisions Daniel reading the second
part of *The Invention of Solitude*. A. dreams that he is dying. Not
having finished "The Book of Memory," he asks his ex-wife to complete it for him and give it to Daniel. His final gift of love for his
child is the book he wrote in solitude, which speaks of experiences
of writing, imagination, and love. The book is his legacy, Daniel's
inheritance, and a symbol of the connection between the generations. It expresses A.'s desire to give his son the gift of solitude, the
capacity for aloneness, at the same time that he gives Daniel the
love and affirmation that Paul never received from his own father.

Yet it is not at all clear how Daniel will react to Paul Auster's
aloneness and his rhythm of intimacy and detachment. Perhaps Daniel
will need more or less solitude than his father, or will understand
solitude in a completely different way, inventing his own version of
aloneness. Perhaps he will experience his father's periods of solitary
work as abandonment. The ending of the book raises the question of

whether Auster will do a better job than did his father at nurturing his son's capacity for solitude and the invention, creativity, and imagination that he hopes it can foster, while also being intimate, connected, and affirming. Auster's assessment of his father has become tied to the ambiguity of solitude, and to his awareness that how a child will react to his parent is always uncertain, and a matter of temperament and values.

Auster's memoir makes the experience of aloneness central to the relationship between fathers and son. His portrait of his father shows the negative side of solitude in Samuel's self-absorption and failure to give his son love in ways that Paul could understand. Auster's portrayal of his own role as father shows him trying to pass on to Daniel the positive meanings of solitude as linked to imagination, memory, and creativity. *The Invention of Solitude* explores the spiritual significance of imaginative writing and of parenting, and the ways that these, his deepest commitments, are rooted in solitude. For Auster, what gives writing and parenting a spiritual dimension is the way in which these activities attempt to encompass and reconcile experiences of solitude and the bonds between self and others.

CONCLUSION

THE VALUE OF SOLITUDE

I HAVE EXPLORED the ways in which solitude has ethical and spiritual value in a range of autobiographies from Augustine's *Confessions* until the late twentieth century. My conclusions are organized in terms of five issues: the nature of the spiritual and ethical values discerned in aloneness; the links between autobiography and solitude; the differences between chosen and involuntary solitude; the question of for whom solitude is valuable; and the question of how to integrate solitude and engagement with others in rhythmic alternation.

Spiritual and Ethical Value

Solitude often brings experiences of serenity and joy; it also led Thomas Merton to times of loneliness, Rousseau to paranoia, and Richard Byrd to life-threatening danger. But whether it is perceived as a positive or negative experience, solitude helps certain individuals to understand and feel connected to the fundamental sources of meaning and value in their lives. Being alone may be associated with discerning God's will, the study of ancient texts, creating works of art or literature, appreciation of the natural world, or forging a singular identity. Some authors explicitly correlate their view of solitude with a conception of God, while secular solitaries' ultimate values are not linked to the divine. Solitude provides an opportunity to pursue the five values discussed in chapter 6: attunement to nature, healing, adventure, creative work, and self-formation. Sometimes aloneness is an escape from the negative aspects of social existence: the boredom, conflict, or anxious striving to please that drain one's energy and spiritual vitality. More positively, solitude allows a person to focus on some dimension of reality that is better appreciated or engaged in when one is not distracted by the need to attend to others. Solitude is both a retreat from unwanted social interactions and a commitment to positive values and dimensions of reality that are best experienced alone.

Marc Chagall's painting entitled "Solitude" depicts a solitude that is not empty but full of potential meaning and sources of value. The pensive posture of the lone human figure, a rabbi, embodies the value of reflection; he may be listening to his conscience or remembering a painful event in the past. He holds a scroll of the Torah, suggesting the need for intense concentration in studying God's word, and perhaps any significant book. Nearby a white cow represents the proximity of the natural world. A violin offers the opportunity to make music. The rabbi is in a field on the outskirts of a town, reminding us that solitude is always bounded by relationships with other people, and for most people a temporary interlude from which they return to responsibilities. Overhead an angel passes, perhaps bringing a divine word of comfort or a new message that the rabbi will deliver to his people. Chagall portrays solitude as an alternative to social engagements and an opportunity to discover rich possibilities of meaning and value that may be significant for other people. Solitude is a door that opens within, permitting introspection; it is also a window that offers a perspective on many aspects of the world.

Solitude is not necessarily antisocial and often has important ethical implications for understanding the relationship between the individual and community. In the introduction I said that the ethics of aloneness encompasses the moral justification of solitude, the role of solitude in criticizing social practices, and the implications of solitude for understanding the good life.

When writers justify their time alone, they do so in three basic ways. They may argue that solitude fulfills their social responsibilities and is an indirect way of contributing to society. Or they may place limits on their moral obligations to others and justify their use of time alone for personal ends. Or they may, as Thoreau and Edward Abbey tend to do, fiercely proclaim their own individual interests and passions as their highest value, rejecting the claims of society as stultifying, inhibiting, and merely conventional or conformist. Of these three general strategies for reconciling solitude with the claims of others, the middle course is the most ethically sound. To justify solitude simply in terms of how it benefits others does not encompass the full range of possibility generated by solitude. To deny that the claims of others set moral limits or conditions on one's pursuit of personal ends fails to heed one of the chief lessons of solitude: our deep human interdependence. There is a genuine moral tension between solitary pursuits and social responsibility that can not be resolved by a theory, rule, or normative system. This tension must be worked out in the details of particular lives, as an individual adjusts her practice of solitude to changing social interactions and needs and makes room in these relationships for periods of aloneness.

In my view, there is no adequate general answer to the most fundamental moral question: how to balance personal interests and needs with the claims of other people, which may take the form of specific obligations, the rights of others, or the general moral imperative to benefit other people's well-being.[1] Yet there is practical wisdom about how to do this in specific circumstances, informed by the example of those who have wrestled with a similar situation. Even when we do not agree with, for instance, Rousseau's way of conceptualizing his solitude in relation to others, there is much we can learn; a good bad example can be highly instructive. The writers examined in this book help us to think about how to combine solitude and social engagements, the advantages and disadvantages of different kinds and amounts of aloneness, and how to balance the values of solitude with other equally important values that cannot be weighed on the same scale. These authors' reflections on solitude involve a critical perspective on their society's values and an alternative vision of the nature of the good life.

From some points of view, the very idea of religious solitude is an oxymoron. If religion is understood as a matter of self-transcendence or commitment to a religious community, and solitude is defined as preoccupation with the self, then aloneness seems the antithesis of genuine spiritual development. This perspective, however, fails to grasp how the purpose of solitude is not necessarily attention to oneself. Even when solitude is devoted to intense introspection—such as the writing of an autobiography—what the author seeks is not only the self, but the world.[2] In solitude some persons practice a certain kind of attentiveness that they cannot achieve when distracted by the presence of other people. Alone, one can concentrate on the natural world, language, conscience, bodily awareness, memory, creative activity, or God, without having to coordinate one's perceptions or thoughts with those of other people. For certain individuals, solitude is a necessary condition of meditative awareness or full concentration on something beyond the self that connects them with the world, and often with what is believed to be sacred, divine, or holy. Solitude at its best—when it realizes its fullest ethical and spiritual value—is not oriented toward escaping the world, but toward a different kind of participation in it, as made possible by disengagement from ordinary social interactions. Solitude is a return to the self, but it is not necessarily narcissitic; it may also be a return to what is most important in one's life and an encounter with sources of meaning and truth beyond oneself.

Autobiography and Solitude

As well as being the explicit subject matter of many autobiographical works, solitude may be construed as a dimension of the writing of autobiography. The act of composing an autobiography is in certain ways analogous to a withdrawal to solitude and has similar spiritual and ethical dimensions. Solitude and life writing may each express a person's search for a freely chosen personal identity. Both involve temporary detachment from a community in order to further the work of self-formation.

In the light of postmodernist critiques of "the subject" and the Enlightenment concept of the individual, the idea that in solitude one is free from cultural influences seems naive. From a postmodernist theoretical perspective, the writer is said to be a "site" where different ideologies, political interests, and discursive practices converge and compete.[3] Yet a time of solitude, like a project of life writing, may play an important role in a person's attempt to claim and exercise agency. Disengagement and detachment from the immediate demands of social roles may allow a person to adjust and revise his understanding of personal identity, perhaps emphasizing or reinterpreting childhood memories, bodily awareness, connections to the natural world, or spiritual intuitions and yearnings. One may reframe one's sense of identity by characterizing oneself in relationship to historical, fictional, or mythic figures. If we understand the self as constituted dialectically through its relationships, rather than as being a self-sufficient atomistic unit, then solitude may help a person choose which relationships are most significant in identity. Both the practice of solitude and the process of life writing may involve an attempt to recover latent sources of the self, deep springs of personal identity that are not expressed in ordinary social roles and interactions. Although self-formation does not happen in a cultural vacuum, solitude and the writing process alike may help an individual to recover a sense of agency, to choose which among many social norms they will affirm, and to decide that personal identity is better understood one way rather than another.

This process of individuation and self-formation need not deny the importance of community, or that most of the values a person affirms are shared with various others. The struggle to interpret one's relationship to intimate others, to formative communities, and to the larger society is a crucial dimension of autobiography. Solitude, too, often involves an attempt to redefine one's relationship to others, to find a way to be engaged in meaningful and intentional ways rather than simply conforming to social pressure or mechanical habit. The solitaries whose insights I have found the most compelling—especially Augustine, Montaigne, and Merton—are highly conscious of the ways in which aloneness and relationship influence each other and depend upon each other to be fruitful. These writers seem to me wiser than others, such as Rousseau and Thoreau, who present their capacity for solitude as a proud declaration of self-sufficiency and indifference to others. Augustine and Merton show that solitude is always bounded by relationships with others, and Thoreau and Rousseau demonstrate, even if they do not admit, that one of the deepest truths taught by solitude is how dependent on others we are even when alone. The ethics and spirituality of autobiography, like those of solitude, are in large part a matter of reconciling and balancing one's individual desires and needs with the claims made by others, and a matter of doing justice to both others' perspectives and one's own. Like the intentional practice of solitude, writing one's autobiography may be an ethical and religious activity, in that a person seeks to transcend being determined by social habits and conventions and to be reoriented toward the values that are most important. In solitude and life writing alike, a person may attempt to understand the deepest sources of vitality and identity and to reorient her life accordingly.

Autobiography can play a significant role for readers by making the values of solitude come alive for us. Life writing shows the conditions in which solitude is fruitful, valuable, and revitalizing and also provides examples of aloneness that provoke criticism. Autobiography helps us to recognize genuine conflicts between the good things that are best pursued in solitude and other good things that can only be achieved by cooperation with other people. Certain works of life writing are like the great works of art that Charles Taylor argues can help us acknowledge and understand those rival goods whose tensions create the characteristic conflicts of modernity: "The great epiphanic work actually can put us in contact with the sources it taps. It can *realize* the contact."[4] Works of art and literature show how the world makes claims on human beings and sets our personal values within a larger context. The sources of goodness are not just good for self-fulfillment; they emanate from the world. We need new ways of encountering these basic sources of value: "As our public traditions of family, ecology, even polis are undermined or swept away, we need new languages of personal resonance to make crucial human goods alive for us again."[5] Autobiographical writing at its best does precisely this, for instance as it represents periods of aloneness. It makes the good things found in solitude come alive for readers, instructing or reminding us of their value. We can share, for instance, the desire Richard Byrd expresses in *Alone:* "to know that kind of experience to the full, to be by himself for a while and to taste peace and quiet and solitude long enough to find out how good they really are" (4). At the same time, autobiographies show what must sometimes be given up for solitude, and how being alone may conflict with other values. Reading how Gibbon, Thoreau, or Merton describes solitude can deepen and shape readers' experience of solitude, help us to imagine its possibilities, make us more deliberate and intentional about our practice of aloneness, and more aware of both its ethical and spiritual value and dangers.

Involuntary Solitude

All of the writers considered in this book chose to be alone. Although Richard Byrd's Antarctic sojourn turned into an ordeal from which he wanted to escape, and many writers experienced periods of loneliness, they all entered into solitude willingly. Aloneness which is not freely chosen is experienced very differently than voluntary solitude. Much of the value individuals find in solitude depends on the freedom they feel from the demands of others: freedom to move at one's own pace, think one's own thoughts, enjoy one's body and the world unselfconsciously, or work according to one's inclination, liberated from the needs and schedules of others. Freely chosen solitude also implies the ability to terminate one's aloneness, to reestablish contact with others when one chooses. It would seem, then, that solitude must be voluntary to be productive, fruitful, and spiritual. Yet forms of involuntary solitude may also bring important spiritual and ethical insights, as can be seen in three forms of autobiographical literature: illness narratives, tales of stranded adventurers, and prison narratives.

Illness narratives often describe the experience and the fear of solitude. Two recent examples are Jean-Dominique Bauby's *The Diving Bell and the Butterfly* and Thomas DeBaggio's *Losing My Mind: An Intimate Look at Life with Alzheimer's.* Bauby, who died in 1996, suffered a massive stroke in December of 1995 that left him completely paralyzed. The only part of his body that he could control was blinking his left eye. Amazingly, he was able to communicate by blinking, and with assistance he devised a code with which he laboriously composed a memoir about his experience. Bauby describes the pain of being cut off from normal social interaction and the usual pleasures of embodied life. He is with other people physically and can understand them, yet he can only communicate fragments of thoughts and feels isolated from his children, lover, and friends. His is a solitude of excruciating loneliness and hopeless longing.

Another illness narrative, DeBaggio's *Losing My Mind*, chronicles the author's gradual loss of memory as he develops Alzheimer's disease. DeBaggio, too, required assistance to complete his memoir, as his ability to formulate words slowly failed. He, too, describes an agonizing loss of human connection, although he suffers gradual diminishment rather than a sudden blow. He looks back on an earlier time in his life when he thought he could live alone happily: "I once thought a person could live alone and devote a life to the mind. I outlined a play with such a theme. The main character was a man on display at a zoo. It has taken thirty years for me to realize why I couldn't finish the play."[6] DeBaggio knows that he will be cared for as his disease progresses but that he will eventually be utterly cut off from other people, unable to communicate or express his emotions: "On a pleasant, sunny day like this several years from now, I will die with no sense of what is happening and surrounded by mourners who can know nothing of my inner travail, a pain I will never be able to utter in my Alzheimer's silence" (174). He presents a truly terrifying vision of unwilling disengagement from other people and permanent solitude with no return. DeBaggio's anticipation of his inevitable final aloneness seeps into the present, making all the more painful and precious his moments of awareness of his wife's comforting presence. He closes his memoir with the prospect of a slow descent into complete isolation: "I must now wait for the silence to engulf me and take me to the place where there is no memory left and there remains no reflexive will to live. It is lonely here waiting for memory to stop and I am afraid and tired. Hug me, Joyce, and then let me sleep" (207).

For Bauby and DeBaggio, illness brings involuntary separation from others and frustrated longing for connection with loved ones. Writing a memoir expresses these feelings, leaves a record of the author that will outlast his physical existence, and testifies to the love that he believes will survive the involuntary solitude of illness. These authors conceive of their works of life writing as spiritual acts. For Bauby, the diving bell of his title symbolizes the weight of his physical condition, "locked-in syndrome," that presses down on, confines, and isolates him. The butterfly is a metaphor for the flight of the mind and imagination, the fragile but beautiful actions of the human spirit that offer moments of transcendence of suffering.

Comparable insights emerge in a second form of narrative about involuntary solitude: tales of stranded adventurers. Daniel Defoe's *Robinson Crusoe,* the fictional ancestor of such narratives, was based on an actual castaway, Alexander Selkirk, who survived more than four years alone on a remote island (visited by Joshua Slocum on his solo voyage around the world). Defoe's story, which many scholars see as the first novel, deals centrally with the experience of solitude, as if that genre's origins were tied to the question of how the solitary individual can make contact with others. Among autobiographical narratives, Byrd's *Alone* is a good example of an adventurer's involuntary solitude, as is Steven Callahan's *Adrift: Seventy-six Days Lost at Sea.* In 1982 Callahan survived eleven weeks on an inflatable life raft drifting across the Atlantic Ocean to the Caribbean Sea, where he was finally rescued. His memoir deals primarily with how he survived hunger, thirst, shark attacks, and broiling sun, but loneliness was not the least of his challenges. He dedicates his narrative to "people everywhere who know, have known, or will know suffering, desperation, or loneliness." Like illness narratives, tales of stranded adventurers may draw important lessons from an experience of unwilling aloneness. Paradoxically, Byrd and Callahan learn how deeply they need, depend on, and love other people at the same time that they discover inner powers of endurance, will, and imagination that probably would never have surfaced without their ordeal.

Finally, prison narratives offer another kind of testimony about involuntary solitude. If solitary confinement was originally seen as a way to encourage repentance, it is now justified primarily as a punishment and to protect others from the most dangerous criminals. Or it is used by totalitarian regimes to break down the resistance of dissenters. Whatever its rationale, solitary confinement is a cruel punishment that rapidly destroys the physical and mental well-being of most prisoners and leads to many painful symptoms and often to utter despair.[7] Within the genre of prison literature, a substantial body of works describes the effects of solitude or can be interpreted in light of what we otherwise know about the author's imprisonment. Such works include Boethius's *The Consolation of Philosophy,* John Bunyan's *Grace Abounding to the Chief of Sinners,* the biography of Robert Stroud ("the birdman of Alcatraz"), Dietrich Bonhoeffer's *Letters and Papers from Prison,* Edith Bone's *Seven Years Solitary,*

Christopher Burney's *Solitary Confinement,* and Arthur Koestler's *Dialogue with Death.* Pivotal experiences of prison solitude shape many religious autobiographies, such as Dorothy Day's *The Long Loneliness* and *The Autobiography of Malcolm X.*

The ethical thrust of these works is somewhat different from those considered in this book because the author is not concerned with defending or justifying solitude but rather with protesting unjust punishment or harsh conditions. The spiritual value of solitary experiences of imprisonment is often central in this kind of writing. The author may find imagination or memory to be a source of inner freedom, may realize anew a feeling of intimacy or union with loved ones from whom he is separated, or he may believe that he witnesses a direct revelation from God. The spiritual value of these experiences does not depend on their being chosen or their leading to serenity or exultation. Like the dark night of the soul, the suffering of enforced solitude may teach the most important lessons about what is truly valuable and what will sustain a person through a terrible ordeal. These three forms of life writing—illness narratives, tales of stranded adventurers, and prison narratives—draw ethical and spiritual conclusions from a time of involuntary aloneness. Ideally solitude should be freely chosen, an expression of a person's values and spiritual practice. But solitude is paradoxical in many ways, often turning into loneliness even when it has been freely chosen, and sometimes generating crucial insights when it has not been chosen. When solitude becomes painful or is endured unwillingly it may still teach vital truths.

A Value for Whom?

This study has been limited to the Western tradition, focusing both on writers committed to Christianity and on secular writers searching for ethical wisdom and spiritual meaning. My focus reflects the limits of my own competence and interests, and also the fact that autobiography is primarily a Western form of writing. Further and contrasting insights would be gained, however, by studying solitude in other religious and literary traditions. For instance, one could examine first-person writing by Westerners learning from Asian solitaries, such as Bill Porter's *Road to Heaven: Encounters with Chinese Hermits.* One could study representations of solitude in the literature of non-Western cultures, such as accounts of Native American vision quests, the scriptures and wisdom literature of many religious traditions, and biographies and hagiographies of Hindu gurus, Buddhist masters, and Chinese sages. Such research would probably find certain continuities with the values that have been sought in aloneness in the West, such as attunement to nature and detachment from the vices of ambition and greed. One would also find distinctive reasons why particular cultures prize solitude. Some Native American tribes, for example, understand the vision quest as an ordeal, and solitude as part of the suffering of this test. In Taoist traditions, according to Philip Koch, solitude is conceived of not as hermetic isolation but as a form of *wu wei*, "inaction," disengagement from striving and self-assertion.[8] I think that solitude is valued by nearly every human culture, yet for somewhat different reasons. This study of solitude in Western autobiography should be supplemented and extended by interpretation of a broader range of literary texts and religious traditions and by analysis of the differing reasons for which various cultures value solitude.

My focus on autobiography may bias my conclusions about solitude toward certain kinds of value, ones that stress benefit to others. Life writing is usually composed in solitude but it is oriented beyond itself, pointed toward other people. It intends to communicate, and an implied or imagined reader is always present in the writer's mind. Life writing implies a clear social justification for extended solitude, because the author's eventual communication with readers depends upon lengthy periods of aloneness. In this respect, the use of solitude for autobiographical writing resembles other kinds of solitary creativity, such as the visual arts, musical composition and practice, and other forms of verbal expression. Some forms of scientific research, recuperation and healing, prayer, and many other solitary practices also eventually lead back to other people and may be ethically justified in terms of whatever meaning and value they eventually offer to others. Some forms of solitude, however, do not provide this kind of ethical justification. One may, like Thoreau, sit in the sun on the front steps, simply basking in the sun, but not write a *Walden*. One may, like Rousseau, float in a boat in reverie, but never try to describe this experience in writing. A person might grow flowers no one else will see, practice playing a guitar with no intention ever to perform, or lie in a hammock watching clouds pass, musing without coming to any conclusions or feelings that seem worth sharing with others.

Do these kinds of solitude have value? I think so; there are many valuable solitary experiences that do not lead to benefits for others, and may not even be fully understood or expressed in words in the ways in which autobiographers characteristically make sense of their lives. Most readers will agree with Thoreau that there are solitary times when one feels that something is happening at a deep psychic level that is crucial to one's well-being but very difficult to put in words: "I grew in those seasons like corn in the night, and they were far better than any work of the hands would have been."[9] The value of solitude is not just what benefits others, what can be articulated, or even, sometimes, what one can understand. If I take the reflections of highly articulate and self-reflective autobiographers as the basis for a normative theory of solitude, I may not adequately account for the solitudes of those who are uninterested in producing polished literary compositions. There is also valuable aloneness that benefits only the solitary, and solitude with benefits which are ineffable, not expressible in words. At the same time, however, I think that those unusually gifted and self-reflective persons who produce life writing can help one recognize and appreciate the intrinsic value of solitude. For instance, Thoreau's allusion to corn growing at night suggests that psychic growth or ripening takes place out of sight, even beneath conscious awareness. He may help one understand and make a place in one's life for this kind of solitude.

Who gets to have solitude? For whom is it a value? An important issue that is seldom raised in any of the books I have examined is the politics of solitude, or the ethical question of the just distribution of solitude in a society. Solitude has usually been a privilege reserved for the wealthy, males, and those whose power allows them to arrange their lives to enjoy periods of aloneness. The writers studied here seem surprisingly unaware of this fact and quite uninterested in the ways in which their lives depend upon others taking care of their needs. If the ethics and spirituality of solitude are not to be irresponsible or self-indulgent, solitaries should be more attentive to the politics of solitude, that is, to such questions as who gets to enjoy it, what it costs, its relationship to structures of power, and why representations of solitude often disguise or mask its political dimensions by presenting the hermit or recluse as having transcended the conflicts of his society. Although Thoreau and Thomas Merton and Edward Abbey conceive of the solitary as a prophetic voice who criticizes social values and political arrangements, even these writers with political concerns are not very self-critical about their own involvement in particular structures of power and their privilege in being able to safely enjoy the role of social outsider and critic.

In chapter 6 I argued that solitude is as valuable for women as it is for men. Solitude seems to me a good thing and perhaps even a right (the right to privacy) to which everyone should have access.[10] Yet opportunities for solitude depend on one's freedom and access to power. A poem by Adrienne Rich, "Yom Kippur 1984," raises important questions about the nature of solitude and who is able to enjoy it:

> What is a Jew in solitude?
> What would it mean not to feel lonely or afraid
> far from your own or those you have called your own?
> What is a woman in solitude: a queer woman or man?
> In the empty street, on the empty beach, in the desert
> what in this world as it is can solitude mean?[11]

Because solitude is dangerous for a woman, a Jew, or a lesbian, Rich desires to find others like herself, and to band together for mutual safety. She confesses that she also loves strangers and craves separateness, and she therefore wonders, on the Jewish day of atonement, whether her people will forgive her. Is her love of solitude a betrayal of solidarity with others? This poem raises the question of whether a desire for solitude is only a luxury and privilege for those safely at the center of society with enough power to drift occasionally to the margins. For these privileged few, Rich shows, solitude is often protected with guard dogs, barbed wire, and guns. The protected privacy of a few is not the same solitude as Rich imagines: a world in which a Jewish lesbian would be free to move about alone safely. "Yom Kippur 1984" concludes with apocalyptic imagery, and with those who have experienced enforced solitude by exclusion finally sharing their stories. Rich ends the poem with this question: "in that world as it may be, newborn and haunted, what will solitude mean?"

Rich's poem makes me aware of my privilege, for I can wander alone in a forest without the sense of apprehension that often colors the aloneness of those who are especially subject to violence. Yet this poem does not reject solitude as an unnecessary luxury or unjustified privilege but rather makes an implicit claim for a world in which solitude would be a good and a right available to everyone. "Yom Kippur 1984" raises far-reaching ethical, political, and religious questions about the conditions necessary for solitude to be enjoyed by every person who desires it. In such a world, where solitude was recognized and affirmed as a crucial value for everyone, what would solitude mean?

Getting the Rhythm Right

There are significant tensions between an ethics of solitude and a spirituality of solitude. Throughout this book I have been concerned

to understand how writers justify solitude and see its moral significance. Yet a preoccupation with justifying aloneness and a constant
awareness of how solitude is bounded by relationships with people
may prevent a person from fully experiencing solitude. My understanding of solitude may be too morally scrupulous and too preoccupied with solitude's social significance to fully appreciate the bliss,
the blessedness, and the serenity of the deepest aloneness, when one
forgets about how one's actions may affect others. Does focusing on
the ethics of solitude destroy the deepest spiritual meaning of aloneness, and undermine the human capacity to be disengaged from other
people while fully engaged in other dimensions of reality?

There are genuine tensions between the ethics of solitude and the
spirituality of solitude, between thinking about how much and under
what conditions solitude is morally justified and experiencing aloneness as a blessed release from just this sort of concern. Still, that is
what we need: both an ethics of solitude and a spirituality of solitude, in fruitful tension. A spirituality without ethics becomes irresponsible self-indulgence, and ethics without spirituality can degen-
erate into joyless duties to others and become disconnected from
much of what gives life meaning, vitality, and beauty.

A poem by Galway Kinnell concisely expresses the idea that solitude and engagement are not antithetical but rather aspects of a
rhythm in natural life:

> When one has lived a long time alone,
> and the hermit thrush calls and there is an answer,
> and the bullfrog head half out of water utters
> the cantillations he sang in his first spring,
> and the snake lowers himself over the threshold
> and creeps away among the stones, one sees
> they all live to mate with their kind, and one knows,
> after a long time of solitude, after the many steps taken
> away from one's kind, toward these other kingdoms,
> the hard prayer inside one's own singing
> is to come back, if one can, to one's own,
> a world almost lost, in the exile that deepens,
> when one has lived a long time alone.[12]

This poem shows the rhythm of withdrawal and connection as part
of nature's way, in this case related to sexual desire.[13] One senses both
Kinnell's attraction to aloneness and his fears that it will become a
permanent exile, that in solitude one can lose the world, and that the

return, "if one can," is not always easy or assured. But if one can get the rhythm right, the alternation of engagement and disengagement is a crucial aspect of living one's life well. That is where the ethics and the spirituality of solitude come together: in getting that rhythm right. The rhythm of solitude and engagement is not entirely within a person's control, nor should it be if living an ethical life includes being open and responsive to the unpredictable needs and demands of others. Ethical and spiritual wisdom involves knowing when to seek solitude and when to turn from it in response to other people.

The bliss of aloneness slowly or suddenly shifts to a hunger for companionship and community, and intense encounter with others often leads to a sensed need for a period of solitary self-appropriation, in an ongoing rhythm of engagement and disengagment. A similar dialectic between separation and connectedness characterizes auto-biography, according to John Sturrock: "The tension in autobiography derives from the conflict in it between the will to apartness and the will to association; and if the evidence of the will to apartness pervades all autobiographical narrative, then the evidence of the will to association lies in the existence of autobiography itself, as the most sociable of literary acts."[14] In an earlier book I argued that both deconversion (the loss of faith) and autobiography involve a search for individuality and autonomy by means of an effort to detach one-self from formative communities.[15] Yet the moment of separation often leads to renewed commitment to a person's original community or a new one and to the affirmation of values shared with others. The dialectic of disengagement and social engagement that I have traced in writers' experiences of aloneness is analogous to the processes of autobiographical writing and religious deconversion. These three human experiences—solitude, writing an autobiography, and criti-cally reevaluating one's faith—may all attempt to define personal values in relation to other people by means of an imaginative separa-tion from and return to community.

Understanding one's relationship to others is, I submit, the central ethical challenge and occasion for spiritual growth. The genre of auto-biography by its very nature embodies the ethical tension between a writer's desire for detachment and critical perspective on particular cultural values and the desire to be understood, to influence others, and to express one's values outwardly. The themes of deconversion and solitude in autobiography reveal the critical assessment of val-ues that is central in the process of individuation, the formation of personal identity that is articulated particularly clearly and coher-ently in life writing.

Autobiography involves both an author's cultivation of solitude for spiritual ends and an assessment of solitude's value and dangers that reveals the author's fundamental ethical concerns. Both of these dimensions of solitude are crucial. We understand the importance of autonomy, individuality, and independence from coercive social pressure. Yet we also yearn for intimacy, community, and social justice. The most discerning autobiographers understand both the spiritual value of experiences of aloneness and the dangers when solitary pursuits are severed from the relationships, social activities, and religious context that give solitude much of its meaning and value.

These writers help us understand that the value of solitude is situational. The meaning and significance of aloneness depend on a variety of circumstances that cannot be put into a formula yet can be explored and critically evaluated in life writing. We need both an ethics of solitude and a spirituality of solitude. Autobiographical narratives offer crucial insights and wisdom about how best to combine solitude and relationship and how to get their rhythm right.

NOTES

Introduction

1. The two scholarly works that most influence my thinking about solitude are Philip Koch's outstanding *Solitude: A Philosophical Encounter* and a psychoanalytic study of creative individuals by Anthony Storr, *Solitude: A Return to the Self*. Other book-length studies include Anson, *The Call of the Desert;* France, *Hermits;* Colegate, *A Pelican in the Wilderness;* and Halpern, *Migrations to Solitude*. Koch's *Solitude* contains a comprehensive bibliography of shorter and specialized studies.

2. Koch, *Solitude*, 15.

3. Ibid., 45.

4. Tillich, *The Eternal Now*, 18, 23.

5. James, *The Varieties of Religious Experience*, 42.

6. Whitehead, *Religion in the Making*, 16–17.

7. Of many works on spirituality consulted, I found helpful Van Ness, *Spirituality, Diversion, and Decadence*, and Evans, *Spirituality and Human Nature*. For a historical perspective on the West see the multivolume series edited by Ewert Cousins, *The Classics of Western Spirituality;* for a comparative perspective, see another series edited by Cousins, *World Spirituality*.

8. Barbour, *The Conscience of the Autobiographer* and *Versions of Deconversion*.

1. Christian Solitude

1. See Wiesel, "The Loneliness of Moses."

2. All biblical quotations are from the New Revised Standard Version (New York: Oxford University Press, 1989).

3. Athanasius, *The Life of Saint Antony*, 19–20.

4. Ibid., 57.

5. Ibid., 60.

6. Ibid., 58.

7. For an interpretation of the value of asceticism, see Miles, *Fullness of Life*.

8. On the history of monastic views of solitude, see Anson, *The Call of the Desert;* Workman, *The Evolution of the Monastic Ideal;* and Lozano, "Eremitism."

9. *Saint Benedict's Rule for Monasteries*, chapter 1.

10. Ibid., chapter 6.

11. Ibid., chapter 42.

12. Modern translations of these collections include Ward, ed., *The Desert Christian;* Ward, ed., *The Wisdom of the Desert Fathers;* and Merton, ed., *The Wisdom of the Desert.*

13. Ward, *Desert Christian,* 35, 19, 36.

14. Ibid., 74.

15. Ibid., 122.

16. Ibid., 145.

17. Gould, *The Desert Fathers on Monastic Community,* 141.

18. Ibid., 157.

19. Ware, "Separated from All and United to All," 30.

20. Louf, "Solitudo Pluralis," 17–29.

21. See Gilpin, "'Inward, Secret Delight in God.'"

22. Lane, *The Solace of Fierce Landscapes.*

23. See Leyser, *Hermits and the New Monasticism.*

24. See, for example, the last chapter of Knowles, *Christian Monasticism.*

25. Ware, "Separated," 44.

26. See Lozano, "Retreat."

27. Brown, *Society and the Holy in Late Antiquity,* 131.

28. Ibid., 131–32.

29. Ibid., 134.

30. Georgianna, *The Solitary Self,* 52. See also "Preface" by Ward and "Introduction" by Savage and Watson in their *Anchoritic Spirituality.*

31. Georgianna, *Solitary Self,* 78.

2. Bounded Solitude in Augustine's Confessions

1. Augustine, *Confessions,* 2.8. Subsequent references to book and chapter appear in text.

2. For Augustine's thinking about Christian life during the years between his conversion and the writing of the *Confessions,* see Lawless, *Augustine of Hippo and His Monastic Rule,* and Zumkeller, *Augustine's Ideal of the Religious Life.*

3. Athanasius, *Life of Antony,* 80.

4. See Zumkeller, *Augustine's Ideal,* 430: "Augustine shifted the notion of community to the center of monastic life. The chief thought behind his ideal of life was to form a community of Christian love and in that community to do everything possible to represent in its perfection the Christian ethic of living. This, above all, is the uniqueness of his monasticism."

5. Ibid., 15.

6. From Augustine's *Commentary on Psalm 132* (which is numbered 133 in most modern English Bibles), quoted in Van der Meer, *Augustine the Bishop,* 216.

7. Ibid., 216.

8. Augustine's *Commentary on Psalm 132,* quoted in Lawless, *Augustine of Hippo and His Monastic Rule,* 158.

9. Brown, *Augustine of Hippo*, 180. The opening sentence of Brown's chapter "Friends" reads: "Augustine will never be alone" (61).

10. Lawless, *Augustine of Hippo and His Monastic Rule*, 3–28.

11. For an analysis of the issues involved, see O'Meara, *The Young Augustine*. O'Meara asserts the historicity of a number of the features of the *Confessions* that have been interpreted by Pierre Courcelle and others as Augustine's condensation of earlier events into one dramatic scene in order to serve his later purposes.

12. Brown, *Augustine of Hippo*, 159.

3. The Humanist Tradition

1. On the poetic tradition that values solitude primarily as a means to achieve the goods of a life of leisure, see O'Loughlin, *The Garlands of Repose*.

2. Petrarch, *The Life of Solitude*, 107–8. Subsequent references appear in text.

3. See "Petrarch's Critique of Self and Society," in Trinkaus, *The Poet as Philosopher*, 52–89.

4. I have used a recent critical edition: *Petrarch's "Secretum": with Introduction, Notes, and Critical Anthology*, ed. Carozza and Shey. For analysis of the *Secretum* in relation to the history of autobiography, see Weintraub, *The Value of the Individual*, 93–114.

5. *Petrarch's "Secretum,"* 39.

6. Sturrock, *The Language of Autobiography*, 62.

7. This letter is contained in the Carozza and Shey edition of the *Secretum*, 153–60.

8. *Petrarch's "Secretum,"* 158.

9. Ibid., 159.

10. Zeitlin, "Introduction" to Petrarch's *The Life of Solitude*, 87.

11. Ibid., 88.

12. Dillon, *Shakespeare and the Solitary Man*, 18.

13. Zeitlin, "Introduction," 55, 57.

14. O'Loughlin, *Garlands*, 231.

15. See Montano, "The *Secretum*," 214: "St. Augustine makes use of examples and admonishments taken from ancient literature, from Cicero, Vergil, Seneca, and Terence, in order to draw Petrarch back to a more righteous life and to more lofty thoughts. So we see that the work is a witness of the poet's humanist trust, i.e., of a Christianity that utilizes classical wisdom to convert the soul." These remarks on the *Secret* are applicable also to *The Life of Solitude*.

16. Frame, *Montaigne: A Biography*, 115.

17. See Ariès, *Passions of the Renaissance*. See also Pollan, *A Place of My Own*, for a contemporary writer's account of why he needed to build a private cabin—a hermitage—not to escape, but to get a different angle on things, a new perspective on life: "The place will house the part of the self that stood a little apart—to get a better view" (42).

18. On old age in Montaigne's essays, see Friedrich, *Montaigne*, 233–39.

19. Montaigne, *The Complete Essays of Montaigne,* 178. Subsequent references appear in text.

20. Frame, *Montaigne,* 113–14.

21. Ibid., 83.

22. Starobinski, *Montaigne in Motion,* 51.

23. On the essay as an exercise of conscience that shapes the writer's moral character, see Barbour, *The Conscience of the Autobiographer,* chapter 4: "Conscience in the Essays of Montaigne and Johnson."

24. Screech, *Montaigne and Melancholy.*

25. Burton, *The Anatomy of Melancholy,* third partition, 432.

26. Screech, *Montaigne and Melancholy,* 33.

27. Frame, *Montaigne's Discovery of Man.*

28. Starobinski, *Montaigne in Motion,* 101.

29. Ibid., 105.

30. In the Foreword to Screech's *Montaigne and Melancholy,* xiii, Marc Fumaroli writes: "It could well be that his greatest originality, and his powerful and lasting influence in France, rests on his successful attempt to work out a perfectly orthodox form of spirituality for the use of laymen and of the gentry, a *liberal* spirituality quite distinct from the models traditionally conceived for clerics bound by constraining vows, inscribed within a narrow hierarchical discipline and thus ill suited to the specificity of an independent lay existence."

31. Gibbon, *Gibbon's Autobiography,* 58. Subsequent references appear in text.

32. On Gibbon's religious views, see Burrow, *Gibbon;* Swain, *Edward Gibbon the Historian;* and Carnochan, *Gibbon's Solitude,* 13–14: "Whatever else he may have come to believe, he never gave up believing in God, or at least wishing he could join the community of believers. . . . Odd though it is to think of Gibbon's as a pious disposition, it is too easy to forget the needs, arising out of loneliness, that inspired his adolescent leap into the arms of the mother church."

33. On Gibbon's relationship to his father see Spacks, *Imagining a Self,* and Craddock, *Young Edward Gibbon.*

34. Carnochan, *Gibbon's Solitude,* 192n18, quotes from Gibbon's letter to his stepmother after his friend Holroyd's maiden speech: "I can only condole with you that a person, in whose fate and reputation you are perhaps more deeply interested, should still continue a dumb Dog."

35. Craddock, *Edward Gibbon,* 369n3, 374n12. Craddock particularly takes issue (375n13) with Carnochan's view of "Gibbon's solitude," which she thinks oversimplifies his complex and changing character.

36. Craddock, *Young Edward Gibbon,* 222–23, concludes that "we cannot know whether the famous scene is historically or only mythically true. . . . We must in some sense respect his judgment of its symbolic importance: Rome, twilight, ruins, and friars in some sense caused the *Decline and Fall.*"

37. Storr begins *Solitude* with the example of Gibbon to illustrate his thesis that creative individuals find their chief happiness and the source of their self-esteem in their work rather than in human relationships: "By most of the standards adopted in the past, Gibbon would be rated as exceptionally well-balanced. It is only

since Freud advanced the notion that heterosexual fulfilment is the *sine qua non* of mental health that anyone would question Gibbon's status as a more than commonly happy and successful human being" (xii).

38. Carnochan, *Gibbon's Solitude*, 3.

39. Carnochan also offers a close analysis of the six drafts of Gibbon's memoirs, which he prefers in their unfinished and inconsistent state to the edited amalgam: "Gibbon's autobiography—that is, his true story—lies in a chaos of rough drafts. A necessary labor of love, Sheffield's editing hides Gibbon's multiplicity behind a veil. When the veil is removed, the monochromatic historian yields to the more richly colored man" (151).

40. Gibbon, *Decline*, quoted in Anson, *The Call of the Desert*, 14.

41. On Barlaam, see Craddock, *Edward Gibbon: Luminous Historian*, 232–33; on Julian, Theodora, and Mahomet, see Carnochan, *Gibbon's Solitude*, chapter 6.

42. Gibbon, in volume 5 of the *Decline*, cited in Carnochan, *Gibbon's Solitude*, 7–8.

43. Weintraub, in *The Value of the Individual*, chapter 11, holds that Gibbon did not have a fully developed sense of individuality, because although he had a keen interest in the time-bound and unpredictable nature of historical development, he shared the eighteenth century's universalizing tendencies and lacked the notion of uniqueness as Rousseau and Goethe would come to understand it.

4. Rousseau's Myth of Solitude in Reveries of the Solitary Walker

1. Starobinski, *Transparency*, 35–36.

2. Rousseau, *Reveries of the Solitary Walker*, 32. Subsequent references appear in text.

3. Stelzig, *The Romantic Subject in Autobiography*, 125.

4. Starobinski, *Transparency*, 354: "The language is not that of the original reverie but its delayed echo or double: a dream of a dream. Not, as Rousseau sometimes insists, a faithful replica but a voice that, moved by the memory of an initial reverie (whose inspiration cannot be recaptured), allows itself to drift, to be swept away in a second reverie as descriptive reflection progresses. The memory of reverie thus becomes another reverie in a process to be repeated ad infinitum as Rousseau rereads what he has written."

5. For analysis of the role of gifts in the *Reveries*, see Williams, *Rousseau and Romantic Autobiography*, 176–80.

6. My interpretation contrasts sharply with that of Rousseau's preeminent biographer Maurice Cranston, who in *The Solitary Self* accepts at face value Rousseau's professions of serenity: "No longer, as in the *Dialogues*, is Rousseau bothered about what other people think or say about him: he accepts his destiny as an outcast from society, and even welcomes the total solitude in which he can make his inward journey undisturbed" (184).

7. See Stelzig, "Rousseau's *Reveries*," 102: "'Reduced to only myself, I feed myself . . . With my proper substance,' Rousseau affirms in the Eighth Walk, yet

his self-possession cannot be absolute or unconditional, like God's, for his 'proper substance,' the professed reversion of his later years, is in fact a function of the anxiety produced in him by 'they,' his shadowy yet omnipresent enemies."

8. Grimsley, *Jean-Jacques Rousseau*, 316.

9. Starobinski, *Transparency*, 46.

10. Barbour, *The Conscience of the Autobiographer*, chapter 2: "Conscience and Truthfulness."

11. De Beer, *Jean-Jacques Rousseau and His World*, 111.

12. See Grimsley, *Jean-Jacques Rousseau*, 290.

13. Starobinski, *Transparency*, 361: "To converse with oneself is not a means to a remote ultimate end but a supreme end in itself, a final goal. And the written word, which *fixes* reverie, becomes the foundation of this encounter of self with self. . . . Clearly the peak of happiness comes just as the mind is about to turn and recognize itself in its fixed image. Rereading and indefinitely repeating the past offers the possibility of pure self-possession, safe from both change and the world's hostility."

14. Olney, *Memory and Narrative*, 208–9. Olney offers a detailed examination of *Reveries of a Solitary Walker* in relation to the themes of memory and narrative (186–203).

15. Ibid., 209.

16. Taylor, *Sources of the Self*, 362. On Rousseau's idea of an inner self as the essence of human nature, and the contrast with Augustine's views, see Hartle, *The Modern Self in Rousseau's "Confessions."*

5. Thoreau at Walden

1. Thoreau, *"Walden" and "Resistance to Civil Government,"* 182. Subsequent references appear in text.

2. Richardson, *Henry Thoreau*, 150. Other biographical studies include Harding, *The Days of Henry Thoreau* and Lebeaux, *Thoreau's Seasons*.

3. See Moller, *Thoreau in the Human Community*.

4. On Thoreau's anarchism, see Drinnon, "Thoreau's Politics of the Upright Man."

5. Cavell, "Words and Sentences," 265.

6. We may recall, however, the scene in Gibbon's autobiography when, musing alone amidst the ruins of the Roman Forum, he is inspired to begin work on his great history. Peck, in *Thoreau's Morning Work*, chapter 6, interprets Thoreau's half-chapter on "Former Inhabitants."

7. On Thoreau's view of Native Americans, see Fussell, "The Red Face of Man," and Sayre, *Thoreau and the American Indians*.

8. For an account of what Thoreau read at various periods of his life and an analysis of its influence, see Richardson, *Henry Thoreau*, and Sattelmeyer, *Thoreau's Reading*.

9. Marx, *The Machine in the Garden*. For another view of Thoreau's place in the pastoral tradition, see Buell, "American Pastoral Ideology Reappraised."

10. Emerson, "Thoreau," 797.

11. Baird, "Corn Grows in the Night," 403.

12. Morris, "To the Woods," 387.

13. Richardson, "The Social Ethics of *Walden*."

14. At least once before, Rousseau has been used as an example of the wrong kind of individualism and contrasted with another autobiographer. Weintraub's *The Value of the Individual* contrasts Rousseau and Goethe as negative and positive outcomes of a concern with defining one's individuality.

15. Richardson, "The Social Ethics of *Walden*," 245.

16. The increasing focus on nature is not only characteristic of the book's structure, but was also true of Thoreau's work on the six drafts of *Walden*. See Shanley, *The Making of "Walden,"* and Sattelmeyer, "The Remaking of *Walden*."

17. Paul, "A Fable of the Renewal of Life."

18. On the interpretation of Thoreau in relation to environmental and ecological concerns, see Marx, "The Struggle over Thoreau" and "The Full Thoreau."

19. Wildness was not the same as wilderness. Thoreau loved the undomesticated land a mile from Concord, but had a very different response to Mount Katahdin; he enjoyed the cozy, protected environs of Walden Pond, but did not stay long in the remote Maine woods and mountains. Ktaadn, as he spelled it, haunted him because of its frightening inhospitality to humans. A wonderful passage in Thoreau's 1848 essay "Ktaadn" records a solitary experience that is simultaneously disorienting and intensely real in its vivid impression of contact with both one's body and the natural world: "I stand in awe of my body, this matter to which I am bound has become so strange to me. I fear not spirits, ghosts, of which I am one,—*that* my body might,—but I fear bodies, I tremble to meet them. What is this Titan that has possession of me? Talk of mysteries!— Think of our life in nature,—daily to be shown matter, to come in contact with it,—rocks, trees, wind on our cheeks! The *solid* earth! The *actual* world! The *common sense! Contact! Contact! Who* are we? *Where* are we?" (in *Henry David Thoreau*, 646).

20. See Gusdorf, "Conditions and Limits of Autobiography," 48.

21. Erikson, *Identity: Youth and Crisis*. In *Thoreau's Seasons*, Lebeaux uses Erikson's concept of a psychosocial moratorium to interpret Thoreau's time at Walden Pond.

22. Lebeaux, *Thoreau's Seasons*, 47.

23. Ibid., 48.

24. Quoted in Harding, *The Days of Henry Thoreau*, 198.

25. For instance, a journal entry in 1857 reads: "This stillness, solitude, wildness of nature is a kind of thoroughwort, or boneset, to my intellect. This is what I go out to seek. It is as if I always met in those places some grand, serene, immortal, infinitely encouraging, though invisible, companion, and walked with him. . . . I suppose that this value, in my case, is equivalent to what others get by church-going and prayer. I come to my solitary woodland walk as the homesick go home" (quoted in Anderson, *The Magic Circle of Walden*, 79).

6. Twentieth-Century Varieties of Solitary Experience

1. Gilpin, "'Inward, Secret Delight in God': Solitude in the Career of Jonathan Edwards."

2. Koch's five "virtues of solitude" are: freedom, attunement to self, attunement to nature, reflective perspective, and creativity. These categories have some overlap with and some differences from the five values of solitude I analyze in this chapter.

3. Thoreau, *"Walden" and "Resistance to Civil Government,"* 85. Subsequent references appear in text.

4. Koch, *Solitude,* 118.

5. See Buell, *The Environmental Imagination;* Roorda, *Dramas of Solitude;* and Slovic, *Seeking Awareness in American Nature Writing.*

6. Abbey, *Desert Solitaire,* 29. Subsequent references appear in text.

7. Dillard, *Pilgrim at Tinker Creek,* 12. Subsequent references appear in text.

8. Koch, *Solitude,* 103.

9. Allister, *Refiguring the Map of Sorrow.*

10. Sarton, *Journal of a Solitude,* 57. Subsequent references appear in text.

11. See several relevant articles in the *Encyclopedia of Life Writing: Autobiographical and Biographical Forms,* ed. Margaretta Jolly: "Loss, Bereavement, and Life Writing," "Shame and Life Writing," "Trauma and Life Writing," and "Recovery, Healing and Life Writing."

12. Barbour, "Shame in the Autobiographies of Mary McCarthy," chapter 7 in *The Conscience of the Autobiographer.*

13. Solo adventure tales include Geoffrey Moorhouse, *The Fearful Void;* Colin Fletcher, *The Man Who Walked through Time;* Francis Chichester, *Gipsy Moth Circles the World;* Steven Callahan, *Adrift: Seventy-six Days Lost at Sea;* Eric Hansen, *Stranger in the Forest: On Foot Across Borneo;* and Jon Krakauer, "The Devil's Thumb," in *Eiger Dreams: Ventures among Men and Mountains.* An interesting question is whether authors accompanied by "primitive" guides or aides consider themselves to be alone. See also Jon Krakauer's reconstruction of the fatal journey of Thoreau-inspired Christopher McCandless in *Into the Wild.*

14. Slocum, *Sailing Alone around the World,* 243, 164. Subsequent references appear in text.

15. On Slocum's relationship to Transcendentalism, especially Thoreau, see Bender, "Joshua Slocum and the Reality of Solitude."

16. Raban, "Walden-on-Sea."

17. Byrd, *Alone,* 4. Subsequent references appear in text.

18. Storr, *Solitude,* 21.

19. Ibid., 122.

20. Kafka, *Letters to Felice,* 155–56.

21. Coe, *When the Grass Was Taller,* 51.

22. Rilke, *Letters to a Young Poet,* 54–55.

23. Sturrock, *The Language of Autobiography,* 14.

24. Trilling, *Sincerity and Authenticity*, 93–94.

25. Taylor, *The Ethics of Authenticity*, 29.

26. This fragment, "presumably a page that belongs to the first days of the collapse," is included as an appendix in Nietzsche's *"On the Genealogy of Morals" and "Ecce Homo,"* 343. Subsequent references appear in text.

27. See Pletsch, "On the Autobiographical Life of Nietzsche."

28. Van Ness, *Spirituality, Diversion, and Decadence*, 227.

29. Ibid., 231.

30. *Memories, Dreams, Reflections* combines diverse materials by Jung and was edited and rewritten by Aniela Jaffe, Jung's assistant during his last years. Because it was censored at different points by Jung, Jaffe, Jung's adult children, and publishing editors, it is difficult to be certain as to how much of this book is really by Jung himself. Biographical studies of Jung that explore his portrait in *Memories* include Noll, *The Aryan Christ*; Hayman, *A Life of Jung*; McLynn, *Carl Gustav Jung*; and Olshen, "*Memories, Dreams, Reflections.*"

31. Jung, *Memories, Dreams, Reflections*, 176. Subsequent references appear in text.

32. Olshen, "*Memories*," 295.

33. On women's understandings of solitude, see Wear, ed., *The Center of the Web*; Sands, "A Room of One's Own"; and Koch's chapter on "Women and Solitude" in *Solitude*.

34. Koller, *The Stations of Solitude*, x. Subsequent references appear in text.

7. Thomas Merton and Solitude

1. Abbreviations of Merton's works cited are as follows:
   AJ: The Asian Journal of Thomas Merton;
   DQ: Disputed Questions;
   IM: The Intimate Merton: His Life From His Journals;
   LL: Learning to Love: Exploring Solitude and Freedom;
   MZM: Mystics and Zen Masters;
   SJ: The Sign of Jonas;
   SL: "The Solitary Life";
   SSM: The Seven Storey Mountain;
   TS: Thoughts in Solitude;
   WD: The Wisdom of the Desert.
Page references to these works appear in text.

2. The official biography of Merton is Mott's *The Seven Mountains of Thomas Merton*. Of many studies of Merton's life and thought, most helpful were Malits, *The Solitary Explorer*; Shannon, *Silent Lamp*; and Cunningham, *Thomas Merton and the Monastic Vision*.

3. See Mott, *Seven Mountains*, 214–16, on conditions at Gethsemani during Merton's early years.

4. Merton's view of solitude has been discussed by Lentfoehr, "The Solitary"; Teahan, "Solitude: A Central Motif in Thomas Merton's Life and Writings"; and

LeBeau, "The Solitary Life." All of these studies were written before Merton's journals began to be published in 1993, and refer primarily to the theoretical essays published in the 1950s and 1960.

5. Shannon, *Silent Lamp*, 179.

6. Seven volumes of Merton's journals have been published since 1993, as he wished. A helpful selection of his most insightful entries is *The Intimate Merton: His Life from His Journals*. Unless a passage is not included in that work I will quote from *The Intimate Merton*, except that all entries during his Asian travels will be cited in *The Asian Journal of Thomas Merton*.

7. Mott, *Seven Mountains*, 438.

8. See Barbour, "Thomas Merton's Pilgrimage and Orientalism."

9. Hampl's *Virgin Time* uses this passage to interpret her spiritual search, which takes her on several pilgrimages, culminating in a silent retreat at a Cistercian women's monastery in California.

8. Solitude, Writing, and Fathers in Paul Auster's *The Invention of Solitude*

1. Eakin, "Relational Selves, Relational Lives," chapter 2 of *How Our Lives Become Stories*.

2. Auster, *The Invention of Solitude*, 15. Subsequent references appear in text.

3. Storr, *Solitude*, 19.

4. McCaffery and Sinda, "An Interview with Paul Auster," *Mississippi Review*, 58. See also McCaffery and Sinda, "An Interview with Paul Auster," *Contemporary Literature*.

5. Bruckner, "Paul Auster, or The Heir Intestate," 28.

6. Rubin, "'The Hunger Must Be Preserved at All Cost,'" 61: "Auster's Jewishness figures in a variety of prominent ways in *The Invention of Solitude*. For example, there is the centrality of the past: . . . His own private past, that of his family, and that of the Jewish people as a whole. There is also the importance of Scripture—of specific texts from the Old Testament, but also of the concept of the Book itself, and of the act of commentary or interpretation, all of which are central to Jewish life, religion, and culture. And then, at the core of Auster's character, of his perception of the self and of the individual's relation to the world around him, is the characteristically Jewish trait of longing, of yearning, of 'hunger.'"

7. Pascal's Memorial may be found in Kerr, *Conversions*, 37–38.

8. McCaffery and Sinda, "Interview," *Mississippi Review*, 59.

Conclusion

1. See Nagel, "The Fragmentation of Value," in *Mortal Questions*.

2. This is the central theme of Eakin, *Touching the World*. See also Hampl, *A Romantic Education*, 4–5: "The self-absorption that seems to be the embarrassment of autobiography turns into (or perhaps always was) a hunger for the world. Actually, it begins as hunger for *a* world, one gone or lost, effaced by time or a

more sudden brutality. But in the act of remembering, the personal environment expands, resonates beyond itself, beyond its 'subject,' into the endless and tragic recollection that is history."

3. For a convenient summary of postmodernist views of agency as they bear on autobiography, see Smith, *Reading Autobiography*, 42–48.

4. Taylor, *Sources of the Self*, 512.

5. Ibid., 513.

6. DeBaggio, *Losing My Mind*, 88. Subsequent references appear in text.

7. See Storr's chapter "Enforced Solitude" in *Solitude*.

8. Koch, *Solitude*, 286–97, discusses Taoist views of solitude in China during the Warring States Period of 700–200 B.C.

9. Thoreau, *"Walden" and "Resistance to Civil Government,"* 75.

10. Ethical reflection on this topic would need to examine the extensive literature on privacy, including legal issues. Halpern's *Migrations to Solitude* avoids the legal controversies as she explores privacy ("the state of being free from the observations, disclosures, and intrusions of others") as a good, but not an unqualified good: "A thoroughly private society would be a cold, disheartening place. Yet privacy, some measure of it, is essential to our souls" (viii–ix).

11. Rich, "Yom Kippur 1984," 75.

12. Kinnell, "When One Has Lived a Long Time Alone, 10."

13. This is one of very few allusions to sexual desire that I encountered in many accounts of solitude (although the desert fathers discuss sexual temptation, and for Merton sexuality was a crucial aspect of the crisis with M.). In solitude one is still a sexual being. An intriguing topic, although peripheral to my central concerns, is cultural attitudes toward "the solitary vice," masturbation. Fear of masturbation reflects many things, including medical theories, religious traditions, gender anxieties, fear of homosexuality, and Victorian worries about waste. Particularly in the eighteenth and nineteenth centuries, fears about masturbation were one reason why solitude was viewed with suspicion. In several of his works, including book 3 of the *Confessions*, Rousseau worries that solitude too easily leads to erotic fantasizing. On Rousseau's anxieties about this and the links between autoerotic fantasy and reading and writing, see Stelzig, *The Romantic Subject*, 53–60.

14. Sturrock, *The Language of Autobiography*, 18–19.

15. Barbour, *Versions of Deconversion*, 208–9.

WORKS CITED

Abbey, Edward. *Desert Solitaire: A Season in the Wilderness.* New York: Ballantine, 1968.

Allister, Mark. *Refiguring the Map of Sorrow: Nature Writing and Autobiography.* Charlottesville: University Press of Virginia, 2001.

Anderson, Charles R. *The Magic Circle of Walden.* New York: Holt, Rinehart, and Winston, 1968.

Anson, Peter. *The Call of the Desert: The Solitary Life in the Christian Church.* London: SPCK, 1964.

Ariès, Philippe. *A History of Private Life,* volume 3: *Passions of the Renaissance.* Trans. Arthur Goldhammer. Cambridge: Cambridge University Press, 1989.

Athanasius. *The Life of St. Antony.* Trans. Robert T. Meyer. New York: Newman Press, 1970.

Augustine. *Confessions.* Trans. R. S. Pine-Coffin. Harmondsworth, U.K.: Penguin, 1961.

Auster, Paul. *The Invention of Solitude.* New York: Penguin, 1982.

Baird, Theodore. "Corn Grows in the Night." In *"Walden" and "Civil Disobedience,"* ed. Owen Thomas, 400–409. New York: Norton, 1966.

Barbour, John D. *The Conscience of the Autobiographer: Ethical and Religious Dimensions of Autobiography.* London: Macmillan; New York: St. Martin's Press, 1992.

———. *Versions of Deconversion: Autobiography and the Loss of Faith.* Charlottesville: University Press of Virginia, 1994.

———. "Thomas Merton's Pilgrimage and Orientalism." In *Literature, Religion, and East-West Comparison: Essays in Honor of Anthony C. Yu,* ed. Eric Ziolkowski. Newark, N.J.: University of Delaware Press, 2004.

Bauby, Jean-Dominique. *The Diving Bell and the Butterfly.* New York: Random House, 1997.

Bender, Bert. "Joshua Slocum and the Reality of Solitude." *American Transcendental Quarterly* n.s. 6 (1992): 59–71.

Benedict. *St. Benedict's Rule for Monasteries.* Trans. Leonard J. Doyle. Collegeville, Minn.: The Liturgical Press of St. John's Abbey, 1948.

Brown, Peter. *Augustine of Hippo: A Biography.* Berkeley: University of California Press, 1967.

———. *Society and the Holy in Late Antiquity.* Berkeley: University of California Press, 1982.

Bruckner, Pascal. "Paul Auster, or The Heir Intestate." In *Beyond the Red Notebook: Essays on Paul Auster*, ed. Dennis Barone, 27–33. Philadelphia: University of Pennsylvania Press, 1995.

Buell, Lawrence. *The Environmental Imagination: Thoreau, Nature Writing and the Formation of American Culture*. Cambridge, Mass.: Harvard University Press, 1985.

———. "American Pastoral Ideology Reappraised." In *"Walden" and "Resistance to Civil Government,"* second edition, ed. William Rossi, 463–79. New York: Norton, 1992.

Burrow, J. W. *Gibbon*. Oxford: Oxford University Press, 1985.

Burton, Robert. *The Anatomy of Melancholy*. New York: Vintage, 1977.

Byrd, Richard. *Alone*. New York: Kodansha International, 1995.

Callahan, Steven. *Adrift: Seventy-six Days Lost at Sea*. New York: Ballantine, 1986.

Carnochan, W. B. *Gibbon's Solitude: The Inward World of the Historian*. Stanford: Stanford University Press, 1987.

Cavell, Stanley. "Words and Sentences." In *The Cavell Reader*, ed. Stephen Mulhall, 260–94. Oxford: Blackwell, 1996.

Coe, Richard. *When the Grass Was Taller: Autobiography and the Experience of Childhood*. New Haven: Yale University Press, 1984.

Colegate, Isabel. *A Pelican in the Wilderness: Hermits, Solitaries, and Recluses*. Washington, D.C.: Counterpart, 2000.

Cousins, Ewert. *The Classics of Western Spirituality: A Library of the Great Spiritual Masters*. New York: Paulist Press, 1978–.

———. *World Spirituality: An Encyclopedic History of the Religious Quest*. New York: Crossroad, 1985–.

Craddock, Patricia. *Edward Gibbon: Luminous Historian*. Baltimore: Johns Hopkins University Press, 1989.

———. *Young Edward Gibbon: Gentleman of Letters*. Baltimore: Johns Hopkins University Press, 1982.

Cranston, Maurice. *The Solitary Self: Jean-Jacques Rousseau in Exile and Adversity*. Chicago: University of Chicago Press, 1997.

Cunningham, Lawrence S. *Thomas Merton and the Monastic Vision*. Grand Rapids, Mich.: Eerdman's, 1999.

DeBaggio, Thomas. *Losing My Mind: An Intimate Look at Life with Alzheimer's*. New York: Free Press, 2002.

De Beer, Gavin. *Jean-Jacques Rousseau and His World*. New York: Putnam's Sons, 1972.

Dillard, Annie. *Pilgrim at Tinker Creek*. New York: Bantam, 1974.

Dillon, Janette. *Shakespeare and the Solitary Man*. Totowa, N.J.: Rowman and Littlefield, 1981.

Drinnon, Richard. "Thoreau's Politics of the Upright Man." In *"Walden" and "Civil Disobedience,"* ed. Owen Thomas, 410–22. New York: Norton, 1966.

Eakin, Paul John. *How Our Lives Become Stories: Making Selves*. Ithaca, N.Y.: Cornell University Press, 1999.

————. *Touching the World: Reference in Autobiography.* Princeton, N.J.: Princeton University Press, 1992.

Emerson, Ralph Waldo. "Thoreau." In *Selected Writings of Emerson*, ed. Donald McQuabe, 779–800. New York: Modern Library, 1981.

Erikson, Erik. *Identity: Youth and Crisis.* New York: Norton, 1968.

Evans, Donald. *Spirituality and Human Nature.* Albany: State University of New York Press, 1993.

Frame, Donald. *Montaigne: A Biography.* New York: Harcourt, Brace, and World, Inc., 1965.

————. *Montaigne's Discovery of Man: The Humanization of a Humanist.* New York: Columbia University Press, 1955.

France, Peter. *Hermits: The Insights of Solitude.* New York: St. Martin's Press, 1996.

Friedrich, Hugo. *Montaigne.* Trans. Dawn Eng. Berkeley: University of California Press, 1991.

Fussell, Edwin. "The Red Face of Man." In *Thoreau: A Collection of Critical Essays*, ed. Sherman Paul, 142–60. Englewood Cliffs, N.J.: Prentice-Hall, 1962.

Georgianna, Linda. *The Solitary Self: Individuality in the "Ancrene Wisse."* Cambridge, Mass.: Harvard University Press, 1981.

Gibbon, Edward. *Gibbon's Autobiography.* Ed. M. M. Reese. London: Routledge and Kegan Paul, 1970.

Gilpin, Clark. "'Inward, Secret Delight in God': Solitude in the Career of Jonathan Edwards." *Journal of Religion* 82 (2002): 523–38.

Gould, Graham. *The Desert Fathers on Monastic Community.* Oxford: Clarendon Press, 1993.

Grimsley, Ronald. *Jean-Jacques Rousseau: A Study in Self-Awareness.* Cardiff: University of Wales Press, 1961.

Gusdorf, Georges. "Conditions and Limits of Autobiography." In *Autobiography: Essays Theoretical and Critical*, ed. James Olney, 28–48. Princeton, N.J.: Princeton University Press, 1980.

Halpern, Sue. *Migrations to Solitude.* New York: Pantheon, 1992.

Hampl, Patricia. *A Romantic Education.* Boston: Houghton Mifflin, 1981.

————. *Virgin Time.* New York: Farrar, Strauss, Giroux, 1992.

Harding, Walter. *The Days of Henry Thoreau.* New York: Knopf, 1965.

Hartle, Ann. *The Modern Self in Rousseau's "Confessions": A Reply to St. Augustine.* Notre Dame: University of Notre Dame Press, 1983.

Hayman, Ronald. *A Life of Jung.* New York: Norton, 1999.

James, William. *The Varieties of Religious Experience.* New York: Macmillan, 1961.

Jolly, Margaretta, ed. *Encyclopedia of Life Writing: Autobiographical and Biographical Forms.* Chicago: Fitzroy Dearborn, 2001.

Jung, Carl. *Memories, Dreams, Reflections.* Recorded and edited by Aniela Jaffe. Trans. Richard and Clara Winston. Revised edition. New York: Vintage, 1965.

Kafka, Franz. *Letters to Felice.* Ed. Erich Heller and Jurgen Born. Trans. James Stern and Elizabeth Duckworth. New York: Schocken, 1973.

Kerr, Hugh T., and John M. Mulder. *Conversions.* Grand Rapids, Mich.: Eerdmans, 1983.

Kinnell, Galway. "When One Has Lived a Long Time Alone, 10." In *When One Has Lived a Long Time Alone,* 68. New York: Knopf, 1990.

Knowles, David. *Christian Monasticism.* New York: Macmillan, 1969.

Koch, Philip. *Solitude: A Philosophical Encounter.* Chicago: Open Court, 1994.

Koller, Alice. *The Stations of Solitude.* New York: Bantam, 1990.

Krakauer, Jon. *Into the Wild.* New York: Doubleday, 1996.

Lane, Belden. *The Solace of Fierce Landscapes: Exploring Desert and Mountain Spirituality.* New York: Oxford University Press, 1998.

Lawless, George. *Augustine of Hippo and His Monastic Rule.* Oxford: Clarendon Press, 1987.

LeBeau, Dorothy. "The Solitary Life." In *The Legacy of Thomas Merton,* ed. Patrick Hart, 133–55. Kalamazoo, Mich.: Cistercian Publications, 1986.

Lebeaux, Richard. *Thoreau's Seasons.* Amherst: University of Massachusetts Press, 1984.

Lentfoehr, Thérèse. "The Solitary." In *Thomas Merton, Monk: a Monastic Tribute,* ed. Patrick Hart, 59–79. New York: Sheed and Ward, 1974.

Leyser, Henrietta. *Hermits and the New Monasticism: A Study of Religious Communities in Western Europe, 1000–1150.* London: Macmillan, 1984.

Louf, Dom Andre. "Solitudo Pluralis." In *Solitude and Communion: Papers on the Hermit Life,* ed. A. M. Allchin, 17–29. Oxford: SLG Press, 1977.

Lozano, Juan Manuel. "Eremitism." In *The Encyclopedia of Religion,* ed. Mircea Eliade. New York: Macmillan, 1987.

———. "Retreat." In *The Encyclopedia of Religion,* ed. Mircea Eliade. New York: Macmillan: 1987.

Malits, Elena. *The Solitary Explorer: Thomas Merton's Transforming Journey.* San Francisco: Harper and Row, 1980.

Marx, Leo. "The Full Thoreau." *The New York Review of Books* 46 (July 15, 1999), 44–48.

———. *The Machine in the Garden: Technology and the Pastoral Ideal in America.* Oxford: Oxford University Press, 1964.

———. "The Struggle over Thoreau." *The New York Review of Books* 46 (June 24, 1999): 60–64.

McCaffery, Larry, and Gregory Sinda. "An Interview with Paul Auster." *Mississippi Review* 20 (1991): 49–62.

———. "An Interview with Paul Auster." *Contemporary Literature* 33 (1992), 1–23.

McLynn, Frank. *Carl Gustav Jung.* New York: St. Martin's Press, 1996.

Merton, Thomas. *The Asian Journal of Thomas Merton.* Ed. Naomi Burton, Patrick Hart, and James Laughlin. New York: New Directions, 1975.

———. *Disputed Questions.* New York: Farrar, Straus, and Cudahy, 1960.

———. *The Intimate Merton: His Life from His Journals.* Ed. Patrick Hart and Jonathan Montaldo. San Francisco: HarperSanFrancisco, 1999.

———. *Learning to Love: Exploring Solitude and Freedom.* Ed. Christine Bochen. San Francisco: HarperSanFrancisco, 1997.

———. *Mystics and Zen Masters.* New York: Farrar, Straus, and Giroux, 1967.

———. *The Seven Storey Mountain.* New York: Harcourt Brace Jovanovich, 1948.

———. *The Sign of Jonas.* New York: Harcourt, Brace and Company, 1953.

———. "The Solitary Life." In Thomas Merton, *The Monastic Journey,* ed. Patrick Hart, 151–62. Kalamazoo, Mich.: Cistercian Publications, 1992.

———. *Thoughts in Solitude.* New York: Farrar, Straus, and Giroux, 1958.

———, ed. *The Wisdom of the Desert: Sayings from the Desert Fathers of the Fourth Century.* New York: New Directions, 1960.

Miles, Margaret. *Fullness of Life: Historical Foundations for a New Asceticism.* Philadelphia: Fortress Press, 1981.

Moller, Mary Elkins. *Thoreau in the Human Community.* Amherst: University of Massachusetts Press, 1980.

Montaigne, Michel de. *The Complete Essays of Montaigne.* Trans. Donald M. Frame. Stanford: Stanford University Press, 1958.

Montano, Rocco. "The *Secretum:* The Awakening of Conscience." In *Petrarch's "Secretum": with Introduction, Notes, and Critical Anthology,* ed. Davy Carozza and H. James Shey, 213–16. New York: Peter Lang, 1989.

Morris, Wright. "To the Woods." In *"Walden" and "Civil Disobedience,"* ed. Owen Thomas, 384–90. New York: Norton, 1966.

Mott, Michael. *The Seven Mountains of Thomas Merton.* Boston: Houghton Mifflin, 1984.

Nagel, Thomas. *Mortal Questions.* Cambridge: Cambridge University Press, 1979.

Nietzsche, Friedrich. *"On the Genealogy of Morals" and "Ecce Homo."* Trans., ed., and with commentary by Walter Kaufmann. New York: Vintage, 1969.

Noll, Richard. *The Aryan Christ: The Secret Life of Carl Jung.* New York: Random House, 1997.

Olney, James. *Memory and Narrative: The Weave of Life-Writing.* Chicago: University of Chicago Press, 1998.

O'Loughlin, Michael. *The Garlands of Repose: The Literary Celebration of Civic and Retired Leisure; The Traditions of Homer and Virgil, Horace and Montaigne.* Chicago: University of Chicago Press, 1978.

Olshen, Barry N. "*Memories, Dreams, Reflections:* The Automythography of Carl Gustav Jung." *a/b: Auto/Biography Studies* 14 (1999): 292–306.

O'Meara, John. *The Young Augustine.* New York: Longman's, 1954.

Paul, Sherman. "A Fable of the Renewal of Life." In *Thoreau: A Collection of Critical Essays,* ed. Sherman Paul, 100–116. Englewood Cliffs, N.J.: Prentice Hall, 1962.

Peck, H. Daniel. *Thoreau's Morning Work: Memory and Perception in "A Week on the Concord and Merrimack Rivers," the Journal, and "Walden."* New Haven: Yale University Press, 1990.

Petrarch, Francis. *Petrarch's "Secretum": with Introduction, Notes, and Critical Anthology.* Ed. Davy Carozza and H. James Shey, 213–16. New York: Peter Lang, 1989.

————. *The Life of Solitude.* Trans. Jacob Zeitlin. Urbana: University of Illinois Press, 1924.

Pletsch, Carl. "On the Autobiographical Life of Nietzsche." In *Psychoanalytic Studies of Biography,* ed. George Moraitis and George Pollock, 405–34. Madison, Conn.: International Universities Press, 1987.

Pollan, Michael. *A Place of My Own: The Education of an Amateur Builder.* New York: Random House, 1997.

Porter, Bill. *Road to Heaven: Encounters with Chinese Hermits.* San Francisco: Mercury House, 1993.

Raban, Jonathan. "Walden-on-Sea." *The New York Review of Books* 42 (April 20, 1995): 21–23.

Rich, Adrienne. "Yom Kippur 1984." In *Your Native Land, Your Life,* 75–78. New York: Norton, 1986.

Richardson, Robert. *Henry Thoreau: A Life of the Mind.* Berkeley: University of California Press, 1986.

————. "The Social Ethics of *Walden.*" In *Critical Essays on Henry David Thoreau's "Walden,"* ed. Joel Myerson, 235–48. Boston: G. K. Hall, 1988.

Rilke, Rainer Maria. *Letters to a Young Poet.* Trans. Stephen Mitchell. New York: Random House, 1984.

Roorda, Randall. *Dramas of Solitude: Narratives of Retreat in American Nature Writing.* Albany: State University of New York Press, 1998.

Rousseau, Jean-Jacques. *Reveries of the Solitary Walker.* Trans. Peter France. Harmondsworth, U.K.: Penguin, 1979.

Rubin, Derek. "'The Hunger Must Be Preserved at All Cost': A Reading of *The Invention of Solitude.*" In *Beyond the Red Notebook,* ed. Dennis Barone, 60–70. Philadelphia: University of Pennsylvania Press, 1995.

Sands, Kathleen. "A Room of One's Own." In *Loneliness,* ed. Leroy Rouner, 218–35. Notre Dame: University of Notre Dame Press, 1998.

Sarton, May. *Journal of a Solitude.* New York: Norton, 1973.

Sattelmeyer, Robert. "The Remaking of *Walden.*" In *Writing the American Classics,* ed. James Barbour and Tom Quirk, 53–78. Chapel Hill: University of North Carolina Press, 1990.

————. *Thoreau's Reading: A Study in Intellectual History with Bibliographical Catalogue.* Princeton, N.J.: Princeton University Press, 1988.

Savage, Anne, and Nicholas Watson. *Anchoritic Spirituality: Ancrene Wisse and Associated Works.* New York: Paulist Press, 1991.

Sayre, Robert. *Thoreau and the American Indians.* Princeton, N.J.: Princeton University Press, 1977.

Screech, M. A. *Montaigne and Melancholy.* Harmondsworth, U.K.: Penguin, 1983.

Shanley, J. Lyndon. *The Making of "Walden."* Chicago: University of Chicago Press, 1957.

Shannon, William H. *Silent Lamp: The Thomas Merton Story.* New York: Crossroad, 1992.

Slocum, Joshua. *Sailing Alone around the World.* New York: Penguin, 1999.

Slovic, Scott. *Seeking Awareness in American Nature Writing: Henry Thoreau,*

Annie Dillard, Edward Abbey, Wendell Berry, Barry Lopez. Salt Lake City: University of Utah Press, 1992.

Smith, Sidonie. *Reading Autobiography: A Guide for Interpreting Life Narratives.* Minneapolis: University of Minnesota Press, 2001.

Spacks, Patricia Meyer. *Imagining a Self: Autobiography and the Novel in Eighteenth-Century England.* Cambridge, Mass.: Harvard University Press, 1976.

Starobinski, Jean. *Jean-Jacques Rousseau: Transparency and Obstruction.* Trans. Arthur Goldhammer. Chicago: University of Chicago Press, 1988.

———. *Montaigne in Motion.* Trans. Arthur Goldhammer. Chicago: University of Chicago Press, 1985.

Stelzig, Eugene. "Rousseau's *Reveries:* Autobiography as Revision." *a/b: Auto/Biography Studies* 4 (1988): 97–106.

———. *The Romantic Subject in Autobiography: Rousseau and Goethe.* Charlottesville: University Press of Virginia, 2000.

Storr, Anthony. *Solitude: A Return to the Self.* New York: Ballantine, 1988.

Sturrock, John. *The Language of Autobiography: Studies in the First-Person Singular.* Cambridge: Cambridge University Press, 1993.

Swain, Joseph Ward. *Edward Gibbon the Historian.* London: Macmillan, 1966.

Taylor, Charles. *Sources of the Self: The Making of Modern Identity.* Cambridge, Mass.: Harvard University Press, 1989.

———. *The Ethics of Authenticity.* Cambridge, Mass.: Harvard University Press, 1991.

Teahan, John F. Teahan. "Solitude: A Central Motif in Thomas Merton's Life and Writings." *Journal of the American Academy of Religion* 50 (1982): 521–38.

Thoreau, Henry David. *Henry David Thoreau: "A Week on the Concord and Merrimack Rivers," "Walden," "The Maine Woods," and "Cape Cod."* New York: Library of America, 1985.

———. *"Walden" and "Resistance to Civil Government."* Second edition. Ed. William Rossi. New York: Norton, 1992.

Tillich, Paul. *The Eternal Now.* New York: Scribner's Sons, 1963.

Trilling, Lionel. *Sincerity and Authenticity.* Cambridge, Mass.: Harvard University Press, 1971.

Trinkaus, Charles. *The Poet as Philosopher: Petrarch and the Formation of Renaissance Consciousness.* New Haven: Yale University Press, 1971.

Van der Meer, F. *Augustine the Bishop.* New York: Sheed and Ward, 1961.

Van Ness, Peter. *Spirituality, Diversion, and Decadence.* Albany: State University of New York Press, 1992.

Ward, Benedicta, ed. *The Desert Christian: Sayings of the Desert Fathers.* New York: Macmillan, 1975.

———. *The Wisdom of the Desert Fathers.* Oxford: SLG Press, 1975.

Ware, Kallistos. "Separated from All and United to All: The Hermit Life in the Christian East." In *Solitude and Communion: Papers on the Hermit Life,* ed. A. M. Allchin, 30–47. Oxford: SLG Press, 1977.

Wear, Delease, ed. *The Center of the Web: Women and Solitude.* Albany: State University of New York Press, 1993.

Weintraub, Karl. *The Value of the Individual: Self and Circumstance in Autobiography.* Chicago: University of Chicago Press, 1978.

Whitehead, Alfred North. *Religion in the Making.* Cambridge: Cambridge University Press, 1926.

Wiesel, Elie. "The Loneliness of Moses." In *Loneliness,* ed. Leroy S. Rouner, 127–42. Notre Dame: University of Notre Dame Press, 1998.

Williams, Huntington. *Rousseau and Romantic Autobiography.* Oxford: Oxford University Press, 1983.

Workman, Herbert. *The Evolution of the Monastic Ideal.* Boston: Beacon Press, 1962.

Zeitlin, Jacob. "Introduction" to Petrarch's *The Life of Solitude.* Trans. Jacob Zeitlin. Urbana: University of Illinois Press, 1924.

Zumkeller, Adolar. *Augustine's Ideal of the Religious Life.* New York: Fordham University Press, 1986.

INDEX

STUDIES IN RELIGION AND CULTURE